Rediscovering the Magic of Music....
for a Song!

CHRISTOPHER LONG

With Bryan Dumas

Foreword by Bella Perron

Bibliozona Books

Tempe, Arizona
2024

Copyright © 2024 Christopher Long

All rights reserved.

No portion of this book may be reproduced in any form without written permission from the publisher or author, except as permitted by U.S. copyright law.

Thank you for your support of the author's rights.

Bibliozona Books

Tempe, Arizona

www.bibliozonabooks.com // info@bibliozonabooks.com

ISBN: 978-1-7332470-4-7 Paperback Edition

*To Rose Petralia —
This book wouldn't exist if not for
her vision and encouragement.*

Contents

Foreword vii
Introduction x

1. Aerosmith – Toys in the Attic 1
2. Alice Cooper – Killer 7
3. The Beach Boys – Endless Summer 13
4. The Beatles – Let It Be 19
5. Tony Bennett – Tony's Greatest Hits 24
6. Blue Öyster Cult – Fire of Unknown Origin 30
7. The Cars – Candy-O 35
8. Cheap Trick – Heaven Tonight 40
9. Chicago – X 46
10. Cinderella – Heartbreak Station 51
11. Crosby, Stills, Nash & Young – Déjà Vu 58
12. Cherie Currie – Beauty's Only Skin Deep 62
13. The Charlie Daniels Band – Fire on the Mountain 69
14. John Denver – Poems, Prayers & Promises 73
15. Eagles – The Long Run 79
16. Earth, Wind & Fire – All 'n All 83
17. Fleetwood Mac – Fleetwood Mac 88
18. Foghat – Fool for the City 95
19. Peter Frampton – Frampton Comes Alive! 101
20. Debbie Gibson – Anything is Possible 107
21. The Go-Go's – Beauty and the Beat 112
22. Daryl Hall & John Oates – Daryl Hall & John Oates 117
23. Heart – Bébé le Strange 121
24. Jimi Hendrix Experience – Smash Hits 125
25. Janis Ian – Between the Lines 131

26. Jefferson Starship – Spitfire 137
27. Elton John – Captain Fantastic 142
28. The Kinks – Low Budget 147
29. KISS – Dynasty 152
30. Led Zeppelin – III 158
31. Paul McCartney & Wings – Wings Over America 165
32. Willie Nelson – Willie and Family Live 170
33. Ohio Players – Honey 175
34. The Ozark Mountain Daredevils – Don't Look Down 180
35. The Partridge Family – Up to Date 186
36. Pretenders – Pretenders 193
37. Bonnie Raitt – Streetlights 196
38. Ramones – End of the Century 200
39. Boots Randolph – Sweet Talk 205
40. Charlie Rich – Behind Closed Doors 211
41. Linda Ronstadt – Heart Like a Wheel 215
42. Bob Seger – Night Moves 222
43. Shalamar – Three for Love 226
44. Nancy Sinatra – Nancy's Greatest Hits 232
45. Rick Springfield – Success Hasn't Spoiled Me Yet 236
46. Stryper – The Yellow and Black Attack 241
47. The Pat Travers Band – Heat in the Street 247
48. Stevie Wonder – Innervisions 254
49. Frank Zappa – Joe's Garage Acts II & III 258
50. ZZ Top – Fandango! 265

Afterword 281
Acknowledgements 283
About the Authors 289

Foreword

When Chris first told me about the concept for *Garage Sale Vinyl*, I was STOKED! One of my favorite writers, writing about one of my favorite things — classic vinyl records.

Listening to vinyl has been a hugely formative part of my musical upbringing. In an era of streaming and instant access to music, there's something extra special about the timeless experience of listening to vinyl. Everything about vinyl immerses you in the artistry of the album. Even flipping through the bins at your local record shop, looking at all of the vivid artwork while searching for your favorite albums. This was one of my favorite things to do growing up, checking out all of the local record shops and then bringing my newfound treasure home; putting it on the turntable right away. The charismatic warmth of the vinyl would fill my bedroom as I listened to classic albums in full. I'd examine the album artwork, reading all of the credits and thank-yous. Looking at the photos of my guitar heroes on the inner sleeve; larger than life and effortlessly cool. The experience of actively listening to vinyl ignites an even deeper love and appreciation for the music.

Now, as a touring musician, it has become my favorite off-day activity to explore local record stores. I love checking out the unique hole-in-the-wall shops in so many different cities. It feels like a continuation of my constant hunt for vinyl as a teenager, now also combined with my love for traveling. Finding a copy of *Axis: Bold as Love* in Philadelphia, *L.A. Woman* in Seattle, *Shangri-La-De-Da* in Los Angeles — to then go home at the end of the tour and experience all of these amazing albums on the turntable.

There's a certain beauty in listening to an album in full, only pausing when it's time to flip to the B-side. You discover so many deep cuts and end up loving them as much (if not more) than the hits. Vinyl is truly a work of art and listening is a ritual.

Chris and I have a wild full circle connection. My mom had become friends with Chris, as they had met at Poison shows in the early 2000's — there are even pictures of them in his book, *A Shot of Poison*. Flash forward 20 years and we connected when Plush's first song was released. Chris was so kind to do an interview and write about our exciting journey as a brand new rock band. He has been incredibly supportive of my journey navigating the music industry since the start!

It has been a rollercoaster since touring with Plush in 2021, a few years packed with surreal experiences opening for so many of my favorite bands. One of the most special moments for me was seeing our debut album on vinyl for the first time. Seeing our photo on a physical album cover and hearing these tracks in that classic warm vinyl sound that I love so dearly. It was a pretty surreal feeling. The album had been out for a while but it just feels so different to have a tangible format; to see these songs now as grooves pressed into wax.

I felt a similar wave of excitement when I heard about *Garage Sale Vinyl*. These 50 albums have undoubtedly had such a profound influence on generations of people from all walks of life. *Garage Sale Vinyl* celebrates these classic albums with not only information on each album, but the personal stories that show how these records have touched so many lives.

FOREWORD

I think the beautiful thing is that the reach and impact of these albums go farther than we can even imagine. We all have our own memories of these albums, whether it's finding your copy on vinyl, being intrigued by the artists sound or image, or discovering your favorite song. Chris really created a special work that ties together all of these unique stories, sharing the love that we all have for these amazing records and showing that vinyl truly is timeless.

—Bella Perron
(Guitarist, Plush)
October 2023
BellaPerron.net

Introduction

Entitled "Jazz Records," it was my favorite episode of the popular, long-running TV sitcom *Everybody Loves Raymond*. The gist of the story was that lead character, Ray Barone, played by Ray Romano, had taken his cantankerous father's old scratchy jazz records and traded them in for shiny new CDs. Played by Peter Boyle, Ray's father, Frank, went ballistic when he learned of the well-intended switcheroo.

Plain and simple, Frank didn't want "crystal clear," he wanted "cozy crackle." And he refused to let the situation go until Ray went downtown and traded the new CDs back in for the old LPs. Finally, we see Frank sitting in his basement, reconnecting with his prized records, peacefully awash in the scratchy splendor. A legit, personal Zen moment.

At the time, it made sense that an out-of-touch curmudgeon like Frank would cling to ancient customs rather than embrace modern technology. *Ugh, old people!* But fast forward a decade, and Frank would prove to be a visionary, a trendsetter — showing current and future generations what the old-timers knew all along — the magic of music is discovered on vinyl.

∙∙

So, there I was, reprising my role as "Cool Uncle Chris," taking my then-16-year-old niece to the Vans Warped Tour. At age 52, I hadn't attended the iconic annual traveling alternative summer music festival in nearly 20 years. I don't think that Mikayla had ever been to one. Given our shared passion for the pop-punk combo, Icon for Hire (who was on the daily bill), the 2015 outing seemed like the perfect op for a little sweat-soaked, ear-splitting, hard-core bonding. *Hey! Race ya to the pit?* The experience would prove quite memorable — especially for me.

INTRODUCTION xi

Upon making our way past the entrance turnstiles, Mikayla bolted with her 17-year-old BF in short order, because NO teenager wants to hang out with their middle-aged uncle at a rock concert, no matter how "cool" he thinks he is. As a result, I would be on my own to explore and experience the sights, sounds, and smells of Warped Tour. And with my ever-constant, monster-sized iced bevy in one hand and an occasional life-sustaining snack in the other, I navigated from stage to stage throughout the sprawling festival grounds for nearly ten sun-scorched hours.

As I waded through the sea of corporate sponsor info tents and band merch booths along the way, I noticed that many of the bands were selling copies of their latest releases — on vinyl. I had to laugh. *Aw, bless their little hearts. The "young people" think they've discovered a new niche novelty.* But this wouldn't be some short-lived fad. As I'd soon learn, vinyl was back.

Honestly, I wasn't completely surprised by this seemingly sudden about-face in format sensibility. Aside from vinyl being simply a superior audio source, the true magic of music is something that must be experienced physically. Our connection to music is personal. And like any healthy personal relationship, there needs to be a physical investment. I've often likened downloading and streaming music to having intimate relations with a blow-up doll, while engaging with records, tapes and even CDs is more like "being" with a real-life babe. Both can result in a happy ending, but the latter is way more rewarding.

The younger generation got the memo loud and clear; consuming music is about more than instant gratification. Time, care, and effort are required — sliding the record lovingly from the sleeve, cleaning it carefully, placing it gently onto the turntable, and then flipping it cautiously from Side One over to Side Two. *Lather. Rinse. Repeat.*

Another recognized component missing from the modern music experience was the all-important sense of community — going out into the real world in search of particular must-have records, then connecting with the perky, quirky gal who owns the funky new music shop downtown, or the old dude with the ponytail who runs the used record concession over at the local flea market. Plus, there's the immeasurable value in hanging out in these stores, engaging with fabulous, like-minded friends. Like during the glorious days of yore.

I'm all too familiar with the authentic in-store experience. A couple of lifetimes ago (1978 to be exact), I was an obnoxiously overzealous music-crazed kid. Just before turning 16, I landed a job at the little neighborhood mom & pop record shop where I lived near Cocoa Beach. It was my first real job, and I worked a couple of days a week after school and on weekends. Soon, I'd graduated to the biggest record outlet in the county. Promoted famously far and wide as, "Your

One-Stop Music Shop," the store was where I would work for much of my retail career throughout the '80s and into the early '90s. Generating gross sales in excess of a million dollars annually, it was THE local go-to destination for records, tapes, CDs, T-shirts, posters, concert tickets, car stereos, smoking accessories, and more.

But by 1991, the nearby mall was thriving, while we barely were surviving. There was one particular night during that summer when I found myself working alone, standing in an otherwise empty shop. As I played Bonnie Raitt's *Luck of the Draw* CD for the third time that night, I walked out onto the front sidewalk. Nearly the entire parking lot of the shopping center was EMPTY — on a Saturday night. Times were a-changin'. And I knew it.

Within six weeks, the once unstoppable, once million-dollar-making "little" record shop would be gone, forever. I was there on the last day, loading fixtures and surplus inventory into a huge moving truck that hauled it all away to who knows where. A huge piece of local history was taken away that day, along with a huge hunk of my soul. More than 30 years later, I've still not gotten over it. In the words of that great American poet, Tom Keifer, "You don't know what you got 'til it's gone."

Along with a couple of investors, I opened my own record shop in 1996. Who knew the mid-'90s would be such a lousy time to start a mid-'80s-style music store? C'mon, now! Stop laughing! Only 18 months and a whopping $250,000 later, my shop came and went. Had we launched just five years later, the business likely would have been a massive success.

In 2016 my girlfriend rediscovered and set up her old home hi-fi set from the '90s. One of the system's components was a rather unreliable turntable. She also soon relocated her modest-sized collection of old, scratchy LPs. After begging ad nauseam for "someone" to get her turntable fixed, I bought her a brand new one for Christmas in 2017. The first record I bought her was the minty-fresh, double white vinyl Gwen Stefani *You Make It Feel Like Christmas* record. What a beautiful album!

From there, it was "game on." We began hitting local garage sales, flea markets and thrift stores everywhere we went, in search of vinyl treasures. I didn't even own a turntable at my place, but that wasn't gonna keep me from getting in on the fun, as I began replacing many of my favorite long-lost LPs for "a song." By rarely paying more than a buck or two for used records, we could afford to become hoarders, snatching up random records we'd never even heard of before — by the bagful! *WOW! Kaptain Kool and the Kongs for only .88¢!* I also became energized by seeking and scoring all kinds of fun, colored vinyl records from many of my favorite current artists. *Oh, that Harry Styles! What a rascal!*

INTRODUCTION   xiii

In 2022, the GF bought me my own home hi-fi set (with a turntable). And lickety-split, I began hoarding more vinyl records than ever — just stashing them off to the side somewhere at my place — often still in the shopping bags, only to forget all about them for months. *Hey, Honey! Where did those Pretenders records go?*

Christmastime 2022. I'd just located a pristine vinyl copy of the 1974 Bonnie Raitt record, *Streetlights,* for less than a buck at a neighborhood garage sale. Overjoyed by the newfound bargain, I reached out to Rose, my longtime editor at Ink19.com to inquire if the magazine would be interested in running a mini retro review of this random 50-year-old record. Rose loved the idea and suggested that it would make for a cozy weekly column, if I was up for it. Heck yeah, I was.

My *Garage Sale Vinyl* series resonated quickly with online readers who shared my genuine passion for old records. Then, a few months later, I heard a little voice inside my head. *Psst! What about Garage Sale Vinyl — the book?*

Be sure, neither the *Garage Sale Vinyl* column nor the book ever was intended to be analytical "Ultimate Albums" content. These records found me, quite organically. And creating both the column and the book has been an incredible, personally rewarding endeavor.

I hope you'll get a kick out of these stories and enjoy the journey, as we rediscover the magic of music, for a song!

1
Aerosmith

Aerosmith
"Toys in the Attic"
(Columbia / April 1975)

Toys in the Attic

Simply put, I was in BIG trouble. In fact, the moment my mother confronted me as I came through the front door, I realized in very short order that, in the words of the late great Cuban philosopher, Ricky Ricardo, I had "a lot of esplainin' to do!"

It was early 1977. I was just 14, and a HUGE Aerosmith fan. At that time, their single "Walk This Way" was a red-hot radio hit. As a naive church boy, waiting patiently for the bowl cut to finally grow out, I thought it was the most incredible record I'd ever heard. Also, I was out of my mind in love with Andrea, the like-minded 13-year-old little rock chick from down the street. When Andrea called me up one night and asked me to write down the "Walk This Way" lyrics for her, I jumped on it, pronto. *Your wish is my command, my queen!*

Be advised, I'll be repeating this point throughout the next 50 chapters, because it warrants the constant reminder — TIMELINE IS EVERYTHING. In 1977, there was NO iPhone technology. There was NO Internet. NO Google search. NO cut and paste. As a result, I had to play my "Walk This Way" 45 rpm seven-inch single over and over at 33 1/3 rpm to decipher each and every one of Steven Tyler's libido-soaked lyrics. *"Down on a muffin?" Jeepers! I love muffins!*

Honestly, I had no clue what the lyrics meant — I just thought it was a groovy tune about spirited teens. However, my mom knew *exactly* what "bleeder" *and* "muffin" meant. And assuming it was a song *I'd* written, she flipped out when she found the copy of my handwritten lyrics lying on the coffee table in the living room. But my prompt clarification did little to dissuade my mom's anxieties, as she remained clearly concerned about that "garbage" I now was listening to. She further suggested that I focus more on church-related social activities. In hindsight, she was probably right.

..

They were magical times, back when rock and roll was honest, pure, and unapologetic. In the studio, the music was created by humans who played instruments and used their actual voices to sing — songs. Microphones were used to record these organic sounds onto reels of two-inch, multi-track analog tape — slice it and splice it, baby! *Wait! What? No Pro Tools? That's impossible!* And while it might blow the minds of many modern-day digital divas, those ancient audio recording techniques actually worked, quite nicely.

It was during that magical period when five boys from Beantown began brewing their unique blend of blues-injected rock. While their first two records met with only marginal initial chart success, Aerosmith was about to blow up worldwide when they dropped a doozie in 1975. Overseen by veteran producer, Jack Douglas, their multi-platinum-selling third studio set, *Toys in the Attic* has since become something of a self-contained "best of" collection.

> "This record always reminds me of why I started playing guitar in the first place… because it's fucking cool."
> —Bella Perron
> Plush
> June 2023

The fact is, LPs *do* sound better than CDs. *Ha — CDs! Remember those?* The format also is totally superior to current streaming options, especially the records created during the glorious analog era. And there are few mightier hard rock examples of vinyl superiority than those early Aerosmith releases — records that are castrated sonically in the digital format.

Filed in among the eclectic selections contained in my GF's modest new millennium record collection were several LPs left behind years ago by one of her former associates — including an abused original vinyl pressing of *Toys in the Attic*. Upon making this wonderful discovery, I pulled the battered record from its tattered cover, gave it a much-needed cleaning, placed it gently onto the turntable and then dropped the needle in the groove. *Snap! Crackle! Pop!*

Even from an old and scratchy vinyl copy, I could still feel the physical presence of Brad Whitford and Joe Perry, slashing through the speakers straight out the gate — as if their Marshall amps were placed strategically between the

GF's hi-fi unit and living room sofa — right next to her recently refurbished, once-resin-coated thrift store coffee table.

> "I grew up obsessed with Brad Whitford's and Joe Perry's playing, especially how they work so seamlessly together!!! It's pure magic."
> —Bella Perron
> Plush
> June 2023

As any sound-minded aficionado can attest, the true secret weapon, the key component to the signature Aerosmith swagger is bassist Tom Hamilton. Go ahead, cue up the title track. Around the 1:30 mark, you can feel the urgency building. *Heart rate revving!* Then, at 1:44, everything goes haywire. But beneath the frenzied ensuing guitar soloing is the track's *real* payoff — that beautifully brutal Tom Hamilton bassline. And he does that kinda thing — relegating the other fellas to the backseat, again and again throughout the record.

"Uncle Salty" still provides a sultry yin to the title track's raucous yang, while the dirty, sexy-feeling riffs of ringleader Tyler's "Adam's Apple" continue to speak effectively to one's nether region. Oddly, the aforementioned hot and horny "Walk This Way" wouldn't find life as a single for a year and a half after the album's initial release, nearly six months following the release of the band's next album, *Rocks*.

Known for its bold, double-entendre lyrics, the boogie-woogie ball buster "Big Ten Inch Record" had been endeared to many since first being released by Bull Moose Jackson back in the 1950s. The revamped 1975 Aerosmith edition was explained to me at the time by a friend's older high school cheerleader sister. "You know they aren't talking about an actual record, right?" she informed me with eyes rolled. Joey Kramer's powerful, funk-fueled, single-kick drum work is magnificent on this one and provides a lasting blueprint for how rock music is meant to be played.

> "I don't know what Joey (Kramer) thinks of me, but I think Joey's God!"
> —Rikki Rockett
> Poison
> September 2003

Only a minor Top 40 hit when first released as a single in '75, the Tyler / Hamilton collab, "Sweet Emotion" remains one of rock's all-time sexiest-sounding tracks. It too would enjoy tremendous success years later as a wildly popular MTV video single. This one comes across so real, you can (almost) feel the gentle spray of Tyler's era-accepted, "mile high"-inspired spittle, as he seemingly reaches through the speakers — grasping for a stray bottle of desperately-needed penicillin. And if you listen *real* close, you just might even hear Tom Hamilton in the background, hocking up a monster loogie. Maybe.

A personal favorite, the Tyler / Perry-penned "No More No More" pins crisp acoustic guitar chords to nasty, electrified riffs as Tyler wrestles lyrically with the realities of rock stardom. The twinkling piano work makes this one sparkle like a diamond, while Tyler and Whitford's "Round and Round" drives into a dizzying, darker direction.

All of the glorious, unabashed cock rock clatter comes to a compelling conclusion with the piano-driven power ballad, "You See Me Crying." A heart-stopping piece of work owning soaring orchestration, this shiny album highlight was cut long before power ballads were a thing. TIMELINE IS EVERYTHING, you know.

Toys in the Attic arrived during a drastically different era. Decades later, it refuses to apologize for its honesty and purity, or for anything else. Nor should it. And it still stands proudly among some of rock's tallest classics.

Toys in the Attic

Track List

SIDE ONE

1. Toys in the Attic (Tyler, Perry) – 3:05
2. Uncle Salty (Tyler, Hamilton) – 4:08
3. Adam's Apple (Tyler) – 4:34
4. Walk This Way (Tyler, Perry) – 3:39
5. Big Ten Inch Record (Weismantel) – 2:10

SIDE TWO

1. Sweet Emotion (Tyler, Hamilton) – 4:34
2. No More No More (Tyler, Perry) – 4:35
3. Round and Round (Tyler, Whitford) – 5:02
4. You See Me Crying (Tyler, Solomon) – 5:12

2
Alice Cooper

Alice Cooper
"Killer"
(Warner Bros. / November 1971)

Killer

One of my all-time favorite flicks is the largely overlooked 1982 cult classic, *Ladies and Gentlemen, the Fabulous Stains*. Featuring acting performances from members of the Sex Pistols and the Clash, as well as a convincing early lead role performance from then-16-year-old actress, Diane Lane, it's a must-see for any (cool) rock aficionado of the era. In the film, there's a particular scene where Lou Corpse, a heavy metal has-been played famously by Tubes frontman Fee Waybill, sits in a sad dressing room prepping for a performance at a run-down Midwest VFW hall. Schooling aspiring teenage rocker Corinne Burns (Lane), the washed-up dinosaur (Corpse) confesses while applying Gene Simmons-style makeup, "There's nothing new, honey."

. .

At the height of the COVID scare, I found myself masked-up and jet setting across the country attending various concert performances by reigning pop superstar, Harry Styles. At one particular show in Portland, Oregon, I noticed two giddy teenage gals holding hands while parading around the arena. Sporting matchy-matchy kindergarten-style Japanese anime backpacks, they giggled and grinned from ear-to-ear, as if they'd stumbled upon something new. *Ooh, Sophie, look at us! We're GIRLS, holding hands — at the Harry Styles concert! We're like, SO shocking!*

Honestly, I found "Sophie" and her sunny Harry Styles concert sidekick, to be *far* from shocking. To me, *their* performance that night was kind of a yawner. Why am I personally so unfazed, even downright bored by the "new" cultural awareness of the 2020s? 'Cuz I was raised by the Alice Cooper group, back in the 1970s.

The album *Killer* was the cornerstone of my adolescent academic curriculum. As a result, today's "shocking" and "controversial" clickbait — sexuality, addictions, gender identities, political perspectives, Kylie, Kendall, Kourtney, Kim and Khloé — are totally tired topics. To quote that great American philosopher, Lou Corpse, "There's nothing new, honey."

> "I was 16 when I came across an old, beat up copy of *Killer* in the .99¢ bin at a record shop in my hometown. Although I had been listening to the album on Spotify for a few years at that point, it's completely different getting to experience the album on VINYL."
> —Bella Perron
> Plush
> June 2023

Times certainly were a-changin' in 1971. Even Peter Brady's voice was changing. Bras were burning, draft cards were burning, and kids got the right to vote. The "telephone was ringing," and the time was right for something truly spectacular. Something ugly, yet beautiful. Something honest and pure, purged from the gutters of Anytown, U.S.A. Something gloriously absurd.

With their collective thumb placed firmly on the pulse of then-current culture, the Alice Cooper group, seemingly by accident, sparked a fabulous social dumpster fire in early 1971 with the surprise platinum-selling breakout record *Love it to Death*. Bold, brazen, and shamelessly irreverent, the Vaudeville-inspired, drag show-style circus freaks dropped their second platinum studio set, *Killer*, later that year.

> "*Love it to Death*, our 3rd Alice Cooper group album, encapsulated all the elements that became the blueprint for our band's success with disenfranchised teens. It had controversy, censorship, grim dark theatrics, heavy rock and our teen alienation anthem and first mega hit, 'I'm Eighteen.'"
> —Neal Smith
> Alice Cooper
> March 2021

The album continues to be regarded by many qualified observers as the band's all-time strongest effort. And when my nail tech GAVE me her ORIGINAL pressing of *Killer* (on ravaged vinyl), I was over the moon, as all of my previous physical copies had vanished over the years.

Overseen by legendary producer, Bob Ezrin, the eight-song collection was a bona fide tour de force. The lead-off single, "Under My Wheels," launched the record with screeching, unabashed, brass-injected cock rock swagger — *The telephone is ringing*, indeed! Equally cocky, yet a smidge more subtle, the second single, "Be My Lover," owns one of the record's greatest lines: "She asked me why the singer's name was Alice. I said 'Listen, baby, you really wouldn't understand.'"

The tragedy of Alice Cooper was that the schtick that made the group iconic — snakes, guillotines, straitjackets, makeup, freaky fashions and paper panty album inserts masked the fact that they actually were master musicians and brilliant songwriters. The dynamic guitar-slinging duo of Glen Buxton and Michael Bruce has yet to be matched. As a lifelong frustrated drummer, I will confirm that during the glory days, super-rock star Neal Smith was America's Keith Moon — only better and cooler. And Dennis Dunaway is THE greatest *rock* bass player, ever. I'll stand behind all of these statements confidently. Need proof of Alice Cooper's uncompromised musical cred? Dig the eight-minute epic "Halo of Flies" and the seven-minute, record-closing title track.

While earnest rockers "You Drive Me Nervous" and "Yeah, Yeah, Yeah" endeared the group further to its enormous adoring youth audience, "Dead Babies" is a prime example of why the fellas also were despised universally by parents. However, for MY money, "Desperado" remains the record's crown jewel. Brimming with mystique and polished to perfection with soaring orchestration, a strong case can be made for "Desperado" being the DEFINITIVE Alice Cooper composition. And I don't deliver *that* endorsement casually either.

> "It's fun. It's weird. Creepy. Catchy.
> Like nothing I've ever heard in my life.
> That's why I love this album so dearly."
> —Bella Perron
> Plush
> June 2023

TIMELINE IS EVERYTHING! Alice Cooper wasn't birthed in a Live Nation boardroom. The group wasn't formulated by a bunch of social media branding experts, and the music wasn't honed by a team of digital songwriting craftsmen or organized by a slew of Spotify curators. *Killer* was created in *1971*. At the time, *Gunsmoke* was still one of the top-rated shows on TV, for Pete's sake! The Alice Cooper group happened organically — a bunch of high school buddies from Phoenix who endeavored to become the biggest rock band in the world. They took crazy chances, gambled big, worked hard, and succeeded HUGE — without the Internet.

In sum, Alice Cooper beat everyone to the punch. They boldly went where no band had gone before, tipping sacred cows and touching on topics considered taboo at the time. And they did it in six-inch pumps and lace-up bustiers. As a result of their impeccable, trailblazing body of work, ONE statement ALWAYS will ring true: "There's nothing new, honey."

Killer

Track List

SIDE ONE
1. Under My Wheels (Bruce, Dunaway, Ezrin) – 2:51
2. Be My Lover (Bruce) – 3:21
3. Halo of Flies (Cooper, Buxton, Bruce, Dunaway, Smith) – 8:22
4. Desperado (Cooper, Bruce) – 3:30

SIDE TWO
1. You Drive Me Nervous (Cooper, Bruce, Ezrin) – 2:28
2. Yeah, Yeah, Yeah (Cooper, Bruce) – 3:39
3. Dead Babies (Cooper, Buxton, Bruce, Dunaway, Smith) – 5:44
4. Killer (Bruce, Dunaway) – 6:57

3
The Beach Boys

The Beach Boys
"Endless Summer"
(Capitol / June 1974)

Endless Summer

Purists typically dismiss compilation releases as less-than-legit albums — and rightfully so. I mean, c'mon, once you own *Honky Château*, it's kinda tough to justify really *needing* Elton John's *Greatest Hits* — no matter how much you might love "Rocket Man." However, in the case of *Endless Summer*, that theory sorta flies out the window. Representing the biggest Beach Boys chart-busters during the band's golden '62-'65 Capitol Records run, the 20-song, two-record set makes a massive statement. The album's undeniable cohesiveness allows it to stand tall all on its own. And I flipped out back in 2020 when a buddy GAVE me his slightly-abused *original* 1974 vinyl copy.

∴

It was the soundtrack to my personal coming-of-age experience, discovering fast cars, bad girls, and rock and roll. But my teenage days didn't play out circa '65, they played out circa '77. Here's the deal — music isn't "timeless" because it continues speaking to the same aging audience in perpetuity. Music is "timeless" because it possesses the ability to speak to new audiences for generations. Hence, the Beach Boys' music has proven to be *truly* timeless.

In January 1977, I was just 14 years old, and it seemed that all of my peers were being allowed to attend rock concerts. Everyone that is, except me. I had to settle for second-hand accounts of amazing performances by legendary artists the following day in the junior high school cafeteria. So, I never got to see the real Alice Cooper group, the original Lynyrd Skynyrd lineup, Bonham, Bowie, Thunders, or Zappa.

After denying my impassioned plea to attend a KISS concert in December 1976, my ultra-conservative parents gave in finally and allowed me to experience my first (wholesome) live rock show the next month — the Beach Boys.

My parents' primary objection to me attending rock concerts was their expectation of people in the audience taking drugs freely and engaging in open sexual activities. I thought that was ridiculous. What did my parents know anyway? They were *over* 30, and by my accounts that made them *really* old and completely *un*-cool. But when I arrived at the concert that night with the three teenage loves of my life; Jackie, Sharyon, and Andrea, I was stupefied by my discovery of throngs of tie-dye-clad hippies scattered throughout the 10,000-seat civic center in Lakeland, Florida, all smoking dope and groping each other. *Holy cow! My parents were right!*

This was during the band's "Brian's Back" era, heralding the return of chief songwriter, producer, and visionary, Brian Wilson. I've often joked that there are *only* TWO kinds of people in the world; "John Lennon people" and "Brian Wilson people." I'm a "Brian Wilson people." I once heard a listener comment on a call-in radio show that Brian Wilson is the "Beethoven of pop music." I loved that one.

Back in the summer of 2013, I'd been on tour, traveling around the country promoting my faith-based book, *C'MON!* The final date on that tour brought me to a book signing event at a music store near my then-hometown of Melbourne, Florida, where I was scheduled to appear with fellow author and old-school surf guru, Balsa Bill Yerkes.

Bill had been an acknowledged kingpin in the bi-coastal American surf community since the '60s, when he met and became friends with the Beach Boys — particularly Brian Wilson. Bill had just released his impressive coffee table-style photo journal book, *THE BEACH BOYS ON TOUR 1966: Surfboards, Stratocasters and Striped Shirts*. It was kinda funny, but for whatever reason, Bill thought I was gonna be some sort of hair band disciple. As a result, he seemed surprised to learn that I actually was a "Brian Wilson people."

Truth be told, I was taken aback a bit when I met Bill, as he was a dead ringer for Brian — *a dead ringer, man!* The poor guy didn't stand a chance, as I pummeled him throughout the event with Beach Boys-related questions. To this day, Bill continues sharing a slew of insider insights with me.

> "We've all seen the reports where they say that the Beach Boys didn't play on their own records. Not true! In fact, on the first four albums, it was *all* Beach Boys and *no* Wrecking Crew. Brian started to add some studio musicians a little at a time, saxophones and then Hal Blaine on timbales. But that was Dennis on drums in *all* of the early hits / albums. The only album that was all Wrecking Crew was *Pet Sounds*."
> — *Balsa Bill Yerkes*
> Beach Boys historian
> July 2023

While making a Charleston, South Carolina appearance in 2021, I had the unexpected tremendous pleasure of discovering Cat Strickland — an absolutely *wonderful* young singer / guitarist who happened to be performing on the outdoor patio at Page's Okra Grill where my crew had popped in for Sunday brunch. In the spirit of full disclosure, I will confess openly that I fell hopelessly in love with Cat the moment I first laid eyes on her. Actually, she has that effect on everybody. When Cat went on break, she approached my table and pulled up a chair. We struck up an instant cozy conversation and became fast friends.

When I returned to Charleston in 2023, I went to see a couple of Cat's gigs, but this time, we also set up a special Monday morning besties "play date." After a stiff cup of "Joe" at her favorite local java joint, Cat took me to a sort of "heaven on earth" destination — the long-famed Monster Music & Movies. I don't know the exact specs, but the place looked to be about 6,000 square feet — packed from wall-to-wall, from floor-to-ceiling with new vinyl, used vinyl, CDs, DVDs, VHS tapes, miscellaneous related accessories, AND MORE! We perused the near-endless bins of records for what seemed like hours. During that beautiful, organic process, Cat picked up a new, factory-sealed LP copy of the Bauhaus EP, *The Bela Session*, while I scored a used LP copy of the first Go-Go's record, *Beauty and the Beat*.

What makes this little anecdote extra relevant to this chapter is that Monster Music & Movies also boasts a bounty of music related books. And in addition to our record acquisitions, I also snatched up a copy of *I Am Brian Wilson*, the 2016 autobiography from Brian Wilson. An engaging, bona fide pager turner, Wilson's honest and transparent-feeling accounts shed considerable light on the Beach Boys' story, as well as his personal relationships, his iconic songs, and his famed production work. For us "Brian Wilson people," it's a must-read.

The 1977 Beach Boys concert that I attended as a young teen was a sold-out event. And from the roar of the crowd and the unique "fragrance" permeating the arena, to the blasting music and colorful light show, the experience proved to be fantastic and memorable.

> "When I was a kid, my dad only bought two records;
> *Harry Belafonte's Greatest Hits* and *Endless Summer*.
> The Beach boys changed my life."
> —*Andrew Marcus*
> Singer, songwriter, musician, producer
> Knoxville, Tennessee
> January 2024

My mom used to sing Beach Boys songs around the house, back when those songs *and* I both were brand new. More than a decade later, in January 1977, *her* music became *my* music. To this day, *Endless Summer* transports me back to a magical time, recalling the sound of Jackie's corduroys whistling as she sashayed from science class, Sharyon's ever-intoxicating perfume, and Andrea's bedroom — don't be a pig, all we ever did was play records.

Endless Summer remains a gorgeous treasure trove. Honest music. Authentic music. American music. Timeless music. Consume it as you see fit. But, for my money, it's best when served on warm, crackly garage sale vinyl. The *only* drag about spinning it on vinyl is that the songs are so short, I often have to go back and flip the record before I even can get to the kitchen and crack a cold cola. Fun, fun, fun, indeed!

Endless Summer

Track List

SIDE ONE
1. Surfin' Safari (Wilson, Love) – 2:05
2. Surfer Girl (Wilson) – 2:15
3. Catch a Wave (Wilson, Love) – 2:15
4. The Warmth of the Sun (Wilson, Love) – 2:47
5. Surfin' U.S.A. (Wilson, Berry) – 2:27

SIDE TWO
1. Be True to Your School (Wilson, Love) – 2:05
2. Little Deuce Coupe (Wilson, Christian) – 1:50
3. In My Room (Wilson, Usher) – 2:11
4. Shut Down (Wilson, Christian) – 1:50
5. Fun, Fun, Fun (Wilson, Love) – 2:16

SIDE THREE
1. I Get Around (Wilson, Love) – 2:14
2. Girls on the Beach (Wilson) – 2:25
3. Wendy (Wilson, Love) – 2:20
4. Let Him Run Wild (Wilson, Love) – 2:21
5. Don't Worry Baby (Wilson, Christian) – 2:45

SIDE FOUR
1. California Girls (Wilson, Love) – 2:37
2. Girl Don't Tell Me (Wilson) – 2:17
3. Help Me, Rhonda (Wilson, Love) – 3:08
4. You're So Good to Me (Wilson, Love) – 2:14
5. All Summer Long (Wilson, Love) – 2:05

4
The Beatles

The Beatles
"Let It Be"
(Apple / May 1970)

Let It Be

This chapter captures the full spirit, heart, and soul of *Garage Sale Vinyl* — from the actual music and the specific format of this classic album to the conversations it still inspires to how this particular copy found me — on the cheap.

Fortunately, a good many current consumers *do* embrace the *true* essence of the modern-day vinyl experience. They understand that it *should* be a lifestyle — one that extends beyond just collecting records. But, *un*fortunately, in today's TikTok culture, there are far too many others who honestly believe that Discogs is a "record store" and that an authentic record shopping experience involves nothing more than a click on the keyboard and a trot to the mailbox.

Truth be told, these (primarily) younger aficionados are missing out on (almost) all of the fun. The beauty of the vinyl experience continues to be mostly about "connection" and "community" — engaging (face to face) with the chill ponytail guy who runs the used record concession at the hometown thrift mall, or the spikey-haired gal who owns the funky new music joint downtown, while also interacting with other like-minded (human) customers in the process. And if you're *extremely* diligent, and you're (physically) in the right place at the right time, you can often discover and score some pretty incredible records, without coughing up a kidney.

In that regard, I'm reminded of a local flea market excursion I made in 2023. While perusing one vendor's "junk" bin, I stumbled across *this* — an early vinyl pressing of *Let It Be*... FOR A BUCK!

"This price can't be right," I said to the snappy-looking, 17-year-old, rainbow-colored pigtail gal with big horn-rims and impressive tatts who was running the lil' retail operation that day. She assured me that the price WAS right, and in short order, she began sharing with me what an amazing record it is (as if I was new) and how much she loved the Beatles — especially Paul. Lickety-split, she pulled out and handed me *another* ONE-DOLLAR vinyl treasure — Paul McCartney & Wings *Band on the Run*. Two classics for two bucks, total. That's the beauty of the vinyl experience — "connection!"

Over the years I've had the good fortune of interviewing a menagerie of multi-media personalities. And somehow, the Beatles pop up frequently, even during non-music-related conversations. In November 2021, I conducted a phone interview with TV's reigning "Queen of Late Night," *Gutfeld!* co-host, Kat Timpf. Simply put, Timpf is a bona fide Beatles buff — a point proven during her 2021 on-air *Gutfeld!* dust-up with radio host, Buck Sexton. Of course, I had to ask her about it.

"I love Buck, that's the thing," Timpf recalled. "Nobody has to like the Beatles. I just don't like when people say, they're 'overrated.' To say they're 'overrated' — they changed music, forever. When a band changes music itself, then they're not overrated for being seen as an important part of music — whether you like them or not."

> "I absolutely love the Beatles. I have so many of their albums on vinyl. They were a huge part of my childhood, a huge part of my life."
> — Kat Timpf
> November 2021

During the fall of 2023, I found myself backstage at Orlando's Hard Rock Live, interviewing 25-year-old UK singer / songwriter, Lauran Hibberd. Known for crafting her own irresistibly catchy pop-rock music, Hibberd discussed the Beatles' legacy from a rather unique perspective.

> "In my later life, as I've kind of grown into music, I've gone back and discovered the Beatles kind of all over again. I'm a fan of music. I love to find whatever — new, old, anything. And I think anything's new if you find it for the first time."
> — Lauran Hibberd
> September 2023

One guy who I particularly love interviewing is Florida-based songwriter and session guitarist, Chuck Lazaras. Ever-faithful in engaging me in spirited music-related conversations, Chuck is known most notably for his work with various members of the iconic goth-rock combo, the Misfits.

> "Nothing in rock and roll is sacred. *Let It Be* comes close"
> — Chuck Lazaras
> November 2023

As for the album, aside from being their last official studio effort, *Let It Be* remains an important Beatles LP for other reasons. Contrary to what many "smart" writers had to say at the time it was released, the record has aged extremely well since first dropping more than half a century ago. It served as a vivid audio snapshot of the biggest band in the world — splintering and ultimately imploding. The oft-lo-fi production factor only added to some of the songs' individual mystique and the album's overall allure.

Five-plus decades later, the three singles; "Get Back," "The Long and Winding Road," and the title track remain as iconic as it gets. However, the soaring "Across the Universe," the funky "I've Got a Feeling," and the blues-injected "For You Blue" still speak to me just a smidge louder. And not for nothin', but "Two of Us" will always be one of my top two (or three) all-time Beatles faves.

This one was a tremendous score, indeed. But, I must confess that it wasn't exactly in the best condition. In fact, I have to play it wet. Yes, that IS a thing. But, HEY — it's a very early vinyl pressing of *Let It Be*, for goodness sake. And I got it… FOR A BUCK!

Let It Be

Track List

SIDE ONE
1. Two of Us (Lennon, McCartney) – 3:36
2. Dig a Pony (Lennon, McCartney) – 3:54
3. Across the Universe (Lennon, McCartney) – 3:48
4. I Me Mine (Harrison) – 2:26
5. Dig It (Lennon, McCartney, Harrison, Starkey) – 0:50
6. Let It Be (Lennon, McCartney) – 4:03
7. Maggie Mae (traditional) – 0:40

SIDE TWO
1. I've Got a Feeling (Lennon, McCartney) – 3:37
2. One After 909 (Lennon, McCartney) – 2:54
3. The Long and Winding Road (Lennon, McCartney) – 3:38
4. For You Blue (Harrison) – 2:32
5. Get Back (Lennon, McCartney) – 3:09

5
Tony Bennett

Tony Bennett
"Tony's Greatest Hits"
(Columbia / 1958)

Tony's Greatest Hits

As a kid, I'd grown up listening to Tony Bennett records. To this day, I actually keep an original 1958 mono pressing of *Tony's Greatest Hits* right next to my modest home office audio setup. Upon hearing the heartbreaking news of Bennett's passing in July 2023, I reached over just six feet, grabbed my prized LP, mugged for a selfie, and posted it promptly on my Instagram and Facebook pages. The simple caption read, "RIP Mr. Bennett. You'll ALWAYS be the greatest!" And I had to smile, as a sea of my "friends" and "followers" soon joined me in this online celebration of life, "Liking" and commenting on the little tribute. Then, I was reminded of the cozy story of how I first was introduced to Tony Bennett's timeless music, more than 50 years ago.

While growing up in the Midwest during the late 1960s and early '70s, I spent as much time hanging out at the Deskin residence as I did at my own house — Joe remains my lifetime bestie. Laney was that understanding "cool" mom in whom all of Joe's friends could confide. To say his dad, Howard, was "obsessed" with music would be to understate the man's passion. And Howard loved to blast his beloved jazz and big band records — loud. *Dude, can you dial it down, just a smidge?* In fact, when it came to music, Joe's dad was what the late American philosopher Rick James would have described as a "Super Freak."

With its multi-big-knob receiver, hi-fidelity turntable, quadraphonic reel-to-reel tape machine and MASSIVE speakers, Howard's stereo system was "state-of-the-art" in 1973. His comprehensive collection of hundreds (and hundreds) of pristine LPs included such contemporary chart-busting artists of the day as the Carpenters, John Denver and Barbra Streisand. It also included classics from the likes of the legendary Sarah Vaughan, the incomparable Nat "King" Cole and — the great Tony Bennett.

Howard's complete audio arsenal and LP collection all was housed in a sizeable closet unit located in the Deskin family room. Even Joe's young, naïve ragamuffin associates knew better than to even look or point in the direction of "the closet" — especially when it was open. *Keep on walking, kids. There's nothing to see here.*

Nearly a decade following Howard's passing in 2010, I found myself visiting the ol' hometown for a few days while on tour promoting my book, *Superstar*. One day, Joe and I drove over to his parents' new millennium condo. Upon walking into a back bedroom, Joe flung the closet door wide open. Angelic trumpets sounded instantly as I squinted from the bright light beaming down from Heaven. *Whoa!* There it was — Howard's complete famed record collection. "It's all yours," Joe announced, grinning from ear to ear.

I couldn't believe it. This was the single biggest, most stupefying blessing I'd received since that time Denise Kirschner agreed to go with me to the high school homecoming dance back in '78. But how on earth was I gonna transport 1,000 LPs from the "Show Me State" to the "Sunshine State?" I was flying home the next day with only one personal carry-on. Regretfully, I had to pass on Joe's very generous offer.

But like a champ, several months later, Joe showed up on my GF's driveway — in Florida, with the ass-end of his minivan nearly dragging the pavement, as he'd hauled the entire load of Howard's LPs cross-country. I was speechless. Among the seemingly endless array of records from Frank, Judy, Nat, Babs, Sarah and so many others, was a SLEW of Tony Bennett titles — including the aforementioned original 1958 mono pressing of *Tony's Greatest Hits*.

A knowledgeable and experienced industry professional, University of Miami Music Engineering graduate, Chris DeAngelis, also is recognized widely as one of the most talented, accomplished, and in-demand stage and studio bass players on the South Florida music scene. I've had the pleasure and privilege of interviewing DeAngelis a few times over the years. And he never fails to offer fascinating music-related insights.

During an August 2023 phoner, I chatted a bit with DeAngelis about Tony Bennett, his then-recent passing, and his legacy. Clearly, not only is DeAngelis an avid Tony Bennett fan, but he's also a massive admirer of classic crooners in general.

> "You need to live, love, and lose a bit before you can appreciate this kind of music, because at its core, it's adult music. The sound of Tony Bennett is a relaxed one. He takes his time and every word in the song counts. Plus, the man had class."
> —Chris DeAngelis
> August 2023

Overseen primarily by bandleader, composer and conductor, Percy Faith, *Tony's Greatest Hits* was packed with many of Bennett's most beautiful early hits and oozed the kind of gorgeous production you still can only experience from orchestral recordings of that era. Enhanced further by authentic cozy crackle, the record instantly became the crown jewel of my newly-acquired classic crooner collection.

Bennett's 1953 recording of "Stranger in Paradise" arguably remains the most popular version of the oft-covered standard. Recorded in April 1951, "Because of You" was Bennett's first major hit, reaching #1, where it remained for more than two months.

> "Most all of the classic crooners (e.g., Tony, Frank, Dean) were first generation Americans and the sons of Italian immigrants. And most of their contemporaries were all Italian American, as was my own father. Maybe somewhere deep inside me there's a touch of nostalgia for my parents built into my love for Tony Bennett. Or perhaps it's an emerging fondness for my Italian American heritage."
> —Chris DeAngelis
> August 2023

The first of the album's two songs written by Hank Williams, "Cold, Cold Heart" was recorded and released by Williams in 1951, not long before it became a #1 hit for Bennett. The second Williams song, "There'll Be No Teardrops Tonight" was a Williams hit in 1949, five years before Bennett's hit version.

Among the many other album highlights was the 1953 chart-topper, "Rags to Riches," along with the less successful "Young and Warm and Wonderful," as well as Bennett's non-charting debut single, the tango-driven "Boulevard of Broken Dreams."

> "Tony Bennett and his fellow crooners — their main musical influences weren't other *singers*, they were *horn players*. The phrasing of a wind instrument is different than that of the typical vocalist. Tony, Frank, and Dean sang long notes even on short words, and the tone of their voices was soft and mellow, like a tenor saxophone or a trombone. The crooners essentially changed the way people sing love songs."
> — Chris DeAngelis
> August 2023

Tony's Greatest Hits would be re-released in a semi-stereo format a few years later, in 1962. However, for my money, you just can't beat the splendor of the original 1958 mono mix.

I truly felt blessed as we unloaded those crates from Joe's minivan that day he rolled up at my GF's. These records were important to me. And I got 'em — ALL of 'em, for F-R-E-E-!

Thanks for the music and the memories, Howard. You'll always be a "Super Freak" in my book!

Tony's Greatest Hits

Track List

SIDE ONE
1. Stranger in Paradise (Forrest, Wright)
2. Cold, Cold Heart (Williams)
3. Because of You (Hammerstein, Wilkinson)
4. Rags to Riches (Ross, Adler)
5. Boulevard of Broken Dreams (Dubin, Warren)
6. Young and Warm and Wonderful (Zaret, Singer)

SIDE TWO
1. In the Middle of an Island (Acquaviva, Varnick)
2. Ca, C'Est L'Amour (Porter)
3. Just in Time (Green, Comden, Styne)
4. There'll Be No Teardrops Tonight (Williams)
5. Anywhere I Wander (Loesser)
6. Sing You Sinners (Coslow, Harling)

6
Blue Öyster Cult

Blue Öyster Cult
"Fire of Unknown Origin"
(Columbia / June 1981)

Fire of Unknown Origin

Not for nothing, but, I blame Blue Öyster Cult. Most of the frustrating and painful auditory issues I suffer from as an old man (I believe) are a direct result of the brutal punishment I endured from attending numerous BÖC concerts as a teenager. The unrelenting kick and snare assault at the hands (and feet) of drummer Albert Bouchard would pierce my skull for 75 minutes at a time — leaving me with (an estimated) 67% hearing loss. Also, the ungodly decibel level at which the keyboard work of Allen Lanier was unleashed over the band's mega-watt sound system ultimately would affect my equilibrium throughout this life, and possibly the next. And as I would learn (the hard way), choosing to purchase and consume pharmaceuticals from unlicensed physicians in the parking lot at any BÖC show never proves prudent.

The band's array of boogie-based, prog-inspired, oft-cowbell-driven arena anthems, including "Cities on Flame with Rock and Roll," "(Don't Fear) The Reaper" and "Godzilla" already had become FM radio staples. Toward the end of their first decade as a major label recording act, BÖC had dropped seven studio LPs, along with one single and a double live set. Although only two of those releases achieved gold status, the fellas had built a massive, loyal arena audience — back when bands could do that kinda thing. And their live shows had become legendary, particularly the following day at high school cafeteria lunch tables far and wide. But despite their notoriety as an enormously popular concert attraction, BÖC needed to really crush it with their eighth studio slab.

Produced by veteran studio ace, Martin Birch (Deep Purple, Rainbow, Whitesnake, Black Sabbath, Iron Maiden), *Fire of Unknown Origin* fought fiercely for the "Class of '81" valedictorian honors. Complicated, yet carefree, sophisticated yet sassy, she was the cheerleader captain who wasn't afraid to sneak out past curfew — the intriguing babe next door who everybody wanted to bang — even the guys.

In the world of big-time rock and roll, if the drum tracks suck, then your record sucks. But, if the drum tracks are world-class, well, then you're cookin' with gas. And in that regard, Albert Bouchard was more than worthy of nabbing

MVP accolades throughout this nine-track maneuver. His drum work and drum *sound* were consistently crisp and punchy as a muther — always on-point, never over-reaching and totally current (at least for the time). And when pinned to the fat and fluid blameless basslines of his brother, Joe Bouchard, a solid rhythm section foundation was laid on which a truly great record could be built. While the dynamic vocal / guitar duo of Eric Bloom and Donald "Buck Dharma" Roeser combined with keyboardist Allen Lanier was a formidable force, the Bouchard boys constructed the platform on which the trinity could be worshiped properly as "Golden Gods."

Free of dinosaur-like distinctions, the opening title track snapped and popped with appealing rock promise, while the leadoff single, "Burnin' for You," was an irresistible summertime sing-along — one of classic rock's most endearing and enduring fearless feel-goods.

Although several of the tunes were intended initially for the 1981 film, *Heavy Metal*, only Bloom's "Veteran of the Psychic Wars" actually made it into the movie soundtrack album. Hypnotic and cosmic, it remains one of the record's tallest standouts. While "Sole Survivor" would likely have felt at home on *Agents of Fortune*, "Heavy Metal: The Black and Silver" definitely would have made for a snug fit on *Smell the Glove*.

Galloping through the intersection of Prog Avenue and Pop Street, "Vengeance" also provided a noteworthy moment, and "After Dark" revealed how BÖC now shared as much common ground with Patty Smyth as with Patti Smith. Arguably the record's crown jewel, "Joan Crawford" stood out from the pack (at first glance) as a result of Lanier's magnificent, Juilliard-caliber piano intro. Conjuring images of apocalyptic doom following the imagined resurrection of the controversial late film star, Joan Crawford, the song was gloriously chaotic. The video would be one of the first banned by MTV for its sexually-explicit nature.

As with most of their LPs, stylistically, this one also was kinda all over the place. But that was back when bands could do that kinda thing too. And at the end of the day, it always worked famously. Four decades later, *Fire of Unknown Origin* remains an impressive and important entry in the impeccable BÖC catalog.

The record had popped back up on my radar after a bit of a playlist hiatus during the COVID thing, when I wrote a 40th anniversary album review for the arts and entertainment news site, V13.net. At the time, I'd never actually owned it on vinyl. But, since the V13 piece wasn't a specific vinyl-related feature, my longtime iTunes copy sufficed just fine. Then, I got hooked on *Fire of Unknown Origin* — all over again. And I *had* to finally get it in my vinyl collection. To my chagrin, it proved to be an impossible flea market find. Tragically, I had to ultimately break down and pony up BIG bucks — a whopping $12 to be exact at a proper local used record joint. And it was worth every penny.

Fire of Unknown Origin

Track List

SIDE ONE
1. Fire of Unknown Origin (Bloom, A. Bouchard, J. Bouchard, Roeser, Smith) – 4:09
2. Burnin' for You (Roeser, Meltzer) – 4:29
3. Veteran of the Psychic Wars (Bloom, Moorcock) – 4:48
4. Sole Survivor (Bloom, Myers, Trivers) – 4:04
5. Heavy Metal: The Black and Silver (Bloom, A. Bouchard, Pearlman) – 3:16

SIDE TWO
1. Vengeance (The Pact) (A. Bouchard, J. Bouchard) – 4:41
2. After Dark (Bloom, Myers, Trivers) – 4:25
3. Joan Crawford (A. Bouchard, Rigg, Roter) – 4:55
4. Don't Turn Your Back (A. Bouchard, Lanier, Roeser) – 4:07

7
The Cars

The Cars
"Candy-O"
(Elektra Records / June 1979)

Candy-O

There I was, "playing possum" in the backseat while my fellow teenage compadre, Jeff, was in the front seat, engaging in a pre-dawn carnal encounter with a 30-something cashier working the graveyard shift at a 24-hour convenience store. *Back in 15 minutes.*

"But there's a guy laying in the backseat," the cashier observed nervously.

"Ugh, trust me," Jeff fired back with certain frustration. "He's completely unconscious."

Looks like I'm gonna be up all night, yeah!

It was the sizzlin' summer of '79. Just 16 at the time, I'd embarked on a carefree, two-week getaway, flying from Orlando, Florida, to reconnect with childhood pals still living in my hometown of Springfield, Missouri, the "Queen City." Jeff owned a late model Oldsmobile, known reverently to our crew as, The Bomb. Jeff had just learned that the trade-in value of The Bomb was a mere $115. However, throw his kickass Jensen car stereo into the deal, and The Bomb was worth over $600.

Historically, it's been the birthright of teenagers far and wide to do stupid stuff, and our crew excelled in "Stupidity 101" successfully and shamelessly. *Hey, we got a bag of M-80s! Let's blow up some mailboxes!*

Our late-night missions typically involved disturbing and terrorizing all sleeping residents within earshot, while blasting Jeff's unapologetic car audio system, as The Bomb chugged along throughout the Queen City. The soundtrack to our summer exploits was magical and memorable: *Get the Knack*, *Van Halen II*, and *Cheap Trick at Budokan* to name just a few.

But our go-to playlist headliner was *Candy-O*, the just-released sophomore set from The Cars. As a result, *Candy-O* was the cassette playing during Jeff's aforementioned pre-dawn carnal encounter. Truth be told, much of my current 67% hearing loss can be attributed directly to *Candy-O* being cranked on Jeff's Jensen tri-axles at a stupid teenage volume night after night during my sizzlin' summer of '79 experience.

A quirky name, (only) 'til they MADE it cool, The Cars was one of the first bands associated with the budding "new wave" sound to roll onto my radar. As their self-titled 1978 debut started gaining traction on the radio, it also began racing up the charts. The band looked cool, and the songs were fresh and fun. By comparison, many of my longtime rock heroes suddenly sounded stale. *If I leave here tomorrow...*

Expectations for the second Cars album were high, and the band dodged the dreaded "sophomore jinx" famously and with gazelle-like swiftness. Overseen by legendary producer Roy Thomas Baker (Queen, Journey, Cheap Trick, Alice Cooper), *Candy-O* was (and is) sonically superb, and it checked all of the boxes with a fat-ass Sharpie. The songs were catchier than ever, the pin-up girl cover was a total tissue-tosser, and the band had become even cooler looking. Heck, in 1979, bassist Benjamin Orr personified "cool." *Step aside, "Space Ace" — there's a new sheriff in town!*

Opening with the urgent and infectious lead-off single, "Let's Go," the Ric Ocasek-penned, 11-song collection felt like an instant pop to the privates. Equally irresistible standouts "Since I Held You" and "It's All I Can Do" proved David Robinson to be the perfect drummer for the perfect songs on a perfect album. The triple-threat combo of "Double Life" and "Shoo Be Doo," along with the title track was a heart-racing banger, to be sure. To this day, the super-sweet suite gives me palpitations, and it remains a qualified infomercial for keyboardist Greg Hawkes and lead guitarist Elliot Easton's ball-busting brutality.

> "'Shoo Be Doo' into the title track is the greatest four minutes and fourteen seconds ever recorded."
> —Freezerp
> Ice Cream Icon
> Boulder, Colorado
> January 2024

Candy-O snapped and popped. It beeped and buzzed. The only thing rivaling the record's massive musical performance was Ocasek's masterful word-crafting, pointing to pictures of "holiday romance," "cadmium cars," and those "ruby rings."

I've bought *Candy-O* numerous times since its initial 1979 release: my original LP copy, then on cassette, then on CD. In recent years, I've scored additional used vinyl copies at various thrift stores and flea markets. Not too long ago, the

GF and I spotted a ravaged vinyl copy at a neighborhood garage sale for just .25¢. The darn thing looked SO sad — like it actually had been pee'd on. For a quarter, I had to buy it. Oddly, it plays great!

> "Elliot Easton is the greatest rock guitarist, ever. And I'll stand by that. He *always* delivered on *every* track."
> —Bryan Dumas
> Co-author, *Garage Sale Vinyl*
> January 2024

Today, 45 years following that sizzlin' summer of '79, *Candy-O* is as tasty (and vital) as ever. In fact, my writing partner, Bryan (Dingus), called me up in 2023 when he picked up a used copy at a joint in Arkansas. Something of an audio geek, Dingus cleaned the record thoroughly, and gave it the ol' studio-quality headphone test. He was flabbergasted by how fresh the songs (still) felt and by how, "such an old album could sound so new."

Candy-O

Track List
(All songs written by Ric Ocasek)

SIDE ONE
1. Let's Go – 3:32
2. Since I Held You – 3:16
3. It's All I Can Do – 3:46
4. Double Life – 4:11
5. Shoo Be Doo – 1:41
6. Candy-O – 2:37

SIDE TWO
1. Night Spots – 3:14
2. You Can't Hold On Too Long – 2:47
3. Lust for Kicks – 3:52
4. Got a Lot on My Head – 2:59
5. Dangerous Type – 4:30

8
Cheap Trick

Cheap Trick
"Heaven Tonight"
(Epic / April 1978)

Heaven Tonight

Ugh! It was pathetic. As a kid, I was hopelessly un-cool. Even as a teen, I remained tragically un-hip. Nearly 50 years later, not much had changed. When it came to the rock idols of my youth, I took their song titles literally. Despite obvious lyrics to the contrary, for the longest time, I really thought that the KISS tune "Deuce" merely was a turbo-charged tennis reference and the Ted Nugent classic "Cat Scratch Fever" simply was a personal tale of tangling with an unfriendly feline.

However, later in life, I began running with more sophisticated associates who happily brought me up to speed in the ways of the world. As a 20-something, I rolled with an enlightened fella named Hank, who ran his own independent pharmaceutical sales and distribution business. Hank shared my passion for catchy, crunchy, guitar-driven pop-rock. He also possessed an uncanny gift for interpreting song lyrics.

One day, while hanging out at my apartment during the late '80s, Hank revealed to me how *every* Cheap Trick song actually was about drugs. When I challenged his assertion, Hank fired back, "C'mon, man! The Dream Police? Are you stupid? What do you think *that's* about?" Then, he shoved a bag of cocaine in my face and encouraged me to, "Wake the fuck up."

Through my numerous vintage vinyl hunting expeditions, I've learned that I don't always have to go to *other* people's garages to find treasures. In 2019, I'd been assigned the task of packing up the contents of our family's longtime Florida beach house, as we were prepping to put it on the market. During this rather arduous process, I found myself rummaging through a few old boxes that had been stored in the garage — since back when I was growing up there. And it was then that I rediscovered a ravaged copy of *Heaven Tonight*. It must have been my brother's copy, 'cuz there's no way I would have discarded any of my old records in a box of garage junk, especially without a cover, and definitely NOT one of my prized Cheap Trick LPs.

Stumbling across that LP gave me pause. And I thought way back to that afternoon in my apartment. What if Hank was right? What if *all* of my beloved Cheap Trick songs *were* about drugs? I still didn't have a turntable at the time, so, I deferred to my then-current CD copy and took a deep dive into *Heaven Tonight* in search of any hidden lyrical narcotics.

• •

Considered by many purists to be the definitive Cheap Trick collection, their third studio release, *Heaven Tonight*, combined the darker punk urgency of their debut LP, *Cheap Trick*, with the sunnier pop sensibility of their sophomore set, *In Color*.

When the record dropped in the spring of 1978, the Rockford-based combo wasn't yet generating massive American radio airplay. However, my local Orlando FM station, WDIZ, did play a couple of early Cheap Trick tracks, a few times. But, this dribble of radio exposure combined with modest magazine coverage was sufficient to get my attention. Hence, I was a Cheap Trick super-fanboy *before* their imminent global takeover. In fact, I already could recite the Cheap Trick gospel, chapter and verse by the time I saw them live, just two weeks following the release of their platinum-selling breakout album, *At Budokan*, in February 1979. Truth be told, despite the enormous popularity of headliners, Aerosmith and Ted Nugent, the primary reason I attended Orlando's "Rock Super Bowl" stadium concert was to see the "new" band that was scheduled to go on at 5pm. Although I only was 16 at the time, it remains one of my most memorable concert experiences.

Heaven Tonight hooked ya straight away with one of guitarist and chief songwriter Rick Nielsen's two most recognizable tunes, "Surrender." Owning an iconic, sing-along chorus, this coming-of-age anthem will probably never die. It's still as fresh and relevant today as ever before. From a distance, "On Top of the World" also seemed like a teen spirit fist-pumper — "You're on top of the world and you can't get any higher." But it soon became clear that it had more to do with hopelessness than hopefulness. Honest and pure pop-punk, before that even was a thing. Before it became a recognized hot topic.

A songwriting collaboration between Neilsen, frontman Robin Zander and bassist Tom Petersson, "High Roller" remains one of my personal favorites, along with the suicidal "Auf Wiedersehen."

A cynical post-relationship earworm, "Takin' Me Back" owned one of my favorite Neilsen lines; "You thought that you could make a fool of me. Don't be so sure that the fool was me," while "On the Radio" recalled a time of innocence, when many of us who were raised during the '60s and '70s lived for radio. As a kid, that "Mister on the radio" really was "my best friend."

As for the title track, well, I might have to give that one to ol' Hank. The haunting, Beatles-tinged tune IS a drug song — and a darn dark one at that. Zander's convincing eerie delivery sounds as if he's only seconds away from choking to death on his own vomit. You can (almost) hear the syringe dangling from his arm and lines of blow being chopped out on the control room mixing console. However, through the thick layers of darkness, an anti-drug sentiment seeps through — at least it helped scare me straight(er) when I was 16.

Neilsen's "Stiff Competition" was a high-octane keeper that packed Toledo-sized riffs, powerhouse vocals, and plenty of poetic brashness; "I screw you, you screw me, they screw us, here we go again!" Another noteworthy stinger, "How Are You?" was a sluttier twin to "I Want You to Want Me," that brought the record to a snappy conclusion.

Over the years I've interviewed a menagerie of famed rock artists. And along with the Beatles, Cheap Trick comes up most frequently as their biggest musical influence — from the band as a unit to the individual members to their unmatched music catalog, particularly *Heaven Tonight*.

> "Cheap Trick are my 'Beatles.'
> *Heaven Tonight* changed my life."
> — C.C. DeVille
> Poison
> June 2006

> "I'm so happy that Cheap Trick is in the world.
> I'm happy that Bun E. Carlos is in the world."
> — Rikki Rockett
> Poison
> September 2003

In sum, the original question stands — was Hank right? Are all of Cheap Trick's songs actually about drugs? *Hmm, doubtful.* While I still don't know exactly what they all really mean, I do know one thing — they still sound great, especially on vinyl. And BTW, although the aforementioned copy in my garage was barely playable, I did score a very playable used vinyl copy of *Heaven Tonight* at a local thrift joint in 2023 for $10. And I was on top of the world!

Heaven Tonight

Track List

SIDE ONE
1. Surrender (Nielsen) – 4:16
2. On Top of the World (Nielsen) – 4:01
3. California Man (Wood) – 3:44
4. High Roller (Nielsen, Petersson, Zander) – 3:58
5. Auf Wiedersehen (Nielsen, Petersson) – 3:42

SIDE TWO
1. Takin' Me Back (Nielsen) – 4:52
2. On the Radio (Nielsen) – 4:33
3. Heaven Tonight (Nielsen, Petersson) – 5:25
4. Stiff Competition (Nielsen) – 3:40
5. How Are You? (Nielsen, Petersson) – 4:21

9
Chicago

Chicago
"Chicago X"
(Columbia / June 1976)

Chicago X

The name is legendary. The logo is iconic. And the tunes — *truly* timeless — even after all these years. Despite reported initial label pressure to ditch the horns, Chicago wasn't the only rock band doing brass during the mid and late-'60s. They just did it better than most. Living without artistic borders, the boys from Illinois seemingly could pull off anything. They could hang with the heaviest rockers and swing with the elite jazzers. They stunk from the funk while oozing classical credibility. Their down-home 1974 ABC TV special, *Meanwhile Back at the Ranch*, suggested the possibly of Chicago even owning a smidge of country appeal.

Arguably the biggest act on the planet by the mid '70s, Chicago was soaring — racking up an impressive string of five consecutive #1's on the *Billboard* Top 200 album chart along with a near-endless slew of Top 10 singles.

I was a goofy-looking, four-eyed 13-year-old when the band's eighth studio set, *Chicago X*, first arrived at my neighborhood Kmart store during the summer of '76. Resembling a partially unwrapped chocolate bar, the eye-catching album cover image could easily have been a legit entry in Series 17 of my massive Wacky Packages trading card collection. Being a bona fide R&B freak, I noticed how the album sounded particularly funky and gritty. As a result, *Chicago X* spoke to me more loudly than the band's previous LPs that my then-16-year-old sister had brought home.

Overseen by celebrated producer James William Guercio at his famed (and now defunct) Colorado Caribou Ranch studio, *Chicago X* was a full-fledged group effort, in which all cylinders were firing fully. Boasting superb songs and brimming with passionate performances, the 11-track collection hosted highlights galore.

Guitarist Terry Kath got down and dirty posthaste on the record-opening "Once or Twice." The semi-dysfunctional love song dripped with Kath's signature style stankiness. His soulful, unassuming lead vocal was a perfect partner for the mighty Chicago horn section — particularly when propped next to the sexy sax solo of Walt Parazaider.

Composer / trombonist James Pankow dropped his vocal debut on "You Are on My Mind" — a smooth groovin', jazzy number that remains one of my all-time Chicago favorites. Another Pankow-penned goodie, "Skin Tight," featured a simply super lead vocal from bassist Peter Cetera. The R&B-fueled romp made for one of the record's funkiest.

The stylistic oddball of the batch, Cetera's romantic ballad, "If You Leave Me Now," became the band's first-ever #1 single. Guercio's engaging acoustic guitar work combined with Cetera's charming lead vocal was pure magic. Kudos to Jimmie Haskell for his lush string arrangements and French horn contribution.

Trumpeter Lee Loughnane stepped up to the vocal mic on "Together Again." Honest and pure, Loughnane's lead vocal owned a quality similar to Kath's. In fact, in later years, following Kath's tragic, untimely death in 1978, Loughnane would recreate the beloved guitarist's "Colour My World" vocals in concert. A straight-up rocker, it was secure enough to get cosmic, yet, sensitive enough to embrace Parazaider's fabulous flute work.

Keyboardist Robert Lamm's, "Another Rainy Day in New York City" was the first of the album's two singles to infiltrate Casey's Countdown. Embracing a world vibe, it featured Cetera on lead vocals, with steel drum performances from Othello Molineaux and Leroy Williams — a happy-sounding song, for sure, or at least as happy as a song can sound that's about spending a rainy day in an over-priced hotel. Lamm's other writing contribution, "Scrapbook," was so fun and funky, it could likely have appeared on an Ohio Players album.

A simple acoustic song reflecting on the pursuit and reality of love, Kath's "Hope for Love" closed the record in a warm and bluesy fashion — arguably one of his most heartfelt works.

I've said it before, but it's a point worth repeating — if your drum tracks suck, then your record sucks. Conversely, if your drum tracks are spectacular, your record has the foundation from which to launch into the stratosphere. Hence, piles of praise should be poured upon the record's dynamic duo of co-founding drummer Danny Seraphine and percussionist Laudir de Oliveira. While nabbing MVP honors is tough on such an all-star team, Seraphine and de Oliveira each popped a nut in that endeavor. Their magnificent performances throughout *Chicago X* made the songs sizzle and sing from start to finish.

For music lovers who are fortunate to be old enough to have lived through the organic tie-dyed '60s and the shag-covered '70s, Chicago was one of those bands whose music touched many of us in beautiful, uniquely personal ways.

CHICAGO 49

Despite all of the more convenient music format options available in today's super-sophisticated iUniverse, the vinyl format remains the most authentic. Pristine-sounding digital just can't compare to human-feeling analog — especially in this case.

I heisted my first vinyl copy of *Chicago X* from my sister's collection decades ago while she was away at college. Where that copy is now, I have no clue. More recently, I discovered a surprise second vinyl copy stashed in a musty box in my own garage. Although I do also own an iTunes version, to this day, that crackly LP is my go-to source — and I "go to" it quite frequently.

In sum, after nearly 50 years, *Chicago X* continues to taste as sweet as a chocolate bar. Just watch out for that guy with the jar of peanut butter!

Chicago X

Track List

SIDE ONE
1. Once or Twice (Kath) – 3:01
2. You Are on My Mind (Pankow) – 3:24
3. Skin Tight (Pankow) – 3:20
4. If You Leave Me Now (Cetera) – 3:58
5. Together Again (Loughnane) – 3:53
6. Another Rainy Day in New York City (Lamm) – 3:03

SIDE TWO
1. Mama Mama (Cetera) – 3:31
2. Scrapbook (Lamm) – 3:28
3. Gently I'll Wake You (Lamm) – 3:36
4. You Get it Up (Lamm) – 3:34
5. Hope for Love (Kath) – 3:04

10
Cinderella

Cinderella
"Heartbreak Station"
(Mercury Records / November 1990)

Heartbreak Station

For their more fervent followers, experiencing the musical evolution of Cinderella felt like a bona fide thrill ride. *You best buckle-up, back there! This baby's turbo-charged!*

Their piston-popping 1986 debut, *Night Songs*, ran circles around the fiercest arena rock competitors of the day. The 1988 follow-up, *Long Cold Winter*, hung a hard left — leading the band in a decidedly more bluesy direction. Given the enormous momentum generated by those first two platinum-selling LPs, the track now was prepped for Cinderella to throttle-up fully with their highly-anticipated third record, *Heartbreak Station*.

A joint production venture between John Jansen (Britny Fox, Faster Pussycat) and the band's founding frontman, multi instrumentalist and chief songwriter, Tom Keifer, *Heartbreak Station* further distinguished the Philly-birthed brigade from the day's pack of less genuine poster boys.

> "I love the Cinderella guys. Onstage they're such a great rock band."
> —Bret Michaels
> Poison
> March 2002

Residing stylistically somewhere near the intersection of Jagger Avenue and Janis Boulevard, *Heartbreak Station* oozed true blue rock and roll swagger and dripped with soulful authenticity. Featuring an array of celebrated session players, including acclaimed percussionist, Bashiri Johnson, and the famed Memphis Horns, the record's street cred was amped-up further by contributions from legendary Uriah Heep organist, Ken Hensley, and string arrangements courtesy of Led Zeppelin bassist, John Paul Jones.

Heartbreak Station hit the *Billboard* Top 20 in short order, and it soon became Cinderella's third consecutive million-seller. But what made the record so successful, and what continues to endear the 11-track collection to so many, was (and still is), the honesty and purity of the songs. Tom Keifer was on his "A" game, and as a result, *Heartbreak Station* was a tour de force.

> "*Heartbreak Station* reminds me of being in high school, burning CDs for girls who I never had a chance with."
> —Freezerp
> Ice Cream Icon
> Boulder, Colorado
> January 2024

Bursting with blues-inspired brashness, "The More Things Change" was a massive opener. A songwriting effort between Keifer and bassist, Eric Brittingham, the funk-fueled "Love's Got Me Doin' Time" was a slave to the groove, while the gospel-tinged "Shelter Me" rode onto the Top 40 with a Buick-sized hook.

A beautifully orchestrated acoustic heart-tugger, the soaring title track remains a career-defining epic. Drummer, Fred Coury, packed plenty of punch and BÖC-style cowbell on both "Sick for the Cure" and "Make Your Own Way"— guitar-driven bruisers, punished to perfection by Jeff LaBar. A countrified coming of age classic, "One for Rock and Roll" harvested layers of lap steel and mandolin — making for a legit "purple sage" moment.

> "Glenn Frey and Don Henley didn't discover alt country. Tom Keifer did."
> —Andrew Marcus
> Singer, songwriter, musician, producer
> Knoxville, Tennessee
> January 2024

Possessing Bad Company-caliber guts, "Electric Love" ranked as another satisfying stand-out, while "Love Gone Bad" was a "long cold" keeper. Delicate and transparent, "Winds of Change" offered heartfelt introspection, and burned as the record's brightest white hot sparkler. But, "that's the way" Keifer rolls.

In the spirit of full disclosure, I will confess openly that Cinderella is my all-time favorite rock band, and that *Heartbreak Station* is my all-time favorite Cinderella album. So, when I got the opportunity to do a phone interview with Tom Keifer prior to the band's 2002 summer tour, I was stoked, to say the least. And of course, among the many topics we touched on was, *Heartbreak Station*.

Communication with Cinderella's organization had proved challenging. Numerous messages left with the band's handlers went unanswered and I was getting nowhere fast. Then, just two days before my deadline, the call finally came through. An interview with Keifer was *confirmed* for the following day at 4PM. Unfortunately, the next day came and went with NO call from Keifer. I'd learned early in my writing career that when it comes to interviewing rock stars, Monday usually means Tuesday, 4PM means 6PM and so on. This time, however, I was getting stressed because my deadline now was only 24 hours away. And I *really* needed to get this story.

I was sleeping-in late on the morning of my deadline after having been out 'til the wee hours DJ-ing at a club the night before. Suddenly, the phone rang. I couldn't imagine who on earth would be so rude as to disturb me at the crack of noon on a Saturday. As I fumbled for the phone, I glanced down at the Caller ID and to my surprise (and relief), Tom Keifer was on the line.

> "Rock and roll is like primal instincts. It appeals to everybody."
> — Tom Keifer
> March 2002

For more than an hour, we discussed various phases of Keifer's incredible career, going all the way back to his teenage years when he made what was to be a life-changing discovery — rock and roll.

"What *is* this music? This is just amazing," Keifer said to himself upon seeing his first live rock band performing at a school dance. "I listened to everything growing up," he continued. "I grew up listening to all of the American rock and roll and all of the music that influenced it — from blues to country to gospel."

While discussing his own record releases over the years, Keifer chuckled in agreement when I told him that *Heartbreak Station* was the best of his career.

"There was a magic going on when we recorded that record," Keifer recalled. "It's my favorite of the ones we've made. We really had a good time making that record."

Plagued by throat problems while in the studio, Keifer described Cinderella's fourth album, *Still Climbing*, as a "torturous" album to make. However, he considers "Bad Attitude Shuffle" and "Through the Rain" to be a couple of their all-time best songs.

Of course, at some point, I had to ask him about the short-lived, yet lethal Seattle grunge movement of the '90s that exterminated the entire good-time arena rock scene, seemingly overnight.

> "I loved Nirvana. I thought they
> were a great rock and roll band."
> — *Tom Keifer*
> March 2002

"What happened in the '90s was not as much of a musical change as it was a fashion change," Keifer said. "A lot of people listen to music with their eyes. Soundgarden and Nirvana — it's loud guitars cranked up through Marshalls with screaming vocals. It all sounded like rock and roll to me. I never got what the difference really was other than the look."

> "There is no doubt that people still want to
> be served rock and roll. It just hasn't
> been on the menu for the last ten years."
> — *Tom Keifer*
> March 2002

I found Keifer's easy-going openness to be quite refreshing and he proved to be as engaging throughout our conversion as he'd appeared to be over the years performing onstage in front of thousands of fans. I appreciated his time, and the experience remains one of my most cherished writing ops.

At 43, an age when too many people are giving up on their dreams and "settling" in life, I got a "dream" gig to go on tour working as a personal assistant for the iconic rock band, Poison. Cinderella also was on the tour. As a result, I saw Cinderella perform live nearly 50 times during that fast-paced, three-month trek.

Simply put, the summer of 2006 was completely surreal. I traveled and lived on the road alongside my favorite band, which exceeds the standard definition of "cool." And I'll be eternally grateful to Poison bassist, Bobby Dall, for giving me that very unique opportunity.

Despite the connection that I thought we'd made during our one-on-one phone conversation in 2002, I found Tom Keifer to be a bit intimidating during our face-to-face excursion in 2006. In fact, we rarely even made eye contact during the tour. *'Sup, dude?* And I never brought up the interview. However, I did get a kick out hearing him in the next door dressing room, almost nightly, doing vocal warm-ups to classic tunes by Rod Stewart and Janis Joplin.

Truth be told, the touring experience ain't quite as cool as most "civilians" might think. But the Cinderella guys always were cool to me — especially lead guitarist, Jeff LaBar. Heck, most of the time, I wished that I'd been traveling on *their* bus, working in *their* world. And I was heartbroken to learn of LaBar's tragic, untimely death in 2021, at age 58.

Since 2013, Tom Keifer has been forging ahead, making vital new music as a solo artist, while decades later, the too-concise Cinderella catalog still sounds fresh. In the span of just four records, the band created an incredible body of work that showcased impeccable songwriting and musicianship that's far more reflective of the old-school classic rock era than the aerosol-sprayed days with which they're too often associated. And *Heartbreak Station* serves as a timeless testament to their true integrity.

When *Heartbreak Station* first arrived in late 1990, LPs merely were a hazy memory from my then-distant past. *Ugh, records! They're like, SO old fashioned!* And I'd only ever owned it on CD. In fact, I wasn't even aware that it ever had been pressed on vinyl until 2021, when I came across a pristine surprise copy at a hometown retro shop. I was so taken aback that I actually plunked down a whopping $12 for the must-have slice of wax.

Heartbreak Station

Track List

SIDE ONE
1. The More Things Change (Keifer) – 4:21
2. Love's Got Me Doin' Time (Keifer, Brittingham) – 5:20
3. Shelter Me (Keifer) – 4:50
4. Heartbreak Station (Keifer) – 4:27
5. Sick for the Cure (Keifer) – 3:39
6. One for Rock and Roll (Keifer) – 4:28

SIDE TWO
1. Dead Man's Road (Keifer) – 6:38
2. Make Your Own Way (Keifer) – 4:17
3. Electric Love (Keifer) – 524
4. Love Gone Bad (Keifer) – 4:23
5. Winds of Change (Keifer) – 5:35

11
Crosby, Stills, Nash & Young

Crosby, Stills, Nash & Young
"Déjà Vu"
(Atlantic / March 1970)

Déjà Vu

The guy was pretty persistent — downright pushy, actually. Having developed a rep as something of a go-to vinyl guru, by 2017, I was getting hit up by folks far and wide, hoping to unload their suddenly seemingly valuable old LP collections. Intrigued by the promise of pure gold, I finally arrived at the guy's Melbourne, Florida home to look at his records. I was shocked (and disappointed) to discover the condition of his box-o-vinyl.

"WTF, dude? This looks like it was sitting in a flood for a month," I commented, posthaste. "Uh, kinda," he replied, grappling with the reality that I wasn't gonna be a pushover. "Just gimme whatever," he conceded quickly. So, I offered him the (very generous) sum of $10 for all 20 LPs. He took it in a heartbeat. For non-mathematicians, that breaks down to .50¢ per record. Among the 20 titles was a factory-sealed copy of KISS *Animalized*, a beat-to-shit copy of Rush *2112*, and a dodgy-looking copy of Crosby, Stills, Nash & Young *Déjà Vu*. The *Déjà Vu* album cover was so waterlogged, I later would *have* to contain it in one of those clear plastic LP sleeves. The vinyl itself was in fairly decent condition — only a slight, cozy crackle. But, like I said, I scored it for only .50¢

• •

Nothing makes me giggle more gleefully than revelations of pontificating pop stars squabbling amongst themselves. *Hey, man! That solo sucked, man!* And that may well describe the scene during the production of the sophomore set from CSN (and sometimes) Y. In fact, it's been reported that the record was less of a self-produced supergroup collaboration, and more of a "four-way street" collision — a patchwork-type mission involving individual solo efforts, glossed over to give a kumbaya vibe. *Hey, fellas! Crosby made S'mores!*

But, at the end of the day, who really cares about intra-band discord and behind-the-scenes struggles? The result was an epic 10-track trove, brimming with timeless treasure. For goodness sake, it's essentially a "greatest hits" album. Even many of the non-singles have become well-known and revered by even casual music consumers.

The iconic acoustic strumming pinned to those tight signature-style CSN&Y harmonies made the Stephen Stills-penned "Carry On" a superb opener. Driven by the pedal steel work of Grateful Dead guitarist Jerry Garcia, the roots-fueled Graham Nash number "Teach Your Children" wrote the definitive country-rock playbook that will be around long after Cher isn't. Conversely, the introspective David Crosby tune "Almost Cut My Hair" still picks you up at the student union center and drops you off at the nearby drug den, every time. Honest and pure, the Neil Young writing contribution "Helpless" provided a lonesome yin to the gregarious yang of the electrified remake of the Joni Mitchell classic, "Woodstock."

Featuring harmonica work from Lovin' Spoonful patriarch John Sebastian, the Legion-like title track was one of the record's shiniest non-single highlights, while the delicate, friendly-feeling "Our House" was (is) a bona fide pop masterpiece. The record-closing "Everybody I Love You" wrapped it all up nicely in a high-octane "Freedom Rock"-caliber style.

In sum, *Déjà Vu* zinged to initial gold status in a jiffy. It reached the top slot on the *Billboard* album chart and crashed Casey's Countdown with three singles. It has since gone on to rack up sales of nearly eight million units and remains a mighty classic rock staple.

Déjà Vu

Track List

SIDE ONE
01. Carry On (Stills) – 4:25
02. Teach Your Children (Nash) – 2:53
03. Almost Cut My Hair (Crosby) – 4:25
04. Helpless (Young) – 3:30
05. Woodstock (Mitchell) – 3:52

SIDE TWO
01. Déjà Vu (Crosby) – 4:10
02. Our House (Nash) – 2:59
03. 4 + 20 (Stills) – 1:55
04. Country Girl (Young) – 5:05
05. Everybody I Love You (Stills, Young) – 2:20

12
Cherie Currie

Cherie Currie
"Beauty's Only Skin Deep"
(Mercury / 1978)

Beauty's Only Skin Deep

What a trip, man! Flashback — 1975. An unsuspecting "roxy roller" is hand-picked from a ripe crop of fresh-faced young'uns, straight out of LA's teen club scene. The "harvester?" — notorious creepy producer guy, Kim Fowley. Lickety-split, she finds herself auditioning for the frontchick gig in a new, up-and-coming all-girl rock project. She passes the audition and joins the band. Along with the other four members of the newly-minted "Fem Five," she tours the world for a couple of years. In the process, the teenage rock siren fuels international frustration among male fans. Then, at the band's white-hot apex, she bails.

Still on the hook with Mercury Records for one more album, Cherie Currie recorded and dropped her first post-Runaways solo set, *Beauty's Only Skin Deep*, in 1978. While Kim Fowley nabbed the producer's glory (and likely the points), credited co-producer, David Carr, reportedly was the guy who actually occupied the studio captain's seat for the ten-track release.

As a crazed adolescent rock dude, I was a somewhat faithful Runaways follower. Then, one night, I went to see *Foxes*, the 1980 coming-of-age feature film starring Jodie Foster, with Cherie making her big screen debut as conflicted high school "fox" Annie Mallick. *Teenage dopers — what a waste.* Cherie thwacked me with her performance in that flick. She's owned me ever since. Don't judge. If you ever see the grocery store scene from *Foxes*, you'll be crashing into canned soup displays too.

My immediate mission was to snatch up a copy of *Beauty's Only Skin Deep*, pronto. But the record wasn't available in America — presenting a particular pickle for a teenage drooler during the pre-Internet era. As a result, the record proved to be something of a "tease" — playing hard-to-get with me for decades. However, there *had* been a couple of close calls.

In the late '80s, a former military brat buddy of mine revealed how he'd scored the record while his dad was stationed overseas back in 1980. Giving into my pathetic pleading, he finally let me borrow and tape his prized LP. It wasn't the ideal fix, but during those prehistoric days, it was the best I could do. I punished that poor TDK SA90 cassette throughout the steamy summer of '88, as it rarely came out of my Sony Walkman. *Fast forward. Rewind. Play. Repeat.* In the booming new millennium iGadget era, I bought the record off iTunes. It was a more satisfying fix, yet my "physical needs" still weren't being fully met.

Ugh! What traditional-type modern-day retail outs are charging for used records can be absurd, and obscene. So, I have a really tough time playing the current vinyl game. I mean, c'mon — $50 for a brutally abused LP, simply because some super-geeker website says that's what it's worth? No thanks! Hence, I remain diligent in my garage sale, thrift store, and flea market vinyl hunting excursions.

Occasionally, though, I will cave.

In 2023, my savvy local record dealer spotted a Near-Mint LP copy of *Beauty's Only Skin Deep* on her in-store Google machine. It would have to be shipped from some exotic, faraway land overseas AND it would cost me $60, but after chasing the record domestically (and for a realistic price) for nearly 45 years, I reasoned that I'd now run out of options. Once in a while, one must splurge.

Knock! Knock!

"Who's there?"

"It's the Amazon guy. And you've got a package!"

"Thanks, dude — marry me!"

Unlike many forward-thinking albums produced during that time, *Beauty's Only Skin Deep* sounds exactly like it was recorded in 1978 — like a vivid Polaroid or a beautiful, self-contained audio time capsule. Real guitars — yep. Authentic drums — yep. Auto-tuned, digitized vocals — NOPE! Dealing with something of an identity crisis, the LP pivoted from rock to pop, from pop to rock, with a splash of new-wave desire.

A bona fide rocker, "Call Me at Midnight" was a crisp, contagious opener — combining Cherie's compelling vocal with crunchy guitars and punchy horns. Not to be confused with the song of the same title on her next record, the heart-tugging "I Surrender," along with the more delicate title track, represented the record's shinier pop fare.

Of the numerous other highlights, "Science Fiction Daze" was a Bowie-inspired standout, while Cherie's duet with twin sister Marie on "Love at First Sight" was a dirty little rocker — sassy and irresistible. Capturing Cherie's "Neon Angel"-style "F-you" energy, "Young and Wild" was a high-octane, corset-worthy closer.

Truth be told, I likely wouldn't be a writer today, if not for Cherie Currie. I was in Los Angeles in the spring of 1990 — pounding the pavement and knocking on doors, promoting my band, Dead Serios. While in town, I popped by a Hollywood bookstore, in a laser-focused pursuit of Cherie's then-newly released autobiography, *Neon Angel*.

At the time, Cherie had been making the rounds on the American TV talk show circuit promoting her book. Having seen her recently on *The Sally Jessy Raphael Show*, I knew that *Neon Angel* was in stores, but I was having no luck locating it in my hometown of Melbourne, Florida. This was years before the birth of Amazon and other online mail-order services, so you'd really have to scour the ol' brick and mortars to nail down certain hard-to-find books and records.

It's amazing what treasures you can discover in LA. I not only found *Neon Angel* in that little Hollywood bookstore, but it was an *autographed* copy — one of a few leftovers from Cherie's recent in-store book signing at the shop. Plus, I scored Japanese import CDs of the first two Runaways records; *The Runaways* and *Queens of Noise*. Had this been the highlight of my 1990 LA adventure I could have returned home completely satisfied. However, this story was just beginning.

As I was packing my bags, preparing for my trip back to Florida the next day, I began examining some of Cherie's printed promo materials that I had received when I purchased her book a few days earlier; bio, 8x10 headshot, contact info, etc. I noticed that the address for her management office was right around the corner from where I was staying off Hollywood Boulevard. Eager to create a truly unique experience that would make this trip particularly memorable, I was struck with a rather crazy and very stupid idea.

Without giving it any thought, and certainly without considering any consequences, I called her management office, masquerading as a music journalist. I had absolutely no idea what I was doing. And I definitely DO NOT suggest this as a way for anyone else to break into the industry. But I "reasoned" that since I was going to be leaving LA the next day, I may as well go out with a bang! After all, what did I *really* have to lose?

Within seconds, I had Cherie's manager, Rick, on the phone. In short order, I convinced Rick of my (bogus) status as an East Coast music journalist. I told him that I was a staff writer for *JAM! Magazine*, a very legitimate and well-respected monthly publication based in Orlando. Realizing that I stood zero chance of ever actually meeting my dream girl, I told Rick that I merely was hoping to schedule a telephone interview with Cherie, sometime soon. After asking me several questions regarding the magazine, Rick told me that Cherie was on her way to his office at that moment, and once he had called the folks at *JAM!* and verified my position with the magazine, I could do the "phoner" with her right away. *Perfect!*

I realized quickly that I probably had less than a minute or two to contact *JAM!* editor, Darrel Massaroni, and apprise him of my scheme before Rick called and found me out. Fortunately, Massaroni was a major supporter of my band and he knew me well. So, when I got him on the phone and told him my story, he actually was pretty amused, and very supportive. Massaroni agreed to vouch for me, but he wasn't gonna play a role in any ruse. So, he encouraged me to "get a good story" and then informed me that my "deadline" for the next issue was just a few days away. *Wait! What?*

Having now covered my bases, I began preparing for my first official interview, jotting down questions frantically, while setting up my buddy's portable cassette tape recorder.

Per Rick's instruction, I called him back around 1PM and within a minute or so, Cherie was on the line. Considering that I had no idea what I was doing, the interview went really well. For more than a half-hour we talked about her time in The Runaways, her solo records, her acting career, and how she had beaten her near life-ending addiction to drugs successfully a few years earlier.

As the interview was winding down, I mentioned to Cherie that I didn't have a very good promo photo of her to accompany the feature and perhaps Rick might want to send a better-quality pic to the *JAM!* office. Then came the *real* bombshell. Instead of opting to mail a photo, Cherie invited me to meet with her *in person* that afternoon at Rick's office and *together* we could go through a box of photos and I could select whichever one I liked. *What the... ?* Without haste, I grabbed a shower, got dressed, jumped in a cab, and within just minutes, I had arrived at Rick's Sunset Boulevard office.

Through a partially opened door, I spotted Cherie in another room as I entered the reception area. Upon introducing myself to Rick's secretary, she escorted me to the room where Cherie was awaiting my arrival and then closed the door behind her on the way out. Only a few hours earlier I was thrilled just to have found an autographed copy of this woman's book — *now* we were alone, face to face, hanging out together — rummaging through a box of promo photos. In my world, this was big. No, it was bigger than big. This was colossal. In fact, I wouldn't have been as psyched had I been invited on a private getaway ski weekend in Aspen with Harry Styles!

In the end, I couldn't believe that I had pulled off such a brazen stunt, and so successfully. Upon returning to Florida, I submitted my first feature story, which appeared in the April 6, 1990 issue of *JAM!* And before long, I found myself being approached by people who had read the piece and they'd often compliment me on my "writing style." *Hmm.* I didn't know that I had a "writing style."

Here's the kicker. The experience wound up being less about pulling off a stupid prank and more about the value of the faith that people often have in us, and the power in the encouragement that they can offer. While my interview with Cherie stemmed from a goof, I do deserve *a little* credit — I knew how to handle myself, and I was extremely familiar with the subject matter. But, Darrel Massaroni believed in me. He encouraged me to "get a good story." He gave me an opportunity — one that I didn't even know I was looking for. And Cherie had faith in me too. She was so kind and so cool, so personable and so easygoing. As a result of that beautiful connection, Cherie Currie ignited a passion inside me — one that I didn't even know existed.

In the summer of 2023, I reached out to Cherie, as I was sharing initial *Garage Sale Vinyl* details with my various industry contacts while the book still was in its early stages. And wouldn't ya know it, 33 years later, Cherie was the *first* to respond (once again) with greatly appreciated words of encouragement.

> "It's thrilling to have a new book about our fortune
> of growing up in the greatest time in music history!"
> — Cherie Currie
> June 2023

After all these years, *Beauty's Only Skin Deep* remains on my personal radar. It said so much, back when rock and roll had something to say. While not sounding exactly fresh and new, it's still a fun one to revisit. However, if fresh and new is your intended destination, you GOTTA check out Cherie's most recent solo set, *Blvds of Splendor* — arguably the strongest, best work of her incredible near-50-year career.

Beauty's Only Skin Deep

Track List

SIDE ONE
1. Call Me at Midnight (Steven T.) – 3:19
2. I Surrender (Bizeau) – 3:43
3. Beauty's Only Skin Deep (Currie, Carr, Fowley) – 3:48
4. I Will Still Love You (Strauss) – 3:32
5. Science Fiction Daze (Steven T., Fowley) – 4:30

SIDE TWO
1. I Like the Way You Dance (Steven T.) – 3:33
2. That's the Kind of Guy I Like (Steven T.) – 2:48
3. Love at First Sight (Bizeau) – 3:12
4. The Only One (Currie, Steven T.) – 3:32
5. Young and Wild (Steven T., Fowley) – 3:47

13
Charlie Daniels

Charlie Daniels
"Fire on the Mountain"
(Kama Sutra Records / November 1974)

Fire on the Mountain

"On the line this morning, I've got Chris Long, from Horace Mann Elementary. Now, Chris, if you can tell me what song is #1 on this week's 1340AM KICK radio Top 30 chart, you'll win a copy of the brand new Bob Dylan album, *Blood on the Tracks*."

PAUSE

"Chris, are you there?"

"Uh, hi! Yes — it's 'Have You Never Been Mellow' by Olivia Newton-John."

"Congratulations, Chris! You're a winner!"

• •

FYI, this wasn't my first (or last) rodeo.

As a music-starved kid growing up during the wondrous quadraphonic mid-'70s, I rarely possessed the funds to purchase the records I craved. While in today's world, $4.98 would be a bargain price for new vinyl, in 1974, that was a whole lotta loot for a nerdy-looking 12-year-old to pony up. However, as a constant radio contest winner, my album library managed to remain comprehensive.

But my fortunes didn't end with just free records. From movie passes and concert tickets to restaurant certificates and sometimes a little cash, my slew of prize winnings kept me rocking, entertained, frequently fed, and occasionally paid. In fact, one time, I snagged a FREE *full* set of new tires for my sister's car from a call-in radio contest. Even my dad was impressed by that one!

A few days following my *Blood on the Tracks* radio score, I won a copy of *Fire on the Mountain*, the new LP from the Charlie Daniels Band. Although Daniels still was an artist on the rise at the time, I already was familiar with the North Carolina-born singer, songwriter, producer, multi-instrumentalist, and session player, as his 1973 Top 10 hit "Uneasy Rider" was one of the crown jewels of my (also) growing seven-inch singles collection.

Fire on the Mountain would be a massive personal eye-opener. Produced by Paul Hornsby (The Marshall Tucker Band, Wet Willie), the record's two singles, the lazy-feeling "Long Haired Country Boy" and the fiddle-fueled "The South's Gonna Do It," both have since become iconic to the classic Southern rock genre; however, Daniels himself was a musical culinary master. Hence, *Fire on the Mountain* offered an array of aural palate-pleasing ingredients, blending rock and country quite beautifully with pop, jazz, and blues. *Come taste the rainbow, baby!*

The first seven of the nine tracks were new studio recordings, while the last two were heart-stopping live tracks recorded in Nashville just a month or so prior to the record's November 1974 release. Fortunately, my first-pressing copy included the limited-edition live three-song bonus seven-inch.

Zinging with zesty Tex-Mex flavor, "Caballo Diablo" was a punchy record opener, while "Trudy" was a true blue, boogie-woogie banger — it remains one of the tallest standouts of Daniels' impeccable catalog. A down-home-style pickin' party, "Georgia" was an authentic feel-good ode to the "Peach State." Penned by CDB guitarist Barry Barnes, "Feeling Free" was a sunny-sounding barnyard stomp, and one of the record's shiniest highlights.

With perennial keyboardist Joel "Taz" DiGregorio providing lead vocals, "New York City, King Size Rosewood Bed" was a down-and-dirty, familiar-feeling, southern-fried gem — Daniels' slide guitar pinned to the dual drum work of Gary Allen and Fred Edwards further fanned the Allman factor.

Scorched by fiery guitars and enveloped in authentic organ, "No Place to Go" was a showstopper, to be sure. *Ain't it good to be alive and be in Tennessee?* Providing my first introduction to bona fide blues, this epic 11-minute live track oozed non-stop walking bass lines from its unsung MVP, Mark Fitzgerald, and offered graveyard shift DJs a well-needed pee break.

Then there was the blistering, record-closing live version of the truly timeless "Orange Blossom Special." While your mileage might vary, personally, this is THE most powerful piece of live recorded music I've ever heard. And I'll stand by that statement until the early-stage Parkinson's develops fully and finally takes me out. Too much passion?

Fire on the Mountain has since sold in excess of a million copies. Tragically, my original LP vanished into the mists of time. And I don't know whatever happened to my 8-track copy, either. *CAH-CLANK!* But I do know the whereabouts of my CD copy. Anyway, I was elated when my nail tech gifted me a FREE, slightly battered original vinyl pressing of the record — but without the bonus seven-inch. Be sure, I'll keep searching those garage sales!

Fire on the Mountain

Track List

SIDE ONE
1. Caballo Diablo (Daniels) – 4:28
2. Long Haired Country Boy (Daniels) – 4:03
3. Trudy (Daniels) – 4:51
4. Georgia (Daniels) – 3:06
5. Feeling Free (Barnes) – 4:10

SIDE TWO
1. The South's Gonna Do It (Daniels) – 4:00
2. New York City, King Size Rosewood Bed (Daniels) – 3:26
3. No Place to Go (Daniels) – 11:24
4. Orange Blossom Special (Rouse) – 3:00

14
John Denver

John Denver
"Poems, Prayers & Promises"
(RCA / April 1971)

Poems, Prayers & Promises

When groovy 50-something elementary school teacher and choir director, Bernice Rephlo began introducing us to John Denver songs in our decidedly square chorus group, it had an immediate "far out" effect on me. More than half a century later, I've yet to come back down to earth.

After a somewhat sleepy start, Denver had gained significant traction in 1971 with the down-home doozie, "Take Me Home, Country Roads." By '72-'73, the song was a staple of our pre-pube vocal ensemble. And I begged my mom to take me to Sears and buy me the full album — my very first Denver LP.

I was ten years old and *Poems, Prayers & Promises* proved to be my gateway — the passage from kiddie-type records cut from the back of cereal boxes in the late '60s to a new informed awareness of the early '70s singer-songwriter era.

Owning two of Denver's most iconic hits; the aforementioned "Take Me Home, Country Roads" (Billboard #2) and "Sunshine on My Shoulders" (Billboard #1), *Poems, Prayers & Promises* was a folksy lil' banger. I had re-purchased the record digitally in the new millennium, as my original LP had vanished to who knows where over the decades. As a result, I was thrilled to discover a reasonably well-cared-for vinyl copy (for a buck) while on a garage sale expedition with the GF in 2022. And I was reminded quickly of just how beautiful the songs were and how well they've aged.

> "'Take Me Home, Country Roads' makes me think of all of my hometown crowds, stretching to West Virginia, requesting this song to relive college times or long-standing love with their spouse."
>
> —Nick Guckert
> Singer, songwriter
> Pittsburgh, Pennsylvania
> (February 2024)

Straight out the gate, the title track provided a vivid portrait of Denver, reflecting on a life well-lived, while all his friends and his old lady sit and pass the pipe around. Long before the "wedding song" genre became unbearably hokey, Denver's heartfelt "My Sweet Lady" was a legit go-to for '70s-era nuptials. And this original version still sparkles like a 60th-anniversary diamond. The urgent "Wooden Indian" and the hopeful "Gospel Changes" also ranked among the record's many highlights

Early in his recording career, Denver possessed a penchant for covering Beatles tunes — efforts that met frequently with tragic results. Conversely, here, his version of "Let It Be" has a custom-tailored feel. Other *Poems, Prayers & Promises* cover successes included remakes of the Paul McCartney solo tune "Junk" and the James Taylor standard, "Fire and Rain."

Prior to achieving massive success as one half of the chart-busting combo, Starland Vocal Band, the husband and wife team of Bill Danoff and Taffy Nivert contributed songs and backing vocals to various Denver albums. One of their finest compositions, "I Guess He'd Rather Be in Colorado," was a super-tall standout, while "Around and Around" was a sunny-sounding treasure.

> "John Denver had this calm, quiet, chaos that songwriters, at best, can only aspire to."
> *— Steve Keller*
> Radio host, WFIT 89.5 FM
> Melbourne, Florida
> (February 2024)

Denver soon would become one of the biggest pop stars on the planet — racking up a staggering string of 14 consecutive gold and platinum LPs, as well as a dozen Top 40 singles by 1979. However, despite all of his incredible career achievements, a strong argument can be made that *Poems, Prayers & Promises* is the mightiest "must-have" in his impeccable catalog.

The album isn't merely one of my personal favorites, it's one of the most important, impactful records to ever find me. The absolute honest truth is, if not for John Denver, particularly *Poems, Prayers & Promises*, my *entire* life would have played out differently. And I have Bernice Rephlo to thank for making that vital introduction.

Bernice Rephlo was much more than just my 5th grade teacher and choir director, she was one of the most inspiring, encouraging, and wonderfully eccentric people I've ever been blessed to know. Sadly, she passed away decades ago, before I had a chance to reach adulthood, figure shit out, and hug her — *and* say, "thank you."

Poems, Prayers & Promises

Track List

SIDE ONE
1. Poems, Prayers and Promises (Denver) – 4:04
2. Let It Be (Lennon, McCartney) – 3:38
3. My Sweet Lady (Denver) – 4:23
4. Wooden Indian (Denver) – 1:38
5. Junk (McCartney) – 1:40
6. Gospel Changes (Williams) – 3:24

SIDE TWO
1. Take Me Home, Country Roads (Danoff, Nivert, Denver) – 3:08
2. Guess He'd Rather Be in Colorado (Danoff, Nivert) – 2:07
3. Sunshine on My Shoulders (Denver, Kniss, Taylor) – 5:10
4. Around and Around (Denver) – 2:16
5. Fire and Rain (Taylor) – 3:44
6. The Box (Lascelles) – 244

15
Eagles

Eagles
"The Long Run"
(Asylum / September 1979)

The Long Run

To be fair, there are both pros and cons to claiming a cast of drinkers and dopers as my closest cronies and colleagues. On the downside, my phone rings frequently at 4AM with: *You have a collect call from a correctional facility. Will you accept the charges?* Sadly, when *you're* the ONE guy in the room with your shit together, *you* get to "clean up" after everybody else. *Listen, man! If my old lady calls, I was with YOU all night. Cool?*

Often, many of my "fun-loving" friends find themselves facing certain "tight spots." *Dude! I really need $43 — TONIGHT!* On the upside, once I finally realized that, contrary to their obligatory heartfelt assurances, they would NOT, in fact, *ever* pay me back, I learned to barter. Typically, they still own at least a few titles from their once-comprehensive vinyl record collections — albeit now all beat-to-shit. And when they REALLY need *that* $43, I'm only too happy to snatch up their classic LPs for just pennies on the dollar. I acquired *this* Eagles staple from a fella down the street for a pack of Camels and a can of Grape Nehi. *Sorry 'bout your luck, brother, but I'm also taking your copy of "Physical Graffiti." Have a great day!*

• •

Despite having sold in the neighborhood of ten million units (to date) worldwide, *The Long Run* has been unfairly maligned by many since the day it dropped back in September 1979. After more than 40 years, it remains the "Jan" of the Eagles catalog.

So much had changed on the pop culture landscape since *Hotel California* checked in three years prior. The music scene had gone from Jimmy bangin' groupies in his hotel room with the "catch-of-the-day" and Stevie swinging from chandeliers in her underpants at 3AM, to diva-driven disco dance floors and goofy guys pogo-ing in skinny ties.

Suffice it to say, many of the day's prominent "Golden God" dinosaurs faced a distinct dilemma in 1979 — either head in a different direction (e.g. Zeppelin, Fleetwood Mac), or own your bloated rock star status and do what you do. As a result of having either 20/20 vision or being totally tone-deaf, the Eagles seemingly chose the latter. Hence, with *The Long Run*, the band developed vivid snapshots of where they were, and what was happening at the time, particularly in the glitzy Hollywood Hills, which often (might have) involved cocaine-fueled after-hours pool parties. And contrary to what some critics have said over the years, along with producer, Bill Szymczyk; Don Henley, Glenn Frey, the new guy, and the other two fellas did a splendid job.

The radio-friendly, Seger-style singles "Heartache Tonight" and "The Long Run" both crashed the Top Ten on Casey's Countdown convincingly. An R&B-flavored adult contemporary track, "I Can't Tell You Why," completed the hat trick, due largely to the engaging electric piano and the honest vocals of newly-recruited bassist and co-writer Timothy B. Schmit.

Proving there's never a bad time for guitar ace Joe Walsh to show up at the party (chainsaw in hand), "In the City" roared like a warrior. It made not only for a record highlight, but it also still stands as one of Walsh's all-time tallest tunes. A natural pair of perfect Henley / Frey-penned "double-Ds," "The Disco Strangler" packed plenty-o-punch, while the less urgent-sounding "King of Hollywood" offered such a spot-on casting couch account, it could have been taken directly from Weinstein courtroom transcripts — "Now look at me and tell me, darlin'. How badly do you want this part?"

> "*The Long Run* is my second-favorite Eagles album.
> Joe Walsh was such a great addition to the lineup!"
> —*Michael G. Yanko*
> Concert photographer
> Cocoa, Florida
> October 2023

According to the ol' GPS, "Those Shoes" traveled way around that Rocky Mountain before landing on Side Two, and "Teenage Jail" still feels as menacing as ever. "The Greeks Don't Want No Freaks" owned the distinction of the record's most disposable track, while "The Sad Café" lives on as one of the band's most poignant compositions. Mad props also are due to the great J.D. Souther for his various masterful songwriting contributions.

I hadn't visited this record in quite a while, but I'm glad we got a chance to get reacquainted. And at the end of the day, *Marsha* will always be hotter, but *Jan* will always have spunk.

The Long Run

Track List

SIDE ONE
1. The Long Run (Henley, Frey) – 3:42
2. I Can't Tell You Why (Schmit, Henley, Frey) – 4:56
3. In the City (Walsh, De Vorzon) – 3:46
4. The Disco Strangler (Felder, Henley, Frey) – 2:46
5. King of Hollywood (Henley, Frey) – 6:28

SIDE TWO
1. Heartache Tonight (Henley, Frey, Seger, Souther) – 4:26
2. Those Shoes (Felder, Henley, Frey) – 4:56
3. Teenage Jail (Henley, Frey, Souther) – 3:44
4. The Greeks Don't Want No Freaks (Henley, Frey) – 2:20
5. The Sad Café (Henley, Frey, Walsh, Souther) – 5:35

16
Earth, Wind & Fire

Earth, Wind & Fire
"All 'n All"
(Columbia / November 1977)

All 'n All

Fall 2023 — I was headed from my Oceanside pad in Cocoa Beach to my 7:00 Sunday night DJ gig, 30 minutes south, at Wid's Place in Melbourne. At least that was my intention, anyway. But I actually wound up at — the Earth, Wind & Fire concert! Unexpected wackiness like this happens in my life all the time. And when it does, I just hang on and roll with it.

Toting my laptops, cables, and mics, I strolled into Wid's Place at 6:30. As I began flipping on the booth lights and firing up the power amps, my phone pinged at 6:35. It was Sam, my longtime drummer buddy from the local music scene. In short order, he explained how he and his celebrated vocalist bandmate, Ana, were with a few other friends at a local venue, attending that night's live performance by the iconic R&B troupe. But there was a tiny "snag" — they had an extra FREE ($75 face value) ticket that needed to be claimed, pronto! *WHAT?* "We jus' gon' leave it fo ya at Will Call," Sam informed me, clearly unwilling to take "no" for an answer.

Lickety-split, I got the club owner, Wid, on the phone and apprised him of the situation.

"So, you're *telling* me that you're bailing on me tonight," Wid replied.

"No," I clarified quickly. "I'm *asking* if I can bail on you tonight."

"What time does the show start?" he asked.

"7:30," I said.

"What time is it now?" he asked.

"6:45," I said.

"Well, what the hell are you doing still talking to me? Go have a good time."

What a kind and compassionate man.

..

Since my earliest recollections as a music-crazed, pre-puber, I've clutched four R&B "aces" close to my chest; Rufus, the Ohio Players, Parliament, and — Earth, Wind & Fire. Truth be told, I even had the MASSIVE group poster from inside the 1977 album, *All 'n All* taped up on my bedroom wall, right up until 1985, when I got engaged and moved out of my parents' house to get my own place. Where that poster is now, I have no idea.

The Earth, Wind & Fire legacy is legendary. Their platinum-selling album catalog is impressive. And their string of chart-busting hit singles — seemingly endless. Can you imagine how ol' CeeLo and André would have gotten by without having Earth, Wind & Fire to lean on for inspiration? I shudder to think.

Despite their incredible achievements, accolades, AND my own extreme personal passion, I'd never actually been to an EWF concert. Yet, oddly, all I could think about as I made the 18-minute commute from Wid's Place to the King Center was, "Holy shit! I'm about to finally see THE Verdine White LIVE!" When I called up my writing partner and pro touring bassist, Bryan Dumas (aka Dingus), while en route to the show, he had only TWO comments; "That's fantastic!" and "Tell Verdine I said, 'Hi.'"

Maybe it's because he just always looked cool. Maybe it's because of the jaw-dropping gatefold album cover pics I used to see of him levitating, onstage. Maybe it's because he's one monster of a musician. But Verdine White always has been MY "guy" — held in the highest regards, along with Bootsy Collins and Bernard Edwards on my (very) short personal list of baddest badass bass players. Heck, even the "smart" writers over at *Rolling Stone* ranked Verdine among their Top 20 all-time greatest.

So, I get to the concert, and my ticket was in fact waiting for me at Will Call. As I made my way through the security checkpoint and into the packed lobby, I couldn't help but notice that there were more fetching 60-year-old kitties cattin' around than I could shake my multiple restraining orders at. PLUS, I was finally about to see THE Verdine White, LIVE. *This is gonna be a GREAT night!*

And it *was* great. Even after more than 50 years, the 12-piece Earth, Wind & Fire lineup still consisted of THREE original members, including vocal powerhouse Philip Bailey and percussionist / vocalist Ralph Johnson. But when I saw *Verdine* step onto the stage, donning glitter tails with matching Oz-like kicks and draped with his prized fire-engine-red Sadowsky bass, I didn't know whether to wet myself or storm the stage and love all over him. *Hmm.* I opted for neither. And he definitely did NOT disappoint. That gorgeous man swaggered, popped, slapped, thumped, and sweat his way through the entire show — like the muther-luvin' superstar he is.

Of course, the band was superb. The 75-minute setlist — totally predictable. And what a beautiful performance and magical experience it was. But it got me to thinking again about *that* record, my much-loved Earth, Wind & Fire album, *All 'n All*. Somewhere along the way, I'd learned that the GF owned TWO, slightly abused vinyl copies. *Really?* My own copy had vanished decades ago — although I did still have it on CD. Don't judge me! So, I'd traded one of my discarded Streisand LPs for one of her EWF duplicates. And I was SO amped to have *All 'n All* back in my personal vinyl collection.

Produced by the band's visionary patriarch, the late Maurice White, *All 'n All* was the eighth Earth, Wind & Fire studio set. Bursting with funk-fueled grooves and oozing jazz-inspired cred while packing plenty of pop-rock appeal, the irresistible 11-track collection crushed the *Billboard* Top Ten album chart. It has since sold more than three million copies.

All 'n All was a particularly important Earth, Wind & Fire record. In addition to owning two (more) wildly popular Top 40 hits, "Serpentine Fire" and "Fantasy," the album further showcased the band's overall world-class songwriting talent, masterful musicianship, and bankable production skills. As a result, *All 'n All* served as a platform from which Earth, Wind & Fire truly was launched into the stratosphere. It remains one of their best and brightest efforts to date. And seeing them live always will be one of my best and brightest concert experiences.

All 'n All

Track List

SIDE ONE

1. Serpentine Fire (M. White, V. White, Burke) – 3:51
2. Fantasy (M. White, V. White, del Barrio) – 4:38
3. In the Marketplace, Interlude (M. White) – 0:43
4. Jupiter (M. White, V. White, Dunn, Bailey) – 3:12
5. Love's Holiday (M. White, Scarborough) – 4:23
6. Brazilian Rhyme, Interlude (Nascimento) – 1:20

SIDE TWO

1. I'll Write a Song for You (Bailey, McKay, Beckmeier) – 5:23
2. Magic Mind (Dunn, Bailey, McKay, M. White, V. White, F. White) – 3:38
3. Runnin' (M. White, Dunn, del Barrio) – 5:50
4. Brazilian Rhyme, Interlude (Nascimento) – 0:53
5. Be Ever Wonderful (M. White, Dunn) – 5:08

17
Fleetwood Mac

Fleetwood Mac
"Fleetwood Mac"
(Reprise / July 1975)

Fleetwood Mac

Wow! People can be so sensitive about their music. Sometimes, *too* sensitive. Truth be told, I was just goofin' with the guy — the fella I'd spotted standing over at the cream and sugar station that one morning.

I recognized "Frank," as he was known as something of a guru on Florida's east coast blues scene. Simply put, he LIVED for the blues.

Having just seen the iconic group perform live, the once-blues-based band was fresh on my mind. So, I approached Frank with a snarky inquiry, sure to elicit a lively response. "Hey, man! What do you think of Fleetwood Mac?" Despite my own decades-long connection to the Florida music community, Frank had no clue who I was, as he shot me an "evil eye" and snarled, "I have ZERO use for Fleetwood Mac in ANY form!"

Conversely, *I've* had TOTAL use for Fleetwood Mac in ALL forms, ever since first discovering the Brit / Yank hybrid back in 1975, when they soared into the stratosphere with their breakout record, *Fleetwood Mac*. While I appreciate much of Fleetwood Mac's blues-inspired '60s-era records and I can even embrace some of the band's less-compelling '90s-era efforts, I possess a particular passion for their mid-'70s "golden" era.

• •

They'd been hovering *just* below the mainstream radar for nearly a decade — slogging through the rock and roll trenches — touring relentlessly while producing several modest-selling albums along with a handful of Top Ten UK singles. But with the release of their self-titled tenth album, Fleetwood Mac's fortunes were changed suddenly, as the band finally seemed to have found the right lineup, the right sound, and the right *songs*. I guess my older sister deserves much of the credit for putting them prominently on *my* radar.

Straight out of leftfield, Fleetwood Mac began generating significant Top 40 radio airplay when the "new" group dropped the soon-to-be Top 20 single, "Over My Head," in the fall of '75. Initially, I found the song to be a catchy, cozy feel-good, and I really liked the lady's voice. C'mon, man — I was 12! And I certainly *wasn't* the only music-crazed kid at the time who thought Fleetwood Mac was a new group. By the spring of '76, they had released their next single, "Rhiannon" — it too received massive airplay and also cracked Casey's Countdown convincingly. This was the same band that did "Over My Head," but the singer on "Rhiannon" was different. *This* lady's voice was darker-sounding than the *other* lady's sunnier-sounding voice.

I now was paying attention to Fleetwood Mac, sorta. Honestly though, with the latest Captain & Tennille album, *Song of Joy*, occupying so much of my headspace, I could muster only minimal interest in other bands — that is, until my sister brought this intriguing new "white album" home on 8-track, just as its cheerful, piano-driven third single, "Say You Love Me" was revving up to complete the Top 20 hat trick.. It was the summer of '76, and in short order, I'd become clobbered by the "Mighty Mac." THWACK!

I've used the words "beautiful," "magical," and "timeless" throughout this book to describe myriad albums. However, in *my* soul, *Fleetwood Mac* is particularly worthy of those endearing terms.

> "Some albums are timeless, and this is one of them."
> *— Anna-Marie O'Brien*
> Author
> Tempe, Arizona
> July 2023

Dig if you will, a picture — a portrait, a painting in progress. If Fleetwood Mac was a blank canvas in 1967, flamboyant founding drummer, Mick Fleetwood, provided crucial rock cred. His partner, founding bassist, John McVie, added blues-fueled authenticity. The arrival of singer, songwriter, and pianist, Christine McVie, in 1970 brought abundant beauty. And the "package" acquisition of singer, songwriter, and guitarist, Lindsey Buckingham, and singer, songwriter, Stevie Nicks, in late 1974 made the magic happen.

A production collab between the band and Keith Olsen (Foreigner, Heart, Bad Company), the *Fleetwood Mac* album just felt beautiful and magical from the get-go — packing WOW factor beyond its three radio singles. The fat bass grooves and warm drum tracks alone set the record apart from most of its thinner-sounding predecessors.

The Lindsey-led "Monday Morning" and "Blue Letter" both were crisp, country-tinged stingers, while Christine's honey-drenched contributions; "Warm Ways" and "Sugar Daddy" were so pure and perfect, nearly 50 years later, they remain among my all-time Fleetwood Mac favorites. Then again, I've always thought that Christine McVie was the band's MVP. Stevie's delicate, introspective "Landslide" not only was an album highlight, but it still stands as one of Fleetwood Mac's tallest, most-loved tunes. Although Lindsey's brooding "I'm So Afraid" made for a moving four-minute record closer, it becomes even more magnificent onstage — a heart-stopping ten-minute tour de force — a certain truth that I'd discover first-hand, many years later.

> "'Say You Love Me' has always been my all-time favorite chorus melody. It gives me a physical sensation of joy. And I must admit, as a kid, I thought a high-voiced boy was singing the song. I didn't know what Fleetwood Mac looked like."
> —Nick Guckert
> Singer, songwriter
> Pittsburgh, Pennsylvania
> (February 2024)

It's kinda crazy that I never actually saw Fleetwood Mac live until 2015. Don't judge me, man! Life doesn't always play out according to plan. But it WAS the "Fab Five" lineup! The result of an extremely generous gift from a very dear friend (with nuclear-strength electronic purchasing capabilities), I found myself seated sixth-row-center. By that time, the band members all were around 70. Heck, I was no kid either — well into my 50s. However, age was of no detriment to any of us. The two-hour-plus performance was superb. The set list was satisfying. And the massive stage production — world-class.

There I was, sitting near one of the many convenient arena concession areas, people-watching, just prior to show time. And as I gnawed away at a giant soft-n-salty $10 pretzel, I noticed something particularly interesting. Of the

20,000 fans attending the sold-out concert, thousands clearly were under 30. And hundreds (maybe more) of them looked to be under 20. *Hmm, "timeless," indeed.*

The aforementioned "extremely generous gift" had included not only those sweet sixth-row-center seats, but also access to Mick Fleetwood's personal meet-and-greet. Attended by 51 *other* disciples, the very exclusive and rather pricey "experience" played out earlier that afternoon. As a longtime drummer, Mick is my all-time hero. Hence, the notion of having a one-on-one encounter with the physical and musical giant was a smidge overwhelming. As we were being lined up in a backstage corridor, we could hear *them* sound-checking. And I soon felt as if I might have a heart attack. Think about it. *They* were just on the other side of *that* wall, and in short order I was going to meet Mick Fleetwood face to face. *Quick! Somebody get a medic! The stylish old guy with the snazzy nails is having a coronary!*

Our group soon was brought into the empty main arena and onto the stage, as "doors" wouldn't be for another two hours or so. It was completely surreal — I was on Fleetwood Mac's stage, with the band's iconic logo blazing across the enormous LED screen that spanned from corner to corner. John's bass rig was to my one side, Mick's drum kit was directly behind me, and Lindsey's elaborate pedal board was at my feet. And in the spirit of full disclosure, I must confess that I *did* run hand gently across the top of Christine's keyboard as we were ushered along.

During the well-organized, hour-long event, each fan got a personal onstage photo op with Mick. As the charismatic then-67-year-old legend arrived on the scene, everyone just stood there, completely awestruck. *Cue the crickets.* And as fans were called front and center for their respective photo, each one remained like the proverbial deer in the headlight, except for me. Mick was *my* "guy." He had been for decades. He still is. So, when *my* name was called out, I made immediate direct eye contact with my hero, and with a spring in my step and arms wide open, I announced in a voice loud enough to echo throughout the entire otherwise quite arena, "I LOVE YOU, MICK FLEETWOOD!" As everyone onstage broke into laughter, Mick bent down and grabbed me around my shoulders. "I love you too, mate," he replied as he gave me a believable hug. *Bucket list, complete!*

An insightful Q&A session soon followed. Sharing various "Behind the Music"-type stories, Mick came across as personable, genuine, and quite likable — an unassuming, old-school blues-rock chap who says, "shit" — a lot! He revealed how his passion for performing was first fueled by his exposure to the theater world as a young lad hanging out with his older, aspiring actress sister. He also referred to the rather unexpected meteoric success of *Rumours* as a "mutant event." Regarding the infamous click-clack balls "dangling about" on the *Ru-*

mours album cover, Mick confessed that to this day, he never performs without them. "I've always got me balls," he said. And although he had no definitive choice, Mick stated that due to his pure rock and roll spirit, the guitar-driven, "Go Your Own Way," *might* be his personal favorite Fleetwood Mac tune.

> "Like Arizona, this album is clean, spare, and yet dramatic. So many good tracks. Perfect for a long desert drive alone, with the moonroof open, listening to the sweet sounds of 'Rhiannon.'"
> —Anna-Marie O'Brien
> Author
> Tempe, Arizona
> July 2023

They created so much beautiful, magical, and timeless music before *and* after their breakout. But to this day, whenever I think about Fleetwood Mac, the first thing that comes to mind is the *Fleetwood Mac* album. I've owned several vinyl copies over the years, including my current garage sale copy. Yet, oddly, I'll always cherish the image of that old *8-track*, warbling and clanking away in the under-dash tape deck of my sister's un-air-conditioned '66 Dodge Dart. Ahh, yeah! The sunny soundtrack to the steamy summer of '76!

Fleetwood Mac

Track List

SIDE ONE
1. Monday Morning (Buckingham) – 2:48
2. Warm Ways (C. McVie) – 3:50
3. Blue Letter (Curtis) – 2:31
4. Rhiannon (Nicks) – 4:12
5. Over My Head (C. McVie) – 3:34
6. Crystal (Nicks) – 5:12

SIDE TWO
1. Say You Love Me (C. McVie) – 4:11
2. Landslide (Nicks) – 3:05
3. World Turning (C. McVie, Buckingham) – 4:25
4. Sugar Daddy (C. McVie) – 4:09
5. I'm So Afraid (Buckingham) – 4:15

18
Foghat

Foghat
"Fool for the City"
(Bearsville / September 1975)

Fool for the City

What a peculiar period — the mid '70s — particularly in the music world. In 1975, the disco craze was revving up, yet the charts still remained dominated by such wholesome, mother-approved pop artists as Barry Manilow, Olivia Newton-John, Donny & Marie and John Denver. Then, Foghat crashed the party. *Hey! Who invited THESE guys?*

Sporting fabulously feathered, shoulder-length coifs and well-cultivated Sam Elliott-sanctioned staches, the blues-based British boogie brigade burst through the door with reckless abandon. Donning glittery jackets, satin scarves and velvet britches, they sparked a joint, spiked the punch and stuck their fingers in the clam dip. Then they grabbed Olivia, Marie and a bevy of John Denver's groupies and trotted upstairs for an all-night soiree. *Hello, front desk? Somebody just threw a TV out the window of Room 817!*

Since 1972, the band had been building a fervent global following with a rapid succession of four impressive, yet modest-selling albums and a fistful of made-for AOR anthems, including "I Just Want to Make Love to You," "Road Fever" and "Honey Hush." By 1975, the stage was set for a major breakout — the landmark slab, *Fool for the City*.

> "I was very proud of that record.
> It was a great record."
> *— Roger Earl*
> September 2020

Following the late 1974 dismissal of original bassist Tony Stevens, co-founding drummer Roger Earl, frontman / guitarist "Lonesome" Dave Peverett and guitarist Rod Price soon arrived at Suntreader Studios in Sharon, Vermont and embarked on their fifth album — a massive, platinum-selling tour de force that not only has become known for its timeless rock anthems, but also for its famous cover depicting Earl sitting on a crate, while fishing from an open manhole in the streets of New York.

As a result of his previous Foghat studio work, resident Bearsville Records engineer, Nick Jameson was tapped to produce *Fool for the City*. The wildly talented 24-year-old multi instrumentalist also played piano and bass throughout the entire seven-song set. And in short order, he was asked to replace Stevens as Foghat's official bassist. He agreed to come on board temporarily — leaving his Bearsville gig for one year to record and tour with the band.

> "He's the singular person who has influenced me.
> I learned a lot from working and playing with Nick.
> He was a very entertaining and funny bastard.
> And he had a huge hand in making this record."
> —Roger Earl
> September 2020

Punching ya right in the privates, *Fool for the City* opened with the hard-hitting, radio-friendly Peverett-penned title track. However, it was another selection on the album that truly opened the floodgates and would enhance Foghat's fortunes forever. Over the years, Ted Nugent has stated that *he* wrote the "sexiest" song of all time. That claim can be disputed. While he *has* written some pretty terrific stuff during his career, the Nuge *ain't* Foghat. And although "Stranglehold" does drip a certain measure of sex appeal, it *ain't* "Slow Ride."

> "Nick and I knew that 'Slow Ride'
> was a single. We knew it was a hit."
> —Roger Earl
> September 2020

According to Earl, when he and Jameson delivered the two-track reel-to-reel master of "Slow Ride" to Bearsville Records, label president Paul Fishkin was less than enthusiastic.

"This *isn't* a hit," Fishkin declared. "It's too heavy. And it's too long."

"Fuck you — this *is* the single!" Earl fired back, standing his ground firmly.

"But we can't put out an eight-minute song," Fishkin countered.

"Fuck you — *yes* you can,"

"Well, can you edit it down?"

"Fuck you — NO!"

The label ultimately gave in, and soon, "Slow Ride" was released it as a single. But to the band's chagrin, radio stations began editing the song anyway. Jameson eventually embraced the harsh reality and edited the song properly — down to just under four minutes.

> "'Slow Ride,' like most of our songs, is about sex. The riff was basically a John Lee Hooker riff played in 4/4 and not in a shuffle. That was a big record for us. It still is today."
> *—Roger Earl*
> September 2020

In addition to the classic title track and the signature Top 20 hit, *Fool for the City* also delivered other soon-to-be fan favorites, including the infectious sing-along, "My Babe." Birthed from Jameson's high-octane arrangement, this riff-heavy rendition of the 1963 Righteous Brothers single continues to appear on Foghat concert set lists.

Earl recounts Jameson's numerous crazy production bits on *Fool for the City* — particularly on "Slow Ride" — from the wooden plank stomping and floor tom flams in the intro to the old school rotary phone effect featured in the funky bridge — you know the part. Listen for it — "I'm in the mood. *(shwak, click, click, click, click, click, click, click)*. The rhythm is right." *(shwak, click, click, click, click, click, click, click)*...

> "We used to have lots of fun doing all sorts of interesting stuff in the studio. Actually, we always had fun in the studio."
> *—Roger Earl*
> September 2020

You can even hear the real life sounds of Earl himself crashing a car into a pile of trash cans during the Jerry Lee Lewis-flavored romp, "Drive Me Home" — a raucous track that was cut in just one take. "The song is all about this chick who's been drinking and she's driving Dave home," Earl recalls. "We went to the top of a mountain and there's this dirt road with trees, about a quarter mile up to the studio. We placed microphones all the way down the hill where we had all these garbage cans for me to hit. As I'm driving down, I hit trees and garbage cans. I did it twice. But on the second one, the car caught fire. If you listen, you can hear me crashing into stuff. It was a lot of fun."

Despite their well-deserved rep as a hard-driving rock band, Foghat always possessed the creative courage to step out of their stylistic comfort zone from time to time and embrace a pure pop song. Hence, the record-closing "Take It or Leave It" was a golden album highlight. Owning a distinctive reggae-tinged bridge, this R&B-inspired gem was a delightful yin to the authentic "Terraplane Blues" yang.

In 1975, *Fool for the City* demanded and attained worldwide attention as a scrappy, exciting, and important new rock release. Even after nearly 50 years, you know the rhythm is right!

Fool for the City

Track List

SIDE ONE
1. Fool for the City (Peverett) – 4:33
2. My Babe (Hatfield, Medley) – 4:35
3. Slow Ride (Peverett) – 8:14

SIDE TWO
1. Terraplane Blues (Johnson) – 5:42
2. Save Your Loving (Peverett, Price) – 3:31
3. Drive Me Home (Peverett) – 3:54
4. Take It or Leave It (Peverett, Jameson) – 4:54

19
Peter Frampton

Peter Frampton
"Frampton Comes Alive!"
(A&M / January 1976)

Frampton Comes Alive!

The mid 1970s was a fascinating period to be a teenager. In 1976, America celebrated its Bicentennial, a peanut farmer from Georgia was elected President, *The Six Million Dollar Man* was a top-rated TV show, and Farrah Fawcett's image was seemingly everywhere. Plus, who could forget the CB radio craze with such catchphrases as "Breaker-breaker, good buddy" and "Hammer down!" From such country artists as Waylon Jennings and Willie Nelson to rock acts including Aerosmith and Ted Nugent to R&B groups like Earth, Wind & Fire and the Ohio Players, there also was an abundance of incredible music in 1976. And I absorbed it all like a fresh quicker picker-upper.

In the spring of '76, I had become friends with two teenage brothers who lived down the street from me in Orlando — Ricky and Ronnie Burns. Unlike myself, the Burns brothers were *very* cool. Ronnie, in particular, smoked cigarettes, rode motorcycles, listened to rock and roll, and was adored by the neighborhood "bad girls." In fact, the Burns brothers were *so* cool that my super-straight-edge mom literally forbade me to associate with them. As a result, I would sneak over to the Burns house and hang out after school while my mom was at work.

It was during these covert rendezvous that Ronnie showed me how to apply Alice Cooper-like make-up and breathe fire, Gene Simmons-style. Ronnie played drums in the school band and had his own kit that he kept set up in his bedroom. From time to time he would give me pointers and even allow me to bang on them — and I loved it! Ronnie also educated me on various "ways of the world" — offering me compelling, step-by-step tips on how to get to "third base." Almost daily we would sit in the Burns living room listening to KISS albums at a ridiculously loud volume. But one day, Ronnie decided to switch up the afternoon playlist and he introduced me to a *new* album.

∙ ∙

> *If there ever was a musician who was an honorary member of San Francisco society — Mr. Peter Frampton!*

The earnest album-opening, live concert intro from Winterland Ballroom general manager, Jerry Pompili, remains as iconic as the songs themselves *and* the classic album cover depicting the rising "Golden God" in all his glory, live onstage.

Having first struck out in 1966, fronting the British rock combo, the Herd, singer / songwriter and guitarist, Peter Frampton, formed the high-octane, blues-based band Humble Pie with singer / songwriter and guitarist, Steve Marriot, in 1968. By 1971, the 21-year-old London native felt ready to spread his creative wings further — signing to A&M Records and launching his career as a solo artist. Frampton's 1972 debut, *Wind of Change*, stalled at #177 on the *Billboard* Top 200. His next two studio efforts, *Frampton's Camel* (1973) and *Somethin's Happening* (1974), also met with minimal fanfare. However, following three years of extensive touring, Frampton's fortunes improved a smidge when his fourth slab, *Frampton*, reached a more respectable #32 on the *Billboard* chart.

Although his record sales were beginning to bubble a bit, Frampton found himself in something of a professional tight spot. An article in *Billboard* indicated that the then-25-year-old musician was $300,000 in debt by the summer of '75. But he'd been cementing a solid rep on the US concert circuit, while the label "suits" grew impatient — pressuring him to *deliver*. Six months later, Peter Frampton finally did deliver — in spades. Only a select few rock records can be described as truly "magical." But "magical" describes *Frampton Comes Alive!* perfectly. And to suggest that Frampton's release merely struck a chord with fervent followers would be an enormous understatement.

It literally quarantined the international rock world.

Recorded during three different 1975 performances (Winterland Ballroom, San Francisco / Long Island Arena, New York / Plattsburgh's Memorial Hall, New York), the budget-priced double-LP captured all the energy, charisma and world-class songs Frampton had become known for as a live solo artist over the last four years.

The self-produced 14-track collection debuted at a dismal #191 on *Billboard* when it was released in January 1976. However, by April, *Frampton Comes Alive!* was THE #1 album in America. In fact, Frampton rocketed so far into rock's stratosphere at such a death-defying rate, by the summer of '76, he even had his own Slurpee cup at 7/11. Of course, I had one!

Despite Frampton's poster boy looks, genuine charm and the record's appealing packaging, what made *Frampton Comes Alive!* an instant sensation and a decades-long classic, was the songs. Sandwiched frequently on Top 40 playlists between "Junk Food Junkie" and "Afternoon Delight," the lead-off single, "Show Me the Way," slashed through car radio speakers like aural beams of golden sunshine — brimming with an engaging ching-a-ling guitar and an infectious sing-along chorus. And seemingly overnight, Frampton had scored a major Top Ten hit single. Organic and irresistible, the Fender Rhodes-fueled ballad, "Baby, I Love Your Way," followed suit, reaching #12 on Casey's Countdown in short order. Driven by Frampton's soon-to-be signature talk box guitar effect, the mammoth arena anthem, "Do You Feel Like We Do" was the album's third single. Edited from its original 14-minute album running time to a (slightly) more radio-friendly seven-minute version, the song hit #10 on *Billboard* that fall.

It can be argued though, that the album's *other* tracks were equally (or more) captivating than the hits. Owning a rib-cracking riff and piano-charged fire, "Something's Happening" was a crunchy, satisfying opener, while "Doobie Wah" was a bouncy, familiar-feeling, funky delight.

The adoring audiences play a prominent role throughout — providing the record's beauty and creating its authenticity — becoming "one" with Frampton — serving as a spiritual extension of the songs. In that regard, Frampton's faithful flock take the reins on the transparent, acoustic standout cut, "All I Want to Be (Is by Your Side)" — *All I wanna be-ee-ee, is... BY-YOUR-SIDE!*

The raucous rendition of the Stones' "Jumpin' Jack Flash" made for another of the many mighty highlights. However, I will contend completely, without fear of contradiction, that anyone who experiences *Frampton Comes Alive!* and *doesn't* become a bit moist by the soaring seven-minute epic, "Lines on My Face," *may* have been born without a heart, or a soul, or even a pulse.

The live concert shots placed inside the album's gatefold cover of Frampton, along with guitarist / keyboardist Bob Mayo, bassist Stanley Sheldon and drummer John Siomos are (still) pretty freaking cool. But there was another component of the record that captured my attention and imagination almost as much as the music — the insightful liner notes. Written by then-teenager Cameron Crowe, the Frampton bio was one of the first bits of rock journalism that I really paid much attention to. Oh sure, I bought a boatload of the day's most popular rock magazines, but with most of them offering near countless puckering pics of Paul Stanley, I couldn't be bothered with text. However, Crowe's contribution to *Frampton Comes Alive* would inspire my *future* writing ambition.

Honest and pure vocals, blistering musicianship and world-class songwriting — the recipe that's made Peter Frampton a rock legend. *Frampton Comes Alive!* would become the #1 best-selling album of 1976, as well as ranking in the Top 20 for 1977. It since has sold in excess of 11 million copies. Nearly 50 years later, it remains faultless and iconic.

Frampton Comes Alive!

Track List

SIDE ONE
1. Introduction / Something's Happening (Frampton) – 5:54
2. Doobie Wah (Frampton, Headley-Down, Wills) – 5:28
3. Show Me the Way (Frampton) – 4:42
4. It's a Plain Shame (Frampton) – 4:21

SIDE TWO
1. All I Want to Be (Is by Your Side) (Frampton) – 3:27
2. Wind of Change (Frampton) – 2:47
3. Baby, I Love Your Way (Frampton) – 4:43
4. I Wanna Go to the Sun (Frampton) – 7:02

SIDE THREE
1. Penny for Your Thoughts (Frampton) – 1:23
2. (I'll Give You) Money (Frampton) – 5:39
3. Shine On (Frampton) – 3:35
4. Jumpin' Jack Flash (Jagger, Richards) – 7:45

SIDE FOUR
1. Lines on My Face (Frampton) – 7:06
2. Do You Feel Like We Do (Frampton, Gallagher, Siomos, Wills) – 14:15

20
Debbie Gibson

Debbie Gibson
"Anything Is Possible"
(Atlantic Records / November 1990)

Anything Is Possible

Simply put, this was a superb piece of work. And had the other shoe not dropped for another 18 months, you'd likely not be giggling right now. But drop, it did.

The first shoe to hit the floor was the arrival of the '90s: a new decade, full of promise. Then, in short order (with a deafening thud), came the second shoe: the mass extermination of music artists who had committed the ultimate unpardonable sin of rising to prominence during the '80s. While many of the Vanilli-flavored, aerosol-sprayed acts of that era deserved to be put out to pasture, many did not. As a result of this sweeping cleansing process, some amazing work created by some amazing artists was pooh-poohed or ignored altogether.

Truth be told, despite her squeaky-clean persona and sunny-sounding songs, in the '80s, Debbie Gibson was a freak. A pop music genius. A powerhouse singer, prolific songwriter, and gifted producer, Gibson racked up two multi-platinum-selling Top Ten albums: *Out of the Blue* (1987) and *Electric Youth* (1989), as well as a string of eight Top 40 hits, including five Top Tens and two #1s ("Foolish Beat" / "Lost in Your Eyes") — ALL before her 19th birthday. By the end of 1989, it seemed as if Debbie Gibson was unstoppable. Then came the '90s. *THUD!*

As *they* say, "timing is everything." In 1990, the 20-year-old Gibson was developing nicely as a singer and a songwriter. However, tragically, her strongest record dropped during the early stage of the aforementioned cleansing process. And although it owned many of her all-time best songs and was promoted fiercely for more than a year with a whopping six singles, Gibson's third studio set, *Anything Is Possible* just couldn't catch fire. The LP ultimately did achieve gold status and it hit the Top Five in Japan, but it struggled to ignite the Top 100 elsewhere — including the US, where it stalled at #41.

But be sure, *Anything Is Possible* was a bona fide banger. Hence, I've taken the liberty of breaking a few sacred rules with this chapter. I didn't "stumble" upon this treasure at a local thrift store, flea market, or garage sale. And I didn't buy it for a buck, either. In fact, for all intents and purposes (in the US), *Anything Is*

Possible doesn't even exist on vinyl. Honestly, I had no idea it ever was pressed on vinyl, period, until 2022 when I was apprised otherwise by a trusted connection at my preferred proper hometown indie record joint.

I had owned the CD version of *Anything Is Possible* since day one. But in the spirit of full disclosure, I must confess that it would be decades before even I recognized its true splendor. Upon revealing this truth to my aforementioned savvy vinyl dealer, she located an LP copy of the record for me in a snap on her in-store Google machine. The used album would cost me $50 (with shipping), and it would have to be ordered from an exotic overseas locale. I agreed to the transaction, posthaste.

After more than a month, the record finally arrived. And it was well worth the wait *and* the absurd price. The LP version contained only 12 tracks, as opposed to the CD's 16 tracks — not a deal-breaker, as there was no way 70-plus minutes of music was going to fit on a single 12-incher. The cover and lyric sheet insert both were surprisingly pristine. The vinyl itself also was clean — just enough crackle to feel cozy.

Produced primarily by Gibson (of course), *Anything Is Possible* possessed a sorta split personality, like that gal with the vodka / Xanax issue who I once dated (for way too long), but without the law enforcement intervention.

Listed on the record's label and album cover as "NRG↑," Side One was upbeat, fun, and funky. For the music snobs still rolling their eyes, be advised that Side One was a songwriting and production collab between Gibson and Motown legend Lamont Dozier. And what screams "CRED" louder than Motown? Not much. Conversely, listed as "Mood Swings," Side Two hung a hard left. And for my money, that's where the real magic happened — soft, yet soaring songs, soaked with soulful and seductive sophistication.

With only a couple of exceptions, *Anything Is Possible* dealt nothing but Aces. Poppy, punchy, and playful, "Another Brick Falls" and the lead-off single, "Anything Is Possible," both showed Gibson maturing naturally as an artist, right on schedule. Additionally, "Reverse Psychology" and "One Step Ahead" established the electro-pop blueprint that continues to define Gibson's current dance club music.

Absolutely heart-stopping, "One Hand, One Heart" made the iron-clad case for Gibson's world-class, across-the-board talent. In fact, I encourage any naysayer to take the "O.H.O.H. Challenge." Clear your head of all distractions, and your heart of any misguided preconceptions, and let the song wash over you. If you're not elevated to an all-new level of spiritual consciousness, well, rest assured that Jesus still loves you. He might be a smidge disappointed, but he'll love you, nonetheless.

Enhanced beautifully by ambient guitar garnish, "Sure" and "Where Have You Been?" both are heart-felt, piano-driven, *Tapestry*-worthy delights that help propel Side Two further into the stratosphere.

Then, there's the record-closing, Gospel-tinged heartbreak ballad, "This So-Called Miracle." Arguably Gibson's single greatest musical achievement, this magnificent, seven-and-a-half-minute epic is so powerful, so honest and pure, it prompts me to curl into a fetal position and sob, every time, like a shattered middle schooler who misplaced their friendship bracelet. Yeah, dudes — it's *exactly* like that!

Anything Is Possible

Track List

SIDE ONE (NRG↑)
1. Another Brick Falls (Gibson) – 3:55
2. Anything Is Possible (Gibson, Dozier) – 3:44
3. Reverse Psychology (Gibson, Dozier) – 4:25
4. One Step Ahead (Gibson, Dozier) – 4:51
5. It Must've Been My Boy (Gibson, Dozier) – 4:19
6. Lead Them Home My Dreams (Gibson) – 5:32

SIDE TWO (Mood Swings)
1. One Hand, One Heart (Gibson) – 4:35
2. Sure (Gibson) – 4:17
3. Negative Energy (Gibson) – 3:40
4. Mood Swings (Gibson) – 3:52
5. Where Have You Been? (Gibson) – 6:07
6. This So-Called Miracle (Gibson) – 7:28

21
The Go-Go's

The Go-Go's
"Beauty and the Beat"
(I.R.S. Records / July 1981)

Beauty and the Beat

UGH! — I've always seen it as a straight-up slap in the face. To this day, you'd be hard-pressed to uncover *any* commentary on the Go-Go's without *that* caveat, something along the lines of, *They hit really good — for girls.* Sure, possessing the balls to be an all-female rock band was pretty impressive, especially back during the late '70s and early '80s. And let's face it, they didn't just show up to the party uninvited, they kicked in the door to *that* ol' "clubhouse" and made the boys their bitches. *Bravo!* Nevertheless, what made (and still makes) the Go-Go's a great band is that they're just a great band — period. BTW, they have great songs, too.

It was an exciting time for music. The dinosaurs were pretty much all becoming extinct, and new carnivorous contenders were consuming the scene. My personal teenage LP collection reflected the changing times, giving refuge to a menagerie of dude-dominated "The" bands — the Cars, the Police, the Clash, and the Knack. Then, a record dropped that totally popped. Instantly, I was thwacked by this *new* "the" band.

Joan Jett and Chrissy Hynde both had released recent dazzling debuts, so when the Go-Go's rolled out of LA and delivered their first album in the summer of '81, they weren't the first or the only belles at my ball. Besides, *my* teenage freak show frustrations were focused fully on Lene Lovich. Yeah, I know. But I like 'em like that. Hence, my obsession for the Go-Go's was genuine, and it was ALL about the music. Well, sorta.

Overseen by budding pop / rock producers, Richard Gottehrer and Rob Freeman, the 11-song set, *Beauty and the Beat,* sounded like sunshine. Straight out of the box, even the cover looked fun, depicting the five members wearing only bath towels and face cream. And the bubble bath pics on the back cover further enhanced the implied fun factor.

Glossed by the angelic lead vocals of Belinda Carlisle and built on guitar work that was crispier than two Denny's side strips, the opening track and lead-off single, "Our Lips Are Sealed," set the stage perfectly, defining the overall record — sassy, yet sophisticated, playfully unpredictable and totally irresistible.

Fueled by the iconic, super-charged hit, "We Got the Beat," *Beauty and the Beat* was a slow burn success, ultimately reaching #1 on the *Billboard* Top 200 in March 1982, where it lived for six weeks. The record now has sold more than two million copies.

But two smash Top 20 singles does *not* a perfect record make. And *Beauty and the Beat* owned highlights galore. "How Much More," was a bona fide beach blanket romp, accented by crunchy guitars and driven by the no nonsense drum work of Gina Schock. Then, before you could wipe the lipstick off your left cheek, "Tonight," planted another smacker on the right.

Penned by the band's co-guitarists, Charlotte Caffey and Jane Wiedlin, "Lust to Love" and "This Town" provided a more mature yin to the carefree "You Can't Walk in Your Sleep (If You Can't Sleep)" and "Skidmarks on My Heart" yang. While Caffey's breakup tune "Fading Fast" and Wiedlin's hypnotic "Automatic" remain personal favorites, bassist Kathy Valentine scored high marks from the Olympic judges for her urgent record closer, "Can't Stop the World."

World-class songwriting and precision production aside, *Beauty and the Beat* succeeded at the time, and it still sparkles today, as a result of the Go-Go's collective appeal — Carlisle's signature Pixy Stix vocals, the inventive Caffey / Wiedlin guitar tag team and Schock's meat and potatoes drum style. Then there's Kathy Valentine. Holy crap, her boss basslines (particularly on "Tonite" and "Lust to Love") were well worth the LP's $6.99 sticker price. Take any one of these five components from the Go-Go's machine, and it would seize up like the engine of my old Dodge pickup truck way back when.

When I think back to when *Beauty and the Beat* was new, I'm often reminded of the time I traveled from Florida back to Missouri for an extended excursion in January 1982. I'd just turned 19, and with high school graduation still a very recent memory, I was psyched about getting back to my childhood hometown and making (more) poor decisions with old friends one last time before being strangled by the ensuing responsibilities of our newfound adulthood.

Beauty and the Beat had only been out for a couple of months and it had become one of my most frequent "play, repeat, play, repeat" favorites. So, before fleeing the "Sunshine State" I taped the album on Side One of a Maxell XLII 90-minute cassette. On Side Two I taped the Rick James album, *Street Songs*. Side One would prove to serve as the primary soundtrack to my month-long getaway in the "Show Me State."

"'Sup, dude?" I shouted through the open passenger window as my buddy Joe and I cruised up Primrose Street, blasting *Beauty and the Beat* along the way. I recognized him easily — the high school senior standing out on his parents' front porch. I hadn't seen Brad since he attended my going away sleepover in '75, so I was eager to reconnect with him during my visit in '82. "I'll call ya later!" I hollered out, as Joe hung a right onto Broadway. I never called Brad during that trip, which I soon regretted because he was one of my favorite elementary school friends.

Brad had given me an Elton John record when he came to my 12th birthday party / sleepover in December '74. There we were, up all night with our sleeping bags lined up on my parents' living room floor, playing cards and listening to records until 4AM when we wound up sitting on the kitchen floor, devouring Pop-Tarts, talking about school, Little League and of course our favorite subject — girls. Truth be told, my other buddies and I would get annoyed whenever Brad showed up at our local roller rink, Skateland, on Friday nights. We all knew that none of us stood a chance with any of the girls from school as long as Brad was hanging around.

A few years later I'd heard that Brad had gone into acting and even landed a couple of small TV gigs. Then, in 1991, Brad caught a BIG break when he appeared the now-iconic film, *Thelma & Louise*. Soon, *Brad Pitt* would become a household name. Despite his enormous subsequent success and international fame, I'd love to chat with Brad again one more time primarily because I'm still dying to find out if he ever made it to second base with Sis Keifer that night at Skateland. As I'm sure he's now well-aware, "Inquiring minds want to know!"

My original *Beauty and the Beat* LP and that Maxell cassette both vanished over the years, and it left a hole in my soul that my CD copy couldn't fill. Fortunately, I did finally score a well-cared for vinyl copy when I traveled from Cocoa Beach to Charleston for a record shopping spree with my favorite green-haired, 20-something in 2023.

In sum, the Go-Go's are just a great band — period. And for me, *Beauty and the Beat* still feels like a party — as fresh and fun as it was when I was blasting it out in front of Brad Pitt's house in '82. *I'll call ya later, dude!*

Beauty and the Beat

Track List

SIDE ONE

1. Our Lips Are Sealed (Wiedlin, Hall) – 2:45
2. How Much More (Caffey, Wiedlin) – 3:06
3. Tonite (Caffey, Wiedlin, Case) – 3:35
4. Lust to Love (Caffey, Wiedlin) – 4:04
5. This Town (Caffey, Wiedlin) – 3:20

SIDE TWO

1. We Got the Beat (Caffey) – 2:36
2. Fading Fast (Caffey) – 3:41
3. Automatic (Wiedlin) – 3:07
4. You Can't Walk in Your Sleep (If You Can't Sleep) (Caffey, Wiedlin) – 2:54
5. Skidmarks on My Heart (Caffey, Carlisle) – 3:06
6. Can't Stop the World (Valentine) – 3:20

22
Daryl Hall & John Oates

Daryl Hall & John Oates
"Daryl Hall & John Oates"
(RCA / August 1975)

Daryl Hall & John Oates

At the risk of sounding like *that* old broken record, I'll say it again: for music artists, you can be the coolest cat in town, oozing more swagger than any other muther around, but if you ain't got *songs*, you ain't got *jack*! And while they have undergone several packaging makeovers since their 1972 major label debut, Daryl Hall & John Oates ALWAYS have had songs — and darn good ones, too. It just took a couple of years and a few records for the masses to catch on. And in the spring of 1976, the masses DID finally catch on, in a very BIG way.

As a naïve Midwest church boy coming of age during the mid-'70s, I didn't have that super-hip older sibling to introduce me to such rock icons as the Stones, Zeppelin, Purple or Sabbath. *My* older sister actually was WAY cooler. Debbie would bring home STACKS of pop singles from the likes of Tony Orlando and Dawn, the Carpenters, Carole King, and David Cassidy. In 1975, she had a thing for a guy who further informed her musical awareness. And whatever Steve recommended, Debbie bought — brought home, and blasted ad nauseam on her portable 1968 Zenith record player.

One of Steve's most righteous recommendations was by a seemingly new Philly-based duo. The album had a slick silver cover with the artists' faces plastered across the front — a glammed-up-looking guy with a fabulous porn stache and his *really* hot-looking chick sidekick. Then, I saw the color pic of the two on the record's inner sleeve. *UGH!* They were BOTH dudes! AND they were BOTH nude! *Some things just CAN'T be unseen!* That album, *Daryl Hall & John Oates* would soon become one of my all-time favorites.

Brimming with pure pop splendor, the opening track, "Camellia" was soulfully irresistible, and it hit me like a 27-pound sack-a-taters. Decades following its initial 1975 in-store arrival, the song still sounds like sunshine to me.

Polished with those skin-tight signature Hall & Oates vocals and driven by authentic R&B-fueled keyboards and punched up by perfect pop / rock guitar work, "Alone Too Long," "Out of Me, Out of You," and "Nothing at All" were warm and cozy, slinky and sexy. At age 12, I wouldn't have known what to do with a girl if I could have gotten one. But I was a quick study. And a few years later, I'd figured some things out and this record served as a faithful go-to soundtrack to my reoccurring carnal teenage exploits.

> "*Daryl Hall and John Oates* is the perfect communion of rock, soul, and pop. The astounding musicianship, perfect arrangements, accomplished songwriting, and the unmatched vocals of Daryl and John make this a spectacular addition to their catalog."
> —Ken Sharp
> Musician, songwriter, producer, author
> Encino, California
> June 2023

Something of a nut-slap directed at their former rep, "Gino (The Manager)" was a particularly catchy standout, while "(You Know) It Doesn't Matter Anymore" pointed to their future '80s brand and "Soldering" brought what at the time was a unique reggae flavor.

Then, there was *that* song — the magical little chart-busting single that was propelling the album into the Top 20, heading quickly to "gold" status. Now, I'm *not* saying this statement is text book accurate, but I *am* saying that a STRONG defense case *can* be made for anyone who would maintain that "Sara Smile" is THE greatest pop song of all time.

I didn't rediscover this LP hiding at a neighborhood garage sale or tucked away at a local thrift store. Shortly after my father passed away in 2022, I was digging through an array of heirlooms in our newly-acquired family storage unit, and there it was — lurking in a box full of my sister's old records, her original vinyl copy of *Daryl Hall & John Oates*. I'm not gonna lie — I stole it from her right then and there. Although I couldn't point to anything specific, I was sure she owed me for *something* from back in the day, so this seemed like appropriate payback.

At the time of the Hall & Oates LP heist, I still didn't have a turntable at my beach house. So, I took the record down to the GF's place to see how well the music had held up. It quickly became our favorite morning coffee soundtrack. In fact, along with the Janis Ian album, *Between the Lines*, it's one of only two LPs that she's flat-out *refused* to give back. I couldn't believe it. My own GF stole a record from me that I'd stolen from my own sister. What gall!

Daryl Hall & John Oates

Track List

SIDE ONE
1. Camellia (Oates) – 2:48
2. Sara Smile (Hall, Oates) – 3:07
3. Alone Too Long (Oates) – 3:21
4. Out of Me, Out of You (Hall, Oates) – 3:28
5. Nothing at All (Hall, Allen) – 4:24

SIDE TWO
1. Gino (The Manager) (Hall, Oates) – 4:10
2. (You Know) It Doesn't Matter Anymore (Hall, Allen) – 3:07
3. Ennui on the Mountain (Hall, Oates) – 3:15
4. Grounds for Separation (Hall) – 4:12
5. Soldering (Beckford, Ranglin) – 3:24

23
Heart

Heart
"Bébé le Strange"
(Epic / February 1980)

Bébé le Strange

Yikes, what a goober! I was a wide-eyed, 17-year-old disciple of ALL things rock and roll. But I couldn't get my parents on board with me attending the full onslaught of concerts that were coming through Central Florida at the time. And even if they *had* given me the green light, my part-time gig at the local record store hardly generated the revenue necessary to cover the cost of tickets, which in those days was approaching a whopping $9 a pop. As a result, in the spring of 1980, I faced a dilemma — I had to choose only *one* of *three* concerts coming to town that week; Journey (with the Babys), Angel (with Mahogany Rush), or Heart (with the Heats).

Given my insatiable appetite for the band's irresistible, super-charged, Fender-meets-Ovation sound (and alluring femme factor), I chose Heart. To this day, I don't regret the decision. In fact, the May 1980 *Bébé le Strange* show in Lakeland, Florida remains one of my most memorable and satisfying concert experiences. Heck, I even bought a tour book *and* twin, full-size, full-color posters of the band's two poodle-coiffed sibling frontchicks; vocalist Ann Wilson and guitarist Nancy Wilson. I *gave* the tour book away to a raging Heart super-fan many years ago. What happened to those once-prized posters, I have no clue.

Christening the new decade with sonic splendor, *Bébé le Strange* was quite a rib-cracker and it quickly became Heart's fifth consecutive Top 20 chart-buster. Fueled by the recent simultaneous breakups between Ann Wilson and longtime manager Michael Fisher, and Nancy Wilson and guitarist Roger Fisher, *Bébé* boasted bold brashness and plenty of passion. *Hell hath no fury, indeed.*

My first copy was on cassette. And for weeks, it might have appeared that I actually had Krazy-glued the sucker directly into my impressive-sized boom box. *Play. Repeat. Play. Repeat. Play. Repeat.*

Crackling with classic surf rock conviction, the title track made for a strong opener, while the gutsy, bluesy "Down on Me" pointed to a relationship on the skids — one of the record's many noteworthy moments. A delicate acoustic guitar instrumental, Nancy Wilson's "Silver Wheels" was a magical yin to the biting "Break" yang. Despite frequently wearing their Zeppelin influences on their sleeves, "Rockin' Heaven Down" proved that Heart was (and is), at their ball-breaking apex when satisfied simply with being — Heart.

It's been said frequently that heartbreak is the best inspiration for great art. And in that regard, "Even It Up" was a total bruiser. Despite achieving only moderate success as a single, it remains a band staple — accented famously by the legendary Tower of Power horn section. Another urgent rocker, "Strange Night" also was a hard-hitting highlight.

An infectious piano-driven number, Nancy Wilson's "Raised on You" danced across the grooves. And pinned to the purity of "Pilot," this dynamic double-shot made for a fabulous 7th inning stretch. Wrapping up the melodic trifecta, the record-closing "Sweet Darlin'" revealed a fleeting relationship that perhaps wasn't all bad — a heartfelt sentiment bathed in a melody that could rip your guts out — arguably one of Ann Wilson's most moving performances.

As a longtime drummer, vocalist, and songwriter, I was in the process of putting together a new music project in 2023, a country trio called Queen City Highway. Along with session guitarist, Chuck Lazaras, the group was set to also include rising blue grass princess, Mary Kate Brennan. I'd already been a huge Mary Kate fan for a few years at that time. As a result, I was psyched about the prospect of with working with her professionally, and I enjoyed hanging out with her as the project was developing.

One afternoon, we went to a popular local joint for chilidogs, because chilidogs are freaking delicious. Afterward, we went for milkshakes, because milkshakes are freaking delicious too. Then, we hit a nearby thrift mall, in pursuit of a couple of old country records. While we *did* discover a bunch of classics from the likes of Johnny Cash, Crystal Gayle, and Lynn Anderson, the only album that I actually felt compelled to purchase was a reasonably well-cared-for vinyl copy of *Bébé le Strange*, for just $3. Holy cow, more than 40 years on, it still packed one heckuva punch and it continues to stand as one of Heart's tallest studio sets.

Bébé le Strange

Track List

SIDE ONE

1. Bébé le Strange (A. Wilson, Ennis, N. Wilson, Fisher) – 3:38
2. Down on Me (A. Wilson, Ennis, N. Wilson) – 4:46
3. Silver Wheels (N. Wilson) – 1:22
4. Break (A. Wilson, Ennis, N. Wilson) – 2:32
5. Rockin' Heaven Down (A. Wilson, Ennis, N. Wilson) – 5:52

SIDE TWO

1. Even It Up (A. Wilson, Ennis, N. Wilson) – 5:10
2. Strange Night (A. Wilson, Ennis, N. Wilson) – 4:16
3. Raised on You (N. Wilson) – 3:21
4. Pilot (A. Wilson, Ennis, N. Wilson) – 3:15
5. Sweet Darlin' (A. Wilson) – 3:18

24
Jimi Hendrix Experience

Jimi Hendrix Experience
"Smash Hits"
(Reprise / July 1969)

Smash Hits

By the time the '60s became psychedelic, the world music scene owned a menagerie of edgy pop heartthrob frontmen, a slew of soon-to-be blood-transfused guitarists with mystique, a bunch of brooding bassists, and even a couple of wildly wacked-out drummers. But in the *truest* definition, it can be argued that there weren't any real *rock stars*, yet — until Jimi Hendrix crashed the party. Elvis was a *pop* star, BTW. Yeah, there's a difference. And not to tip anybody's "sacred cows," but truth be told, Keith, Mick, and their cast of contemporaries only became genuine rock stars *after* Jimi Hendrix gave them permission and mapped out the blueprint.

Dressed head to toe in beautiful crushed velvet, Hendrix was a branding genius, decades before that was a thing. Donning several evolving doos, along with an impressive collection of groovy headbands and fabulous feathered boas, he slashed his way onto the international rock stage with shamelessly flamboyant abandon — upside down Fender Strat in-hand, and all against a backdrop of ear-splitting Marshall amps. In the process, he changed everything and influenced everybody.

> "Hendrix's soul and feel cannot ever be replicated. You can hear just a second of his playing and know immediately that it's him. Pretty much every rock guitar player in the world has been influenced by Jimi Hendrix, whether they know it or not!"
> —Bella Perron
> Plush
> December 2023

Jimi Hendrix played guitar like no one else before (or since). His style was as brutal and sexual as it was musical. Ferocious feedback was his friend. But, so were sweet melodies. At the height of the "Peace and Love" era, he smashed his fair share of those prized Strats into piles of splintered kindling. Then, with his trusty can of lighter fluid always nearby, and his ever-faithful Zippo, he set that shit on fire! Remember, TIMELINE IS EVERTHING. It was the late '60s. The weekly *Smothers Brothers Comedy Hour* was considered controversial television. And bowl cuts and skirts above knees were downright unacceptable to decent folks.

> "Jimi Hendrix is Chuck Berry on acid. And once you realize it, every song is even better."
> —*Jimmy Failla*
> TV / radio host, comedian, author
> December 2023

Even as a wide-eyed tween hearing Hendrix for the first time on my monster-sized headphones circa '75, I recognized that his music was unique. "Purple Haze" wasn't "Smoke on the Water," "Slow Ride," or "Whole Lotta Love" for that matter. I'd never heard such an honest and pure guitar tone. As a now less wide-eyed little old man, I've still not heard anything like Hendrix.

The first time I experimented with drugs (strawberry rolling papers with a DIY roach clip and a dab of black tar on a tiny piece of aluminum foil), *Are You Experienced* was playing on my buddy's turntable. Although in 1978 it already had been out for nearly a decade, the album sounded fresh, innovative, and exciting, despite being stoned shitless and the comparatively primitive production techniques back in those days. Even lyrically, Hendrix had his thumb placed firmly on the pulse of current *and* future pop culture perspectives.

> "With such iconic albums as *Are You Experienced* and performances so wild, they're still talked about nearly 60 years later, Jimi Hendrix laid the foundation for all future generations of rock guitarists... while also defining what it means to be a total rock star."
> —*Bella Perron*
> Plush
> December 2023

I get such a kick out of watching TV music talent show contestants being showered with impulsive praise from celebrity judges who should know better — like that time the karaoke champ from Duluth skipped up to the mic and delivered a barely adequate rendition of a Journey staple. In short order, the kid was told by a platinum-selling pop star judge that they're "the whole package." Giddy with delight (and right on cue), the contestant then was complimented further by a different judge for being "an amazing *artist*" and "a gifted *storyteller*." Why did I find all that so amusing? Because, in reality, *Jimi Hendrix* actually was "the whole package." *Jimi Hendrix* was "an amazing artist." *Jimi Hendrix* was "a gifted storyteller." Funnier still, if Hendrix was to walk onto one of those shows today, he wouldn't pass the audition process. And even if he did, he definitely wouldn't get a single "turn." But I digress.

> "This record was always leaning up against the turntable cabinet, and I grew up hearing those songs with all the hisses and pops of the vinyl. When I bought the Hendrix catalog on CD, it took me a long time to appreciate the sharper, cleaned up versions of those songs. To this day, I prefer to hear the crackle during the opening riff of 'Purple Haze.'"
> — Scott Itter
> *Dr. Music* podcast host, concert photographer
> September 2023

I've included only a couple of compilation titles in this 50-chapter cavalcade, as "Greatest Hits" collections typically feel like less-than-legit albums to me. However, when I found this surprisingly well-cared-for, two-dollar vinyl copy of *Smash Hits* buried at a rummage sale in 2022, it gave me a cause for pause, a reason for reflection, and inspiration to share.

While Jimi Hendrix was the renowned "rock star," the album artist was credited as a band — the Jimi Hendrix Experience. Personally, I'm not so sure that bassist Noel Redding and drummer Mitch Mitchell truly got their deserved credit for just how much they brought to the Hendrix musical "experience." I'm certainly not a "guitar guy," but I absolutely am a "drum guy." And I'm more than qualified to comment without fear of contradiction, that Mr. Mitchell's talent, his skill and his rock-ribbed style made him as valuable of an asset as Mr. Hendrix.

> "Jimi Hendrix paved the way for so many great artists and bands. How could you not love this album?"
> —*Michael G. Yanko*
> Concert photographer
> Cocoa, Florida
> October 2023

The UK version of *Smash Hits* was released in 1967. My copy is the modified US version that dropped in 1969. Despite being a sliced-up showcase for Hendrix's most celebrated early work, the album remains a shining beacon, a bold testament to his timeless artistry. In sum, Jimi Hendrix was "the whole package," indeed.

Smash Hits

Track List

SIDE ONE
1. Purple Haze (Hendrix) – 2:46
2. Fire (Hendrix) – 2:34
3. The Wind Cries Mary (Hendrix) – 3:21
4. Can You See Me (Hendrix) – 2:31
5. Hey Joe (Roberts) – 3:23
6. All Along the Watchtower (Dylan) – 4:01

SIDE TWO
1. Stone Free (Hendrix) – 3:33
2. Crosstown Traffic (Hendrix) – 2:15
3. Manic Depression (Hendrix) – 3:30
4. Remember (Hendrix) – 2:47
5. Red House (Hendrix) – 3:48
6. Foxey Lady (Hendrix) – 3:15

25
Janis Ian

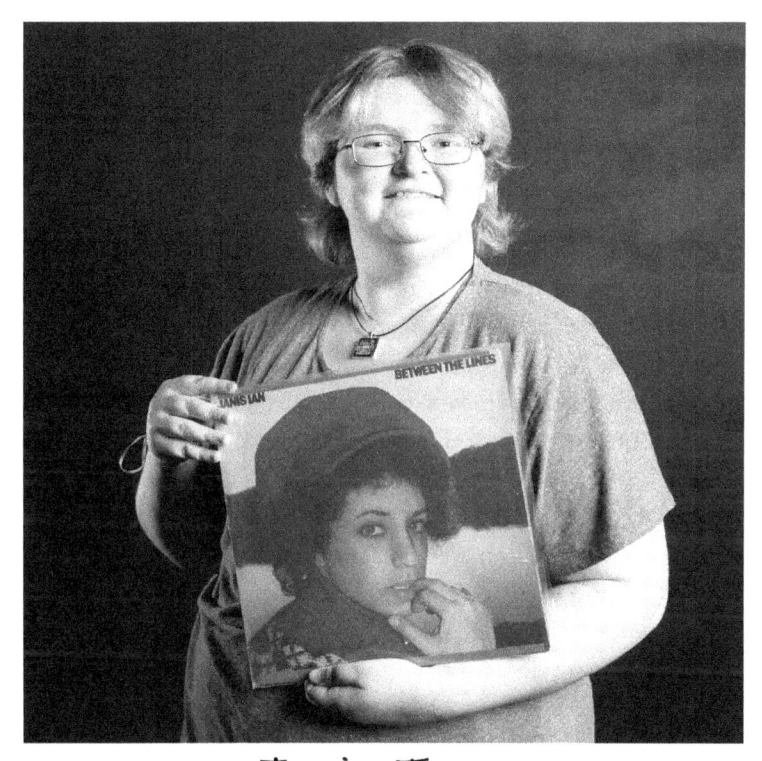

Janis Ian
"Between the Lines"
(Columbia / March 1975)

Between the Lines

There's a memorable scene in the Oscar-winning 2000 Cameron Crowe film, *Almost Famous*, in which the fictional rock band Stillwater is being schooled by their big-time music manager on the importance of mystique. The cool thing about prolific singer, songwriter, and author Janis Ian is, she *oozes* mystique. She always has. As a naïve church boy growing up during the late '60s and early '70s, even I could spot her undeniable mystique factor. You could see it in her eyes, especially in her various early TV appearances — Janis Ian was transmitting from an entirely different dimension from her contemporaries.

And she wasn't playin'. A fresh-faced teen at the time, Ian stirred a mighty shitstorm when she dropped her debut single, "Society's Child." Clearly, in 1966, America wasn't nearly ready to embrace the then-taboo topic of interracial romance. I was too young to feel the effect of Ian's first tsunami in the '60s. However, as a devout pre-pube parishioner at The First United Church of Casey Kasem, I nearly drowned during Ian's second massive wave in the '70s.

Following a few of her leaner years, Ian's seventh LP arrived in stores during the spring of 1975, and by the summer, *Between the Lines* was bubbling up as one of the season's hottest album releases.

My family had just relocated from the Ozark mountains of Missouri to the sunny beaches of Florida. Suddenly, I found myself in an unfamiliar place, with no friends. The few people with whom I did connect were way too cool, too pretty, and too popular to have much need for a nerdy, 12-year-old "new kid." As a result, Janis Ian became my one "friend," offering me solace via the little AM radio tucked under my pillow at night. Through the lyrics of her chart-busting single, "At Seventeen," we seemingly understood each other — at an incredibly difficult and awkward time.

Fast forward nearly 50 years, and there we were, the GF and I, hauling off a bag-o-budget-priced used LPs at the Mount Dora, Florida flea market — super-scores from the likes of Bob Welch, Dave Edmunds, Leo Sayer, and *that* Janis Ian album.

Upon arriving back at the GF's funky abode, I placed the "seasoned" copy of *Between the Lines* onto the turntable, posthaste. *Wow, this record is still SO beautiful!* Then, a few nights later, I popped by the GF's for dinner, when I received the tragic news. Poking her head out from the kitchen, she proclaimed boldly, "BTW, you're NOT getting that Janis Ian album back, ever."

Ugh! I now would have to seek out a *second* vinyl copy of a decades-old LP that ain't exactly easy to locate. Oddly, I somehow accomplished the perceived impossible mission.

In early 2023, I reached out to Janis Ian to get *her* thoughts on this magical record.

∴

Overseen by Brooks Arthur (Neil Diamond, Van Morrison), Between the Lines still feels good, from start to finish. It had to have been incredible, working with such a celebrated producer.

"Brooks was amazing. I've been very lucky that I had two great producers in my life. I've had very good producers like Jim Cregan, but Shadow Morton and Brooks Arthur were great producers. Shadow went from the Shangri-Las to me and 'Society's Child' to 'In-A-Gadda-Da-Vida.' Brooks engineered 'Society's Child' and then produced 'At Seventeen.' He really taught me how to sing in the studio. He had an ear for how to combine sounds so that the singer's voice was never obscured, but all the instruments were heard. It's nice that people remember how involved he was, because without Brooks or Ron Frangipane, to be fair, that record never would have been what it turned out to be. We stayed close friends until literally, he died a few months ago."

Any particular "fly on the wall" recollections from the recording sessions?

"There was a little stress between me and Brooks because the studio was operating 24 hours. I was swapping off times with Bruce Springsteen, who would come in when I was done, and Melanie, who would come in after Bruce. Brooks was trying to engineer everybody, so you can imagine how stressful that was. But on top of it, we all knew we had something special going on. I remember going to Brooks at the end and begging him to try and find enough money that we could afford to record another six songs, because I felt like the band we had, the studio we were in, the timing of everything was just right and we would never be able to replicate it. And I was right. We never were."

Between the Lines soared to #1 on the Billboard chart and moved over a million copies quickly. Were you surprised by the album's overnight success?

"That's a funny question, because none of us had time to be surprised. 'At Seventeen' and the Between the Lines album looked like they suddenly came out of nowhere and shot up the charts, but we worked that record for six months before it really went anywhere. And by 'worked,' I mean I got up at 6AM every day to do the morning news shows, and then I'd do the afternoon shows, then I'd do the afternoon radio, and the drive-time later, and then go to soundcheck, and try to eat something, do the show, meet the mayor and his family afterward, and fall into bed at midnight or one or two in the morning. We all — all the CBS promotion people, all of my band members, everybody on my team, we worked and worked and worked."

Oddly, "At Seventeen" was not the first single released from the album. Was that some sort of label goof?

"That was very calculated. The executive producer was Herb Gart, a very smart fellow. And he said, 'At Seventeen' is gonna be a tough record to break. It's too long. They're gonna say it's depressing. They're gonna say it's not a drive-time record. So, let's lead with 'When the Party's Over' and have all the DJs come back to us and say, 'Are you nuts? This song is the single.'"

"At the same time, to get it on TV, he sent copies to all the television news anchors' wives. At the time, pretty much all of the news anchors were male. So he sent the producers' wives and the news anchors' wives copies of the record, which was really smart, because then they'd say, 'Why isn't she on your show?' I don't know that the record would have broken without that kind of outside-the-box thinking. Because that album was, in hindsight, pretty radical."

Honest and pure, cozy and compelling, Between the Lines found you at the top of your game. Were there any other personal song highlights besides the monster hit single?

"'From Me to You,' I think really shines on that album. I think 'Watercolors' is a standout. That's (about) a relationship that has splintered, except nobody knows it yet. To tell you the truth, I didn't know what that song was about, 'til years later when an ex-boyfriend said to me, 'I can't believe you wrote that about us.' And I thought, 'Oh my gosh, I did.'"

Nearly 50 years following its initial release, Between the Lines remains one of the most sought-after titles in your impressive catalog. Given the additional renewed interest in vinyl, are there any plans to perhaps reissue the record?

"We're trying at some point to put something together to release the remastered version on vinyl. We just managed to re-release it on CD, completely remastered with all the correct artwork, and I'm hoping to release it again on vinyl, because the vinyl everybody's hearing is the original vinyl. Which is great, except there's not a lot of it around."

∴

Still oozing mystique some 60 years into the game, Janis Ian continues to transmit from that different dimension. Her best-selling 2009 autobiography *Society's Child* is an absolute must-read for diehard *and* casuals fans alike, and her 2022 album *The Light at the End of the Line*, not only was one of her strongest efforts in years, it also was nominated for "Best Folk Album" at the 2023 Grammy Awards. And the shitstorm continues!

Between the Lines

Track List
(All songs written by Janis Ian)

SIDE ONE
1. When the Party's Over – 2:57
2. At Seventeen – 4:41
3. From Me to You – 3:19
4. Bright Lights and Promises – 4:17
5. In the Winter – 2:29
6. Watercolors – 4:58

SIDE TWO
1. Between the Lines – 4:03
2. The Come On – 3:56
3. Light a Light – 2:45
4. Tea & Sympathy – 4:28
5. Lover's Lullaby – 5:25

26
Jefferson Starship

Jefferson Starship
"Spitfire"
(Grunt / June 1976)

Spitfire

T-I-M-B-E-R-R-R-!

If hacked down in a musical forest, an experienced logger could easily count the many rings of this nearly 60-year-old rock and roll Monterey cypress. During their high-flying early days as the Jefferson Airplane, the group defined the psychedelic San Francisco sound of the '60s. Boasting a revamped lineup, the band transformed into the cosmic Jefferson Starship and rocketed further into the stratosphere during the '70s. Under the stripped-down moniker, Starship, the former pioneers of the peace and love movement became purveyors of platinum-selling pop during the '80s. Today, various tribute-type incarnations of the famed franchise still tour across the country.

∴

As a rock-crazed 11-year-old, I'd completely missed my flight on the Jefferson Airplane. However, I totally was on board (E-ticket in-hand) when Jefferson Starship launched their debut LP, *Dragon Fly*, in '74.

Truth be told, lo-fi protest songs by shabby-looking hippies never was my thing. But, polished, quadraphonic rock tunes by sweet-smelling "Golden Gods" definitely *was* up my alley. As a result, I fell to my knees at the rock and roll altar at age 12 when Jefferson Starship dropped their chart-topping, multi-platinum-selling sophomore set, *Red Octopus*, in '75. *Go, Papa John! Go!*

By the time their third album, *Spitfire*, hit stores in '76, Jefferson Starship had become MY band. Now age 13, I was hooked hopelessly on their irresistible, made-for-FM sound. And the band's fetching, unfiltered co-vocalist, Grace Slick, was a tremendous source of personal teenage inspiration. *Boy Howdy!*

I was traumatized when, as a kid, my family relocated from Springfield, Missouri to Orlando, Florida. Decades later, as a little old man, I still haven't gotten over it. I *never* felt like a Space Coast kid. I'll *always* be a kid from the

Ozark Mountains — one who just never found my way back home. However, once the COVID thing happened, I quickly became considerably more grateful to be living in the "Sunshine State."

Simply put, Floridians don't like being told what to do. And while most states were "taking a knee" in 2020, locking down and masking up, Florida was "open for business." Don't get me wrong, COVID was real. People got sick, and tragically, people died. Believe me, I don't make light of that. It was the government's "peculiar," over-the-top *response* to the "random" virus that I found *truly* scary. But that's a conversation better suited for another place and time.

My point is, most Americans merely were existing — helpless prisoners held hostage in their very own homes, yet us "deplorable" Floridians actually were, *living*. While we *did*, to a degree, have to "play the game" for a short period, we were pretty much free to travel, go shopping, go to restaurants, go to the beach — whatever the heck we wanted. The "mouse" had to eat, ya know.

For a guy whose revenue stream was connected directly to the nightclub industry, residing in Florida proved to be a blessing. Another wonderful thing was that after only a brief "pause," record stores in Florida also were open — a HUGE deal for a guy whose professional writing endeavors frequently required accessing physical music in a jiff.

It was during that time when the GF and I made a pilgrimage down to Vero Beach where we discovered an amazing indie music shop, Wax Records Inc. From new and used vinyl and CDs to in-the-box *and* vintage home audio gear, as well as other related accessories, this place had so much cool stuff it took the first hour just to process all the possibilities.

Unlike too many modern-day outlets, Wax Records wasn't gouging people — like charging $50 for an unplayable piece of trash vinyl simply because some geeker website says that's what it's worth. Not only was their overall pricing generally reasonable, they also had boxes and bins of budget-priced records that were as pristine as most of their "top shelf" inventory. After a couple of hours rummaging around the joint, the GF and I scored BAGS *full* of LPs on the cheap, including *this* "VG" copy of *Spitfire*, which I nabbed for just $3 — a particularly sweet score considering that, like so many other records I'd bought as a teen, my original vinyl copy of *Spitfire* somehow vanished over the years to who knows where.

A production collab between the band and studio vet, Larry Cox, *Spitfire* raced straight out of the box and shot to the *Billboard* Top Ten. The colorful, eye-catching album cover depicting a mystical-looking woman riding a wild-looking dragon captured my young imagination instantly and demanded a place in my personal growing LP collection.

Driven by "more cowbell," a swanky bass groove, and funky guitar riffs, "Cruisin'" set the stage amid swirling orchestration. Co-frontman, Marty Balin, commandeered the mic and took the wheel, as he breezed up the freeway — windows down. And with complete cock-rock confidence, he confessed, "You're lookin' so foxy by my side." #OnlyInThe70s

Without missing a beat, "Dance with the Dragon" was another delight. The piano contribution from Pete Sears twinkled, while the ripe guitar work of Craig Chaquico tasted oh-so-sweet. The Paul Kantner-led, signature-style call-and-response group vocals made it sound like a raucous house party — one to which we *all* were invited. *"Call it macaroni," baby!*

Slick stepped up to the mic and amplified the "inspiration" factor further on the super-sexy, high-octane rocker, "Hot Water." Whether the water was hot or cold, *that* was a tub I needed to be in. Although "team Starship" certainly was an all-star operation, the track presented a convincing case for how (with sticks-a-twirlin') drummer, John Barbata, was totally worthy of taking home the record's MVP honors. His kick foot and ride wrist alone were worth the price of admission.

"St. Charles" sounded like a romantic fantasy playing out in an exotic locale. Balin's lead vocal accented the group vocals wonderfully. The marvelous keyboard work of David Freiberg made this one a particular treasure, as guitar chaos ensued, revving into a massive crescendo.

The two-part "Song to the Sun: Ozymandias / Don't Let It Rain" was a mystical seven-minute masterpiece that could have coexisted harmoniously on the same record with "Hyperdrive" back in '74, while Balin's honey-smacked ballad, "With Your Love" served as a "101" blend of radio-friendly AM pop and FM rock — a perfect follow-up to the band's 1975 chart-buster, "Miracles."

A beautiful heartache ballad, "Switchblade" felt painfully honest. An unassuming love letter, it was one of Slick's all-time most powerful performances. Pete Sears earned mad props here for his warm organ accompaniment and space age moogin'.

"Big City" was an unexpected honky tonk-style rock and roll feel-good. Featuring Barbata on lead vocals, it led perfectly into the soaring, record-closing "Love Lovely Love" — none more '70s, to be sure.

In sum, the impeccable body of work created by Jefferson Starship was magical and timeless. Even after nearly 50 years, *Spitfire* remains a mighty stinger of a record.

Spitfire

Track List

SIDE ONE
1. Cruisin' (Hickox) – 5:27
2. Dance with the Dragon (Kantner, Slick, Balin, Chaquico, Sears) – 5:02
3. Hot Water (Slick, Sears) – 3:17
4. St. Charles (Kantner, Balin, Barish, Chaquco, Thunderhawk) – 6:38

SIDE TWO
1. Song to the Sun: Pt I Ozymandias / Pt II Don't Let It Rain (P. Kantner, Chaquico, Barbata, Freiberg, Sears, Slick, C. Kantner) – 7:15
2. With Your Love (Balin, Covington, Smith) – 3:33
3. Switchblade (Slick) – 4:01
4. Big City (Barbata, Hill, Ethridge) – 3:20
5. Love Lovely Love (Barish) – 3:31

27
Elton John

Elton John
"Captain Fantastic and the Brown Dirt Cowboy"
(MCA / May 1975)

Captain Fantastic and the Brown Dirt Cowboy

It had been one heckuva wild ride — a five-year run that saw massive success — 14 US Top 40 singles and eight US Top Ten studio albums. In fact, including the recently-released *Greatest Hits* record, the British songwriting partnership of pianist / vocalist Elton John and lyricist Bernie Taupin had seen their last five consecutive LPs all hit #1 in America. By early 1975, it was hard to imagine the dynamic duo blowing up any bigger. But they did. And in May 1975, they released what would become arguably their most celebrated set, *Captain Fantastic and the Brown Dirt Cowboy*. The first pop-rock album ever to debut at #1 on the *Billboard* album chart, *Captain Fantastic* was a personal retrospective — a musical diary that reflected Elton and Bernie's unassuming beginnings working together in the late '60s. The record shipped gold (500,000 units) and then turned platinum (1,000,000 units) within days.

There's a scene in director Cameron Crowe's award-winning film, *Almost Famous*, in which 11-year-old William Miller gazes wide-eyed as he peruses his older sister's vinyl album collection, circa 1969 — classic LPs from The Who, Neil Young, Crosby, Stills & Nash, Joni Mitchell and others. That scene is particularly spot-on, as in those wondrous days, record releases were beautiful, magical works of art — from the songs to the musicianship to the production to the album covers to the liner notes to the photography. And in that regard, *Captain Fantastic* offered the whole package — spectacular cover art created by Alan Aldridge, *two* booklets and a "fantastic" poster of the entire opened outer gatefold jacket — ALL for the (now) unheard of bargain price of just $5.99 (maybe $5.49 if your mom took ya to Kmart).

Music consumption always has been a very personal, spiritual experience. As it's been said, our music chooses us — not the other way around. At age 12, many of my closest compadres had older siblings whose personal album collections included classics from the likes of Deep Purple, Black Sabbath, Jimi Hendrix, and Led Zeppelin. For a good many of my pre-teen peeps, *Captain Fantastic* was one of the first rock-oriented albums targeted to the older high school crowd that seemed to speak to *us* too.

I once had a dear friend named Greg. We both were the same age, and as kids, we both loved *Captain Fantastic* — a lot. More than 20 years later, Greg was one of my frequent customers where I was a bartender. Every night at closing time, I'd lock up, restock the bar, and Z-out the register while Greg kept me company — knocking back Jose Cuervo shots, one by one, as if they were Kool-Aid. Frequently, we would get into something of a battle, quoting random lyrics from various *Captain Fantastic* songs.

Greg's favorite tune from the album was the title track. Bathed in Elton's warm electric piano and glossed with his honey-soaked vocals, the song was accented by Davey Johnstone's crisp acoustic guitar work, as it gave way to a racing bridge and soaring crescendo. Greg often would wave his empty shot glass in the air to get my attention and holler out, "Hey! 'Two teas. Both with sugar, please!'"— an iconic line from the song.

There have been very few people in my life who I've loved as much I loved Greg. He was such a great guy. And I was humbled and honored when I was asked to officiate Greg's funeral a decade or so later. The eulogy I gave was emotional and deeply personal. I brought Greg's 20-something son up to the front of the service, and *together* we toasted his father. Our beverages? That's right, two teas. Both with sugar (please).

Elton's longtime producer, Gus Dudgeon once stated, "There's not one song on it (*Captain Fantastic*) that's less than incredible." Elton himself has stated, "I've always thought that *Captain Fantastic* was probably my finest album." Hence, to dissect the record properly, could fill an entire book. However, there is an array of stand-out bullet points.

On "Tower of Babel," Elton's vocals were wonderfully soulful, while Johnstone's solo was gloriously gritty. "Bitter Fingers" was packed with playful verses and crunchy choruses — *I'm sick of tra la las and la de das!*. "Tell Me When the Whistle Blows" remains a delicate, bluesy treasure, while the record's sole single, "Someone Saved My Life Tonight" has become one of the most endearing Elton John staples — a Top Ten smash that Elton has referred to as, "one of the best songs that Bernie and I have ever written together."

If you're not absolutely moved by the heart-racing, guitar-driven urgency of "(Gotta Get A) Meal Ticket," it's probably time to call an EMT, 'cuz you're clearly flat-lining. Conversely, "We All Fall in Love Sometimes" remains a heartfelt masterpiece.

In addition to Johnstone's brilliant guitar playing, the record also benefited equally from Dee Murray's rock-ribbed basslines. Nigel Olsson's dry, yet fat-sounding, signature-style meat and potatoes drumming was superb as always. Olsson knows when to smash a note, and he knows when to simply let it breathe.

Sometimes less IS more. For Ray Cooper, his percussion work dances from the left to right speaker — making these songs pop with utmost precision.

There are few within my personal circle whose lives *haven't* been touched by the *Captain Fantastic* record. My (now) grown son also was raised on the record. Even a couple of my closest current teenage cronies know and love the album, from start to finish. Elton John and Bernie Taupin may have intended for *Captain Fantastic* to tell *their* story, but, for me and the people in my world, nearly a half-century later, it's (still) telling *ours*.

My original LP copy disappeared years ago. While I've owned two different CD configurations of the album since then, digital just didn't provide the same satisfaction as vinyl. The GF owned TWO vinyl copies, but CLEARLY, *neither* of those were *ever* gonna leave her house. So, after purchasing a new high-end hi-fi for my place in 2023, I began poking around for my own *Captain Fantastic* replacement LP. And I found one, for just $4 at a local joint near Cocoa Beach. Tragically, even in my garage sale vinyl excursions, sometimes, you do get what you pay for. And in this case, $4 didn't buy me much. In fact, even after a thorough cleanly, it was 100% unplayable. *Aw, rats!* And so, the search continues.

Captain Fantastic and the Brown Dirt Cowboy

Track List
(All songs written by Elton John and Bernie Taupin)

SIDE ONE
1. Captain Fantastic and the Brown Dirt Cowboy – 5:45
2. Tower of Babel – 4:28
3. Bitter Fingers – 4:32
4. Tell Me When the Whistle Blows – 4:20
5. Someone Saved My Life Tonight – 6:45

SIDE TWO
1. (Gotta Get A) Meal Ticket – 4:00
2. Better Off Dead – 2:35
3. Writing – 3:38
4. We All Fall in Love Sometimes – 4:15
5. Curtains – 6:12

28
The Kinks

The Kinks
"Low Budget"
(Arista / July 1979)

Low Budget

Have you ever been high? Be honest. I mean *really* high. I'm talking about being so freaking obliterated that your tongue becomes two-feet-thick as you achieve a drooling level of bloodshot, dumbass paranoia so extreme that *every* sound is a cop siren, *every* flash in the rearview is a cop light, and *every* stranger standing behind you in line at 7-Eleven MUST BE — a cop. That was me, on an all-too-frequent basis. But, that was a VERY long time ago. Fortunately, it's *never* too late to get your shit together.

• •

It was 1979. And the soundtrack to my near-nightly "hit parade" of poor adolescent decisions was *Low Budget* blasting from the 8-track tape deck that my dad had installed under the front driver's seat of the family Chevy Chevette.

The Kinks undeniably were one of the "Big Four." Along with The Beatles, The Stones and The Who, they helped to define the British pop-rock sound of the psychedelic '60s. And in the process, they also designed the blueprint that angry punk and hungry metal acts would follow for years to come. Led by singer / songwriter, Ray Davies, and his guitarist brother, Dave Davies, the band enjoyed an impressive initial string of successful street-smart singles. "You Really Got Me," "All Day and All of the Night," "Tired of Waiting for You," "Sunny Afternoon" and "Lola" all made cannonball-size splashes on both sides of "the pond" from '64-'70.

As the 1970s played on, The Kinks were concentrating more on creating lofty theatrical albums and less on producing snappy hit singles. As a result, the band's popularity had waned considerably by 1975. Upon signing The Kinks to his newly-formed Arista Records label, music industry mogul, Clive Davis, encouraged the band to refocus on radio-friendly fare. Hence, they scored their first US hit album in years, reaching #21 with *Sleepwalker* in 1977. However, their next set, *Misfits*, stalled at #40 in 1978.

Us "seasoned" folks can recognize what a dumpster fire the world has become in recent years. And we have the good fortune to have been around long enough to reflect fondly on what we *believe* were the "good ol' days." But, truth be told, the late '70s weren't all about lava lamp-lit exploits in carpeted custom vans, while the carefree chorus of "Mu-Mu-Mu-Mu-Mu-Mu-Mu-Mu-My Sharona" serenaded horny teens to premature ecstasy. In fact, 1979 was a troubled time. Economic tension was global. There was a perceived energy crisis, gas was becoming a scarce commodity, the Middle East cats were going bonkers and a peanut farmer from Plains, Georgia was in the US presidential hot seat. Musically, disco was heading for its demise and the rock market was being flooded by crunchy new wave combos, all with spiky haircuts, skinny ties and the word, "The" prefacing their band names.

The Kinks had that "crunch" factor, for sure. They even had some spiky hair, a couple of skinny ties and the word "The" in their trademark logo. So, what would this once influential British band from the '60s do in the '70s to remain relevant in the upcoming '80s? They took up residency at the famed Power Station recording studio located in the congested, clattering streets of New York City. They climbed neck-deep into the cultural muck of the big city, ingested the stench, and then allowed that "inspiration" to seep from their artistic pores. And it's that streetwise authenticity that drips from the grooves of *Low Budget*, arguably the sexist, most exciting record of The Kinks' storied career.

Even the *Low Budget* album cover was kind of dirty and sexy — a super-tight close-up of red spandex-wrapped ankles seemingly belonging to a presumed "professional" gal standing on a cement street corner, with tootsies contained tightly in red heels and crushed, lipstick-stained cigarette butts scattered about. Painted on the asphalt between her feet... that classic Kinks logo.

Produced by Ray Davies, the 11-song set found the band with its collective fingers placed firmly on the pulse of the culture at the time. Kicking off with legit punk rock fury, "Attitude" served as a blistering bitch slap; a four-minute "self-improvement" seminar courtesy of Ray to an individual apparently steeped in an "alternative" lifestyle — "It's not your manners, that you gotta improve. Ooooo, it's your attitude!"

Opening with a delicate piano intro, "Catch Me Now I'm Falling" quickly borrows a little "mo" from "Jumping Jack Flash." Addressing how the US had few global allies at the time, Ray announces, "This is Captain America Calling — calling!" Crisp and compelling, this one was a stand-out, for sure. Kudos to Nick Newall for the superb sax work.

"Pressure" flashes a brief glimpse of Chuck Berry's "School Days," just before surrendering to a wall of Ramones-inspired riffage. Pointing to a certain preferred physical "tension" release method exercised primarily by teenage boys far and wide, "National Health" proclaims, "It sure beats Quaaludes. It sure beats cocaine. Even Freud recommends it, 'cuz it relieves the strain."

"(Wish I Could Fly Like) Superman," offers an Everyman confession of facing real-life struggles. This disco-flavored earworm charted semi-respectfully, just missing Casey's weekly countdown and it remains a *Low Budget* highlight.

Grounded by Dave Davies' signature guitar chug, the 200-pound title track was the real deal then, and it's the real deal now. Free of privileged rock star pretense, Ray admits transparently, "I'm just a cut-price person in a low budget land." When pinned against the melodic "Celluloid Heroes"-style charm of "Little Bit of Emotion," one can truly appreciate the wide array of aural paints used to create this vivid social portrait.

Reminiscent of some of the band's early work, "Misery" was catchy, fun and bouncy, while "Moving Pictures" resembled the bubbly, giggly drunk gal at the office holiday party. Possessing a particularly unique stylistic DNA, it was an irresistible record-closer.

Even without the drugs, *Low Budget* still packs a powerful personal punch. Its buzzy riffs and biting social commentary remain as fresh and relevant as ever. Oddly, I never owned the LP version of the album — I'd only ever owned it on 8-track. So, I was super-psyched to finally discover a semi-low budget-priced $8 copy at a local joint in 2019. And it's one of the cleanest and quietest of my garage sale vinyl finds. *Score!*

Low Budget

Track List
(All songs written by Ray Davies)

SIDE ONE
1. Attitude – 3:47
2. Catch Me Now I'm Falling – 5:56
3. Pressure – 2:45
4. National Health – 4:02
5. (Wish I Could Fly Like) Superman – 3:35

SIDE TWO
1. Low Budget – 3:46
2. In a Space – 3:43
3. Little Bit of Emotion – 4:50
4. A Gallon of Gas – 2:41
5. Misery – 2:57
6. Moving Pictures – 3:33

29
KISS

KISS
"Dynasty"
(Casablanca Records / May 1979)

Dynasty

The scent of Monica's perfume was intoxicating. Her delightful fragrance cut through the undeniable aroma of local reefer blended with the bouquet of fresh Budweiser that hung in the air. It was an end-of-the-school-year "hoo-ha," attended by nearly 100 kids I knew from Satellite High. At age 16, I could have been described best as a scumbag. At 15, Monica could have been described best as an angel. A total Coppertone cutie, Monica looked adorable that night in her surfer shirt and painter's pants, accented by a stylish puka shell necklace. And I was stoked about being on our first date.

I was no stranger to these types of backyard soirees. I'd often bring my albums from home and play DJ — forcing "real" rock and roll onto the predominately pabulum-crazed teenage attendees — a selfless, humanitarian effort that typically met with shouts of "KISS sucks!" from many of my Jimmy Buffett-loving classmates.

But much had changed over the last couple of years. My kabuki-faced heroes no longer were seen as dark and dangerous. In fact, given their exploding merchandise empire — dolls, makeup kits, lunchboxes, and such, KISS now was perceived by many as a "kiddie" band. And their new pop-fueled album, *Dynasty*, did little to reignite KISS' fading street cred. Of course I bought the record on its first day of release in May 1979 and I absolutely loved it from the first spin. However, it was NOT a record that I brought to *this* night's social gathering.

> "When I was little — little, like younger than five, I was really drawn to KISS. I just thought Ace Frehley's smoking guitar, the outfits and makeup and everything was the coolest thing. That's why I wanted to start playing."
> —Bella Perron
> Plush
> October 2021

Since releasing their self-titled debut in 1974, KISS seemed to have done everything right — building a bankable international reputation as the "Hottest Band in the Land." But, by the spring of 1979, cracks were appearing in their platinum pavement. It had been two years since KISS hit the Top Ten with their last studio LP, *Love Gun* — a lifetime in the days when rock bands often released two albums per year. Despite projecting the intended image of unity, the band members' 1978 solo album releases actually served as a further indicator of how KISS was splintering behind the scenes. And their recent TV movie, *KISS Meets the Phantom of the Park*, was seen as an embarrassing bungle, even by me. As a result, KISS needed a BIG hit — NOW.

> "*Dynasty* demonstrated KISS' seasoned and often overshadowed pop sensibility. Paul Stanley was the reigning king on this album, delivering the smash hit, 'I Was Made For Loving You' and the equally brilliant pop-infused powerhouses, 'Sure Know Something' and 'Magic Touch.'"
> — Ken Sharp
> Musician, songwriter, producer, author
> Encino, California
> June 2023

The band was imploding, but most fans wouldn't have guessed it by the looks of *Dynasty*. All four original members appeared prominently on the cover and shared in the songwriting and lead vocals. Only later was it revealed that drummer Peter Criss had been replaced on the entire album by Anton Fig — the powerhouse who had played so famously on Ace Frehley's solo record.

Overseen by Vini Poncia, the celebrated songwriter who also had produced Peter Criss' solo record, *Dynasty* was EXACTLY the album that KISS needed — at that time.

Despite being branded over the years as a disco record, *Dynasty* merely was a super-polished, guitar-driven pop-rock record, much like other chart-busting releases of the day from such established artists as The Stones, Rod Stewart and Queen. In fact, it can be argued that KISS was far more effective as a pop group in the '70s than it was masquerading as a hair band in the '80s or as a grunge band in the '90s. But all arguments aside, *Dynasty* became a worldwide smash, particularly in the US, where it achieved platinum-selling, Top Ten status and birthed a monstrous Top 20 single — the infectious Paul Stanley / Vini Poncia / Desmond Child collab, "I Was Made for Lovin' You."

> "There was some good stuff on this album, like the quiet parts between songs."
> *– Chuck Lazaras*
> Songwriter, session guitarist
> Cocoa, Florida
> December 2023

With honest lead vocals provided by lead guitarist, Ace Frehley, the remake of the Mick Jagger and Keith Richards-penned, "2,000 Man" felt more like an authentic KISS tune than a Stones classic. Frehley spread his creative wings further with his additional two *Dynasty* contributions — the street-smart "Hard Times" and the crunchy break-up track, "Save Your Love."

Not to be outshined by the "Spaceman," the "Starchild" also contributed three tracks to *Dynasty*. In addition to "I Was Made for Lovin' You," Paul Stanley also offered up a pair of perfect pop-rock gems — "Sure Know Something" and "Magic Touch."

> "Syncin' Stanley here, people... AND LISTEN! I love *Dynasty*, ESPECIALLY the 'Paul' songs. 'Sure Know Something' is one of my favorite KISS songs, EVER!"
> *– Syncin' Stanley*
> Parody character
> October 2023

As for Gene Simmons, the "Demon" contributed two impressive chest-thumpers — the irresistible, ego-driven, "Charisma," and the equally satisfying sing-along, "X-Ray Eyes."

Residing stylistically somewhere between his previous *Love Gun* track, "Hooligan" and the Donna Summer hit, "Hot Stuff," Peter Criss' sole vocal / songwriting contribution, "Dirty Livin'" was the cat's meow.

My affection for *Dynasty* lasted way longer than Monica's affection for me. Decades after the demise of my original LP, I was gifted a slightly scuffed vinyl copy from a friend for FREE. Currently, it's residing at the GF's, not because I'm an ultra-sweetie guy, but because KISS music just doesn't speak to me as loudly in my sixties as it did in my teens. Truth be told, for me, the band stayed at the "party" WAY too long. In the process, the iconic KISS mystique was exterminated completely, forever. But, I will offer mad props to Paul Stanley for forging into the future fearlessly. With his latest project, Soul Station, Stanley combines R&B classics with authentic, Motown-inspired originals. And his 2021 debut album, *Now and Then*, was his best and brightest work since his faultless '78 solo album. Yeah, I own it on vinyl. But *that* one lives at *my* place!

Dynasty

Track List

SIDE ONE

1. I Was Made for Lovin' You (Stanley, Poncia, Child) – 4:30
2. 2,000 Man (Jagger, Richards) – 4:54
3. Sure Know Something (Stanley, Poncia) – 4:00
4. Dirty Livin' (Criss, Poncia, Penridge) – 4:19

SIDE TWO

1. Charisma (Simmons, Marks) – 4:25
2. Magic Touch (Stanley) – 4:41
3. Hard Times (Frehley) – 3:30
4. X-Ray Eyes (Simmons) – 3:46
5. Save Your Love (Frehley) – 4:41

30
Led Zeppelin

Led Zeppelin
"Led Zeppelin III"
(Atlantic / October 1970)

Led Zeppelin III

Don't ya just love *The Brady Bunch*? I sure do! But you gotta feel kinda bad for Jan Brady. Despite being a good-natured go-getter, Jan never seemed to get her props. Her presence was overshadowed constantly by her older Prom Queen sister, Marcia. And she wasn't as bubbly as her precocious younger sister, Cindy. Even competing for attention among her newly-adopted brothers proved challenging for Jan. She was less outgoing than Greg and she lacked Peter's quirky charm. However, Jan *did* outshine her younger brother, Bobby. But then again, *everybody* outshined Bobby. Everybody, *except* Sam the butcher — he was plain creepy. In that regard, *Led Zeppelin III* could possibly be perceived as the "Jan" of the iconic Zep catalog.

> "I've loved Led Zeppelin since I was a 4th grade, four-eyed nothing growing up in the hills and valleys of Ohio rock n' roll suburbia. This third album — we only listened to certain tracks; 'Immigrant Song,' of course and 'Gallows Pole.' It really was the 'Jan Brady' of albums, now that I think about it. Overlooked and underappreciated."
> —Anna-Marie O'Brien
> Author
> July 2023

Designed by multi-media artist Zacron, the original pressing *Led Zeppelin III* LP resided in a gatefold sleeve. With its eye-catching, built-in interactive spinning wheel, the album boasted one of the most elaborate and expensive cover designs of the day. Yet, at the time, it still went for a very reasonable $5.48 down at Sears.

"It was my cousins who actually got me into Led Zeppelin. I remember going over to their houses and going through their records and playing the *Led Zeppelin III* album... spinning it and stuff."
—Charlie Benante
Anthrax
July 2023

"One of the coolest album covers of all time! Every time I look at my vinyl copy I notice something new among all of the random images. The art contributes so much to the vinyl experience. The cover gives the visual of how wildly creative the album is. I still love to turn the wheel in the album cover and look at all of the changing images!"
—Bella Perron
Plush
June 2023

"Metallica were going to be inducted into the Rock & Roll Hall of Fame, and they invited Scott (Ian) and myself to the festivities. The night before the ceremony, they had a party at the Hard Rock and Jimmy Page was there. For me, Jimmy Page is the ultimate rock star. I was introduced to him by the photographer Ross Halfin. Immediately, I went right into something, and caught his attention because I asked, 'Jimmy, back on Zeppelin III, I've always heard, and I've read that the engineer erased a major part of a song that was going into 'Celebration Day,' it was this whole musical piece.' Jimmy went right into it and started talking about it. I just stood there, in amazement, that I was talking to Jimmy Page — about this! He was so eloquent in explaining how it happened — it just made my year!"
—Charlie Benante
Anthrax
July 2023

Stylistically, the songs presented a rainbow-like array of aural colors — a massive and appealing ten-track palette, indeed. Fast and furious, the record-opening "Immigrant Song" moved quicker than Miss Pamela ironing Jimmy Page's satin wizard pants before a *Rolling Stone* photo shoot. *Hurry along, darlin'! Annie's gonna be here any minute!*

The hypnotic orchestration and unapologetic fret buzz of "Friends" pitted against the soul-cleansing crunch of "Celebration Day" provided a powerful double-whammy. Page's blues-soaked guitar swagger cozied up nicely with John Paul Jones' organ allure on "Since I've Been Loving You" — a track that still stands as one of Zep's all-time tallest, along with "Out from the Tiles" and "Hats Off to (Roy) Harper."

> "*Zeppelin III* — the second I started listening to it, I said, 'Wow!' I never heard hard rock mixed with old blues before. There's also a good amount of great acoustic songs."
> — Anthony Bramante
> Nuclear Assault
> July 2023

> "I love this record because it shows the difference between a hard rock band, an acoustic band, a folk band, a heavy metal band. There are so many movements on that record that I could say 'Immigrant Song' is a fuckin' heavy metal song, 'Tangerine' is a beautiful pop song, 'Since I've Been Loving You' is a blues song that's just SO awesome. Then the folky-stuff that's on that record too — 'Hats Off to (Roy) Harper,' 'Friends,' it's just all those songs — there were NO limits to that band."
> — Charlie Benante
> Anthrax
> July 2023

Digital versions of *Zeppelin III* clearly reveal the Speed King kick pedal squeak once buried within the massive drum tracks from the mighty John Bonham. I'm still not sure if that's a good thing or a bad thing. There's often a fine line between authenticity and annoying.

> "The thing I love most about this album is that it's so REAL
> — like how you can hear the faint squeaks of Bonham's
> kick pedal in 'Since I've Been Loving You.' There was
> no 'cleaning up' in ProTools, just real and raw chemistry
> between four of the greatest musicians to ever live."
> —Bella Perron
> Plush
> June 2023

Director Cameron Crowe gave new life to two of the record's finest creations when he placed "Tangerine" and "That's the Way" prominently in his award-winning film, *Almost Famous* — decades after they'd received their gold retirement watches. Truth be told, these two tracks still hit me with such a wallop, it's very difficult to listen to either and breathe at the same time.

Bare-chested, "Golden God," Robert Plant, provided poetic perfection throughout: "Her face is cracked from smiling. All the fears that she's been hiding." Doggonit, man — that's some mi-tee good stuff right there. "Measuring a summer's day, I only find it slips away to grey." Wow, that one ain't half-bad, either.

> "I didn't really discover *Zeppelin III* until I moved to California
> when I was 18, finding myself in the hills and valleys of Los Angeles.
> With its folksy busking, medieval-ish vibe, clapping and stomping,
> twangy guitars and big vocals, this album is the equivalent to a peaceful day
> on the beach and an evening spent around a fire with friends in Topanga."
> —Anna-Marie O'Brien
> Author
> July 2023

Produced by Mr. Jimmy Page, the record was, to my ears, a crisper and sunnier affair than its two predecessors. And it still sounds fresh. So many mandolins, so little time!

I nabbed this copy during the summer of 2023 for just $6 from what was referred to as the "sad box" — a crateful of "misfit" records that had been shamed into a less-than-prime floor space at one of my go-to local dealers. Here's the kicker; not only did I rediscover this lil' treasure for "a song," the cover had the spinning pinwheel feature, the vinyl was super-clean, and it played, PERFECTLY. Ah, not so "sad" after all!

Decades later, *Led Zeppelin III* has proven that she ain't NOBODY'S "Jan." Even today, as a super-sexy 50-pluser, she does things that "Marcia" never would have dreamed of doing — not even under the bleachers at the dance with Davey Jones.

Led Zeppelin III

Track List

SIDE ONE
1. Immigrant Song (Page, Plant) – 2:26
2. Friends (Page, Plant) – 3:55
3. Celebration Day (Page, Plant, Jones) – 3:29
4. Since I've Been Loving You (Page, Plant, Jones) – 7:25
5. Out on the Tiles (Plant, Page, Bonham) – 4:04

SIDE TWO
1. Gallows Pole (Page, Plant) – 4:58
2. Tangerine (Page) – 3:12
3. That's the Way (Page, Plant) – 5:38
4. Bron-Y-Aur Stomp (Page, Plant, Jones) – 4:20
5. Hats Off to (Roy) Harper (Obscure) – 3:41

31
Paul McCartney & Wings

Paul McCartney & Wings
"Wings Over America"
(Capitol / December 1976)

Wings Over America

Back in 2018, I was contracted to co-author the autobiography of a former famous rock star. Living up to his infamous reputation, he flaked, PDQ. In hindsight, I recognize how that short-term disappointment actually was a long-term blessing in disguise. Throughout the course of that ill-fated project, I worked with a passionate, prominent publishing agent. Whenever she spoke to me about well-written, high-quality literary works, she always referred to them as, "beautiful" books. In terms of classic albums, that description certainly applies to *Wings Over America*.

..

For kids like me, music-crazed little freaks coming of age during the shagadelic '70s, Wings was Paul McCartney's white-hot "modern" band, after that old-timey band he was in during the psychedelic '60s. *Abbey Road*, *Sgt. Pepper*, *The White Album* — those albums were *okay*, but they really "belonged" to our older siblings. *Band on the Run*, *Venus and Mars*, *Wings at the Speed of Sound* — THOSE albums belonged to US!

In the span of six years, Paul McCartney had ascended fully into the stratosphere; from an unimaginable place of prominence as one the defunct Fab Four to the undisputed, unchallenged El Jefe of the intergalactic music scene — brandishing a slew of Top Ten LPs and a string of chart-busting singles as the patriarch of his own band.

Paul McCartney & Wings was my gateway drug — a sort of cosmic vessel that transported me and my like-minded compadres from adolescent pop to adult rock. I'd bought and became subsequently obsessed with the band's *Wings at the Speed of Sound* album (on 8-track) during the summer of 1976. Six months later, *all* I wanted for Christmas was the combo's newly-released, chart-topping *Wings Over America* album. With her patience wearing noticeably thin, my mom indicated with considerable disdain that I wasn't likely to find the triple-record treasure tucked under the tree. *Keep it up, little man, and you'll get NOTHING!*

Recorded live at various locales during the band's well-publicized, wildly successful recent US concert tour, the 30-song collection was plain cool, not to mention, exhaustive. Along with the cavalcade of established Wings hits, the deeper album cuts also suddenly felt more magical than ever. The 1976 live version of the 1970 studio track, "Maybe I'm Amazed" assumed a whole new life as it soared into the Top Ten on Casey's Countdown. I rushed out and bought the single, just to hold me over until I'd saved up enough allowance and lunch money to get the entire LP. Even the album's Beatles classics felt fresh, as if *those* songs now belonged to "us" too.

With soon-to-be "Sir" Paul leading the charge in this live concert setting, Wings finally seemed like an actual "band." Musically speaking, Linda McCartney was no Yoko Ono. And I don't believe that up until then, she'd received her rightful props for what she brought to the table. But with *this* record, she definitely earned her "wings." Co-founding member, former Moody Blues guitarist; singer / songwriter, Denny Laine, delivered additional authenticity to the album, along with the uncompromised street cred of newer recruits; blues-inspired Scottish singer / songwriter and guitarist, Jimmy McCulloch, and American meat-and-potatoes drummer, Joe English.

Another beautiful aspect of *Wings Over America* is that it was a *live* album recorded during the prehistoric era when *live* bands played — *live* — a truly wacky concept in today's super-tech-savvy touring world. *ATTENTION ALL TOUR STAFF: Tonight's show is canceled! Nikki lost his laptop!* While *some* overdubbing *may* have occurred, the numerous crash-and-stomp song endings were pretty reliable indicators that this was, indeed an authentic *live* album. For my money, English's sack-cracking snare, chest-popping kick, and overall rock-ribbed style were well-worth the price of admission.

Wings Over America has been released (and re-released) several times, in various configurations over the years. I've owned it personally on LP, 8-track, and CD. I even bought it digitally from iTunes in 2018. I located a $3 vinyl copy at a local rummage sale in 2014. Quite selflessly, I allowed it to live at the GF's. However, in 2023, I scored my very own well-loved vinyl copy for just $8 at a nearby beachside thrift joint. While that's WAY more than I'm usually willing to pay for pre-owned vinyl, it *was* a TRIPLE record. PLUS, it was fairly clean and it only skipped once. Also, it came with the original, full-color pull-out poster that didn't appear to ever have been touched. *SCORE!*

After nearly 50 years, *Wings Over America* still stands up, really well. In short, it remains a "beautiful" record!

Wings Over America

Track List

SIDE ONE
1. Venus and Mars / Rock Show / Jet (McCartney) – 9:56
2. Let Me Roll It (McCartney) – 3:51
3. Spirits of Ancient Egypt (McCartney) – 4:04
4. Medicine Jar (McCulloch, Allen) – 4:02

SIDE TWO
1. Maybe I'm Amazed (McCartney) – 5:10
2. Call Me Back Again (McCartney) – 5:04
3. Lady Madonna (McCartney, Lennon) – 2:19
4. The Long and Winding Road (McCartney, Lennon) – 4:13
5. Live and Let Die (McCartney) – 3:07

SIDE THREE
1. Picasso's Last Words (Drink to Me) (McCartney) – 1:55
2. Richard Cory (Simon) – 2:50
3. Bluebird (McCartney) – 3:37
4. I've Just Seen a Face (McCartney, Lennon) – 1:49
5. Blackbird (McCartney, Lennon) – 2:23
6. Yesterday (McCartney, Lennon) – 1:43

Continued on next page...

PAUL MCCARTNEY & WINGS   169

Wings Over America

Track List, continued...

SIDE FOUR
1. You Gave Me the Answer (McCartney) – 1:47
2. Magneto and Titanium Man (McCartney) – 3:11
3. Go Now (Banks, Bennett) – 3:27
4. My Love (McCartney) – 4:07
5. Listen to What the Man Said (McCartney) – 3:18

SIDE FIVE
1. Let 'Em In (McCartney) – 4:02
2. Time to Hide (Laine) – 4:46
3. Silly Love Songs (McCartney) – 5:46
4. Beware My Love (McCartney) – 4:49

SIDE SIX
1. Letting Go (McCartney) – 4:25
2. Band on the Run (McCartney) – 5:03
3. Hi, Hi, Hi (McCartney) – 2:57
4. Soily (McCartney) – 5:10

32
Willie Nelson

Willie Nelson
"Willie and Family Live"
(Columbia / November 1978)

Willie and Family Live

In her 1981 #1 hit, then-music and TV star, Barbara Mandrell sang, "I was country when country wasn't cool." Truth be told, that now-famous lyric could have been applied more accurately to Willie Nelson. Actually, the iconic Texas-born singer / songwriter's unique brand of butter-churnin' good-time music is BIGGER than "just" country. His signature outhouse-meets-roadhouse-meets-bighouse-meets-coffeehouse "outlaw" style is more reflective of Americana. In fact, it could be said that, "Willie Nelson was Americana when Americana wasn't cool."

Although I was raised on authentic, traditional country music as a little kid, by the time I hit my late teens, I'd become obsessed with such Camaro cock-rockers as Aerosmith, Foghat, and the Nuge. As a result, despite the passionate persuasion of Harold, my boss at the local record store and my uncle Gary's super-fine new wife, Rita, I didn't really "get" Willie Nelson — at least not until my uncle Floyd convinced me to see Nelson's silver screen feature film, *Honeysuckle Rose* in 1980. As a guy who's now worked professionally as a personal assistant on several arena concert tours, I can say with complete confidence that, along with *The Rose* and *Almost Famous*, *Honeysuckle Rose* was one of the most accurate sex, drugs, and rock & roll flicks ever. *I got you now, you pigtailed son of a bitch!*

So, with the *Honeysuckle Rose* soundtrack providing sound inspiration, I started paying immediate attention to Willie Nelson and diving deep into his exhaustive catalog — a pursuit that led me ultimately to what I believe to be the definitive Willie Nelson album, the two-record set, *Willie and Family Live*.

Released in November 1978, *Willie and Family Live* was recorded earlier that spring at Harrah's in Lake Tahoe, Nevada. At the time, the self-produced album was a career-spanning collection, boasting a bounty of Nelson's best-known material, from his earliest songwriting successes, including the Patsy Cline classic, "Crazy" and the Faron Young #1 smash, "Hello Walls" to such more recent hits as, "Mammas Don't Let Your Babies Grow Up to Be Cowboys" and "Georgia on My Mind." The album also featured several of my personal favorite Nelson staples; "Uncloudy Day," "If You Could Touch Her at All," and "'Til I Gain Control Again," as well as what I consider to be the "Ace of Spades" of the Nelson repertoire, "Whiskey River." Country sensation, Emmylou Harris, provided sassy, chicken-fried backup vocals on "Will the Circle be Unbroken" and "Amazing Grace," while *real* outlaw, Johnny Paycheck, dropped a solid rendition of *his* classic hit, the David Allan Coe-penned, "Take This Job and Shove It."

Bringing more bang for my hard-earned buck, Nelson's band members were the same as the "Golden God" lineup from *Honeysuckle Rose*; Bobbie Nelson on piano, drummers Paul English and Rex Ludwick, guitarist Jody Payne, bassists Bee Spears and Chris Ethridge, and longtime MVP, Mickey Raphael on harmonica. All that was missing was Amy Irving laying down some tasty "Vanilli" guitar.

After buying (and losing) several copies of various configurations of the album over the years, I discovered a reasonably clean, reasonably cheap vinyl copy at a local thrift joint in 2018. Being an acknowledged ultra-sweetie guy, I allowed it to live at the GF's — until I bought her a shiny-new 45th anniversary copy on springtime fresh violet vinyl for her birthday in 2023. I immediately snatched back the scratchy old black vinyl copy. I'm sweet, but I'm not *that* sweet.

A few months later, just a smidge before Christmas, I found myself working my weekly Sunday night DJ gig at a little hometown sports bar. Among the array of big screens showing the Ravens / Jaguars game was the televised 90th birthday celebration for Willie Nelson. Paying heartfelt tribute to the music legend was current country artists Jimmy Johnson and Miranda Lambert, along with such "seasoned" artists as George Strait and Keith Richards. And it got me thinking. It's an oft-overused term, but Willie Nelson truly *is* a timeless American treasure. And the album *Willie and Family Live* remains one of his all-time best.

Willie and Family Live

Track List

SIDE ONE
1. Whiskey River (Shinn) – 3:40
2. Stay All Night (Stay a Little Longer) (Wills, Duncan) – 3:24
3. Funny How Time Slips Away (Nelson) – 2:45
4. Crazy (Nelson) – 1:47
5. Night Life (Nelson, Buskirk, Breeland) – 3:55
6. If You've Got the Money (I've Got the Time) (Frizzell, Beck) – 1:44
7. Mammas Don't Let Your Babies Grow Up to Be Cowboys (E. Bruce, P. Bruce) – 3:33
8. I Can Get Off on You (Jennings, Nelson) – 2:06

SIDE TWO
1. If You Could Touch Her at All (Clayton) – 3:00
2. Good Hearted Woman (Jennings, Nelson) – 2:57
3. Time of the Preacher (Nelson) – 2:13
4. I Couldn't Believe It Was True (Arnold, Fowler) – 1:03
5. Blue Rock Montana / Red Headed Stranger (Nelson, Stutz, Lindeman) – 2:40
6. Blue Eyes Crying in the Rain (Rose) – 2:29
7. Red Headed Stranger / Just as I Am (Stutz, Lineman / Arrangement Nelson) – 4:31
8. Under the Double Eagle (Arrangement Nelson) – 2:43

continued on next page...

Willie and Family Live

Track List, continued

SIDE THREE
1. 'Til I Gain Control Again (Crowell) – 5:59
2. Bloody Mary Morning (Nelson) – 3:33
3. I'm a Memory (Nelson) – 1:52
4. Mr. Record Man (Nelson) – 2:01
5. Hello Walls (Nelson) – 1:29
6. One Day at a Time (Nelson) – 2:05
7. Will the Circle Be Unbroken (Carter) – 2:18
8. Amazing Grace (Traditional / Arrangement Nelson) – 5:12

SIDE FOUR
1. Take This Job and Shove It (Coe) – 2:52
2. Uncloudy Day (Traditional / Arrangement Nelson) – 3:40
3. Only Daddy That'll Walk the Line (Bryant) – 1:29
4. A Song for You (Russell) – 2:43
5. Roll in My Sweet Baby's Arms (Flatt, Wilson) – 1:56
6. Georgia on My Mind (Carmichael, Gorell) – 4:09
7. I Gotta Get Drunk (Nelson) – 1:22
8. Whiskey River (Shinn) – 2:43
9. Only Daddy That'll Walk the Line (Bryant) – 2:12

33
Ohio Players

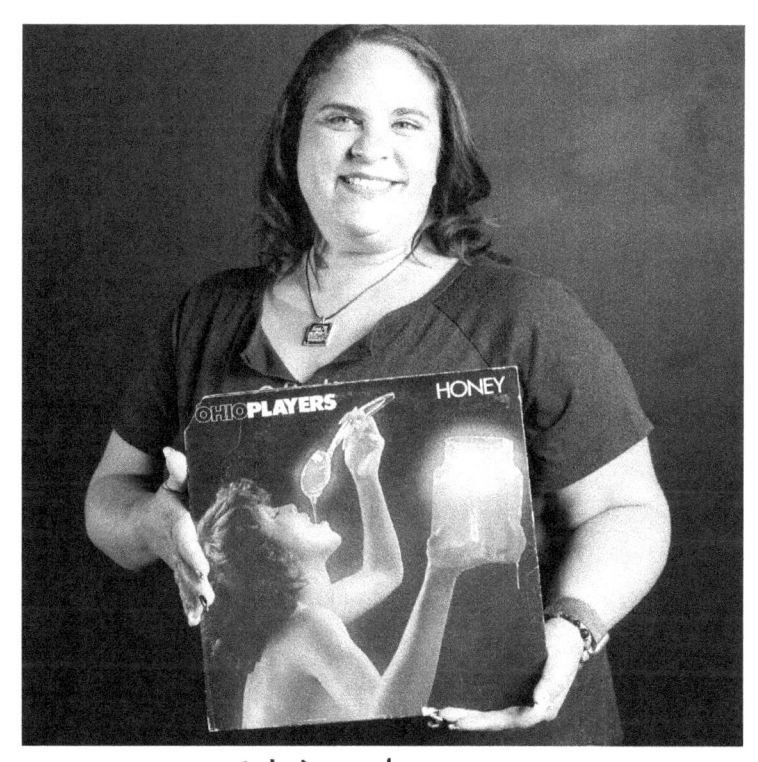

Ohio Players
"Honey"
(Mercury Records / August 1975)

Honey

Oh, baby — I sure miss the bell-bottomed, shag-carpeted, zodiac-crazed '70s! During that wonderfully wide-eyed era, us young people didn't have (or need) Spotify to inform us of what was cool. *Our* curators were compelling, iconic radio DJs. *Keep your feet on the ground and keep reaching for the stars!* And our influencers were TV talk-show hosts and producers, such as Don Kirshner, Dick Clark, and Burt Sugarman — visionaries who brought many of the latest and greatest artists right into our living rooms via televised music programs. Sugarman's weekly Friday night series, *The Midnight Special*, presented live concert performances from an array of artists as eclectic as David Bowie, Wilson Pickett, and Helen Reddy — in a single 90-minute episode.

As a result of being exposed to *truly* open-minded content as a kid, I developed a certain lifelong, organic awareness. I've never recognized musical genres. And I still can't "hear" race or gender. To quote the carefree character, Christine Sixteen, from the 1999 box office flop, *Detroit Rock City*, "Good tunes is good tunes."

During my early junior high school days, I was a fortunate beneficiary of colorblind AM radio. And I gravitated gleefully toward such R&B artists as Curtis Mayfield, Rufus, and the O'Jays. At age 12, I had THE maddest "thing" for Gladys Knight. I mean, Tina Turner had a sizzle factor, but she was no Gladys Knight.

It was around that time when I was introduced to an amazing music act via *The Midnight Special*. Combining heavy rock riffs with legit funk rhythms, the band was brutal. I was wrecked by their high-energy performance, and throughout my ensuing teenage years, the Ohio Players would be MY "Led Zeppelin."

Monster musicians and prolific producers, the Ohio Players checked all the boxes — a fantastic collision of rock, R&B, and jazz. Their funky horn arrangements scratched a personal itch that Chicago just couldn't reach. And they transformed free-form studio jams famously into infectious radio songs. Darker than Earth, Wind & Fire, more dangerous than Kool & the Gang, and (way) dirtier than the Commodores, the Ohio Players were the real deal.

While more than a few of my peers spent their Study Hall time carving KISS logos into their desktops, I was busy drawing full-color, live-performance pictures of the Ohio Players on sheets of notebook paper. I'd usually add a caricature of myself to their lineup, as I fantasized about having an afro and donning a sequined jumpsuit with platform shoes and jamming onstage with my dudes from Dayton. *Gee whiz, Mom! You mean I'm gonna STAY this color?*

In those days, for the casual observer perusing record bins down at the local Kmart, one image likely came to mind PRONTO at the mention of the Ohio Players — nekked ladies. But, for their more faithful followers, it wasn't the sexual imagery depicted on their album covers that made the Players so appealing — it was what was oozing from the grooves. Truth be told, the names Diamond, Billy, Merv, Jones, Sugar, Pee Wee, and Satch were as revered to me as sports All-Star names were to the "normal" boys in my neighborhood.

After dropping several less-than-spectacular-selling LPs on the Detroit-based indie Westbound label, the group ultimately signed with major label Mercury Records. In short order, their 1974 album *Skin Tight* moved a million units and spawned the hit single "Jive Turkey," as well as the Top 20 title track. Fueled by the chart-busting hit, "Fire," their follow-up release, *Fire*, scorched the *Billboard* top spot. However, their *next* album, *Honey*, proved even sweeter — going platinum and delivering three massive chart-busters: "Sweet Sticky Thing," "Fopp," and the iconic #1 smash, "Love Rollercoaster."

> "The first time I ever made a
> 'stank face' was when I heard 'Fopp.'"
> — Freezerp
> Ice Cream Icon
> Boulder, Colorado
> January 2024

Aside from the hits, the seven-track collection boasted a bounty of other highlights, including the seductive, smooth groovin' opening title track and the unapologetic, down-n-dirty, "Ain't Givin' Up No Ground."

Ultimately *Honey* would inspire a slew of prominent rising artists. Soon-to-be platinum-selling noisemongers Soundgarden covered "Fopp" on their 1988 EP, *Fopp*. The Red Hot Chili Peppers contributed a well-intended remake of "Love Rollercoaster" to the 1996 *Beavis and Butt-head Do America* movie soundtrack. And in 2005, pop-soul princess Vanessa Williams included a beautifully faithful recreation of "Let's Love" on her album, *Everlasting Love*.

> "No 'Love Rollercoaster,' no Prince.
> *Or* Chili Peppers, for that matter."
> —Bryan Dumas
> Co-author, *Garage Sale Vinyl*
> January 2024

Nearly 50 years later, I still can't fathom how my ultra-conservative parents ever allowed a record in their home with a honey-dripping nekked lady on the cover. Where that original *Honey* LP is now, only my ex-wife's attorney knows for sure. Since the early '90s, my CD copy had remained within an arm's reach at all times, until 2020, when the GF and I snatched up a solid used vinyl copy at the local flea mall, for just $3.

I'm reminded of that old axiom, "The apple doesn't fall far from the tree." Many years ago, while accompanying me on one of my book tours, my then-teenage son was over the moon to spot and score his own LP copy of *Honey* at a used record joint in Chattanooga, Tennessee. Clearly, a shining example of incredible, effective parenting.

Honey

Track List
(All songs written by Williams, Satchell, Bonner, Jones, Middle-brooks, Pierce, Beck)

SIDE ONE
1. Honey – 5:15
2. Fopp – 3:45
3. Let's Love – 5:15
4. Ain't Givin' Up No Ground – 1:45

SIDE TWO
1. Sweet Sticky Thing – 6:13
2. Love Rollercoaster – 4:52
3. Alone – 4:40

34
The Ozark Mountain Daredevils

The Ozark Mountain Daredevils
"Don't Look Down"
(A&M / October 1977)

THE OZARK MOUNTAIN DAREDEVILS

Don't Look Down

The GF and I never miss finding a treasure. As a result, "Joe" has become one of our favorite vendors down at the local flea market. Truth be told, the guy's little concession *barely* rates "vendor" status. It's actually just a huge, rotting wooden table, out in the open at the end of Row Z. And it's always piled with all sorts of random crap for sale — rusty power tools, mismatched plastic dishware, well-worn hand-me-downs, etc. But what makes this our go-to flea market spot is the box of ravaged vinyl LPs that's usually tucked *under* Joe's table.

So, there I was, that one Sunday afternoon, rifling through Joe's old records (trying carefully to avoid contracting tetanus), when he announced, "Everything in that box is a quarter." In my hands at that moment was a completely destroyed copy of *Don't Look Down*, the 1977 release from the Ozark Mountain Daredevils. The cover was totally tattered — not even a paper inner sleeve. But for .25¢, how could I go wrong? I had it on CD and iTunes, but this was an *original* vinyl copy. *SOLD!* As it turned out, despite also being warped as shit, the record played nicely — darn near mint-sounding, in fact. You just never know.

· ·

As the saying goes, there really was, "gold in them thar hills." And the Ozark Mountain Daredevils panned for precious metals successfully — both gold and platinum. The cool thing about this Springfield, Missouri-based collective is they've always remained committed to two key creative components: integrity and authenticity. The country-rock hybrid thing had been brewing for a few years, but the Daredevils took *their* rootsy, down-home music to another level — blending folk, bluegrass, and country with rock and pop — effectively defining the Americana genre decades before the patchouli-soaked hipsters claimed it as their own deal.

The band's initial five-title string of A&M Records studio LPs ('73-'77) all were simply superb pieces of work, to be sure. And over the years, those albums have aged beautifully. To this day, the massive hit singles, "If You Wanna Get to Heaven" and "Jackie Blue" remain classic rock radio staples. But at the time of the 1977 release of *Don't Look Down*, the music scene had changed drastically, as disco dominated everything and new wave was pogo-ing onto the horizon. As a result, the record went largely unnoticed — a particular tragedy given that *Don't Look Down* found the Daredevils firing on ALL cylinders, moving forward while maintaining their unique identity.

Produced by David Kershenbaum (Duran Duran, Joe Jackson, Bryan Adams), the album owned some of the Daredevils' finest and freshest songs to date. The shoulda-been-a-single "Following the Way That I Feel" was a pure pop treasure, while the funky-feeling "The Fox" was a chunky, Jamaican-flavored treat, and the fiddle-fueled "Giving It All to the Wind" was a delicate, signature-style standout.

The album has been a personal favorite since back when I had great hair and cut abs, which was a *really* long time ago. But I was curious about what the *band* thought of it. So, in 2023, I reached out and left a voice message for co-founding bassist, Michael "Supe" Granda, in hopes of getting *his* take on *Don't Look Down*. And I'll be dipped — the dude called me back. Apparently, he digs the album too.

• •

So, Supe, what's the scoop on Don't Look Down?

"When we began to record Don't Look Down, we'd also added a new guitar player, a new piano player, and a mandolinist. With the addition of the mandolin, we were able to include my bluegrass tune, "Stinghead." With Rune Walle's searing slide guitar, we were able to do a country tune, "On the Rise," and several all-out rockers; "River to the Sun," "Snowbound" and "Backroads."

The Ozark Mountain Daredevils possessed a prominent presence on the international rock scene. Caribou Ranch Studios was one of the pre-eminent facilities of the day. I'm sure it made for quite an interesting environment.

"Located right up the mountain from Boulder, Colorado, Caribou Ranch Studios was notorious for late nights and a "let's go see who's recording" attitude. Artists, in town to play Red Rocks, would stop in. Ann and Nancy Wilson of Heart, Dennis Wilson and Al Jardine of the Beach Boys, America, and the Sons of Champlin all stuck their heads in the door. All were welcomed. None impeded progress."

The Daredevils had a longstanding reputation for being party-hardy, hell-raising hillbillies. That probably was blown out of proportion. Surely, you fellas were "all business" while making the record. Right?

"The general feeling of the place (Caribou Ranch) was upbeat and up-tempo. This is what we attempted to inject into our music. The sessions were fun, festive, and full of life. One highlight was a drinking contest we held. On an off night from recording, we gathered in the dining room and drank one shot of beer every sixty seconds, until the last man was standing. The first hour was funny. The second hour began to get wobbly. The third hour was psychedelic. When guitarist Steve Canaday won after 216 shots, the rafters rang with laughter."

More than 45 years after its release, Don't Look Down might be endeared to fans as much for its memorable cover as for its impeccable songs.

"Though the album contained no big hits and found no real commercial success, we had an absolute blast making it. This conviviality can be seen on the cover. As we all balanced on a 2×4, superimposed onto a taut rope, dangling in mid-air, the camaraderie was wonderful."

∙∙

In sum, *Don't Look Down* was a stinger of a record. In fact, if "Stinghead" alone doesn't make a *true* believer out of ya, well buddy, I'll keep prayin' for ya.

Don't Look Down

Track List

SIDE ONE
1. River to the Sun (Cash, Dillon) – 3:25
2. Crazy Lovin' (Cash, Dillon) – 3:53
3. Giving It All to the Wind (Lee) – 4:13
4. The Fox (Cash) – 2:45
5. Backroads (Canaday) – 3:13

SIDE TWO
1. Snowbound (Cash, Dillon) – 3:30
2. Following the Way That I Feel (Lee) – 3:35
3. Love Makes the Lover (Cash, Dillon) – 3:21
4. True Believer (Lee, Cash) – 4:13
5. Moon on the Rise (Lee, Cash) – 3:05
6. Stinghead (Granda) – 2:09

35
The Partridge Family

The Partridge Family
"Up to Date"
(Bell / February 1971)

Up To Date

The late '60s and early '70s — what an amazing time to be alive in America. Those wonder years were particularly beautiful for us little kids. For the most part, we still lived in our first houses, still had our first pets, still rode our first big-kid bikes, and our parents were still alive *and* married — to each other. And it was during those wide-eyed early vinyl days when most of my young friends also were discovering their first bands; The Beatles, The Stones, Zeppelin, the list could go on and on. But, those were the *cool* kids' first bands. Then, there was me.

Even at age seven, everybody in my world knew the truth — I was a hopeless nerd. It was as painfully obvious as my porcupine-looking, half-grown-out flattop and my frequent socks-n-sandals fashion statement. The horn rims would be coming soon enough. On the upside, my parents took great comfort in knowing that my certain future was bright, as I most assuredly was destined to land some type of important, respectable, high-paying super-geeker gig with the ACME Technology Corporation or as an IRS agent or maybe even as a local TV weatherman. Yep, I was a shoe in for success, that is, until The Partridge Family hit the scene and I discovered MY first band. I became so instantly obsessed with their music and with David Cassidy's chick magnet image, I couldn't think straight. And any chance I had of achieving a stable and secure future sailed straight out the window. Heck, even as little old man, now in my sixties I still want to be David Cassidy — when I grow up.

∴

An immediate ratings champ, the iconic sitcom, *The Partridge Family*, debuted on the ABC television network in September 1970. The show was based on a fictional pop group made up of three brothers and two sisters, along with their widowed mother, Shirley Partridge, played by veteran stage and screen actress, Shirley Jones. This was back in the glorious pre-Internet days when there only were three networks and three channels — period. Consequently, I'd never before seen or heard anything like this "band." Of course there was The Monkees, another made-for-TV pop group, but they didn't "speak" to me like The Partridge Family.

The band was fronted by Keith Partridge, played by real-life rocker, David Cassidy. He had a fabulously feathered, shoulder-length coif and he wore cool clothes. He also sang lead and played an electric guitar, and chicks went crazy every time he opened his mouth. *Jeepers, Ma! I want cool hair and hot chicks too!*

Another alluring aspect of The Partridge Family for me as well as throngs of other adoring pre-tweenage boys was Keith's lip-syncing sister, Laurie Partridge. Played by then-relatively unknown 18-year-old actress / model, Susan Dey, Laurie Partridge was an exquisite beauty and my first pin-up girl. She was tall and slender with long straight brown hair. Even I could sniff out her intriguing and mysterious qualities.

I succeeded in persuading my mom to buy me every Partridge Family record that came down the pike — until 1973, when the show's storyline and the ratings began to sputter. I wore those LPs into vinyl dust on my sister's trusty 1968 Zenith record player, before graduating to Elton John, Alice Cooper, and Paul McCartney & Wings, *and* a more sophisticated 8-track hi-fi.

Fueled by the massive #1 single, "I Think I Love You," the debut Partridge Family album dropped in October 1970 and it stirred an instant sensation. The first of six Partridge LPs to achieve gold status, it reached #4 on the *Billboard* Top 200. Released via Bell Records just four months later, in February 1971, their sophomore set, *Up to Date*, soared to the Top Ten and also "went gold" in short order.

Overseen by Bell art director, Beverly Weinstein, the eye-catching album cover resembled a calendar, with photos and birth dates of the "family" members. Having just turned eight, by only complaint was that the cover pic of Susan Dey wasn't larger.

I dissected and analyzed each of the albums featured in these 50 chapters along with my longtime writing partner, high school pal, occasional bandmate, and fellow vinyl enthusiast, Bryan Dumas. Although he's known as "Richard" down at the DMV, his closest confidants call him, "Dingus."

Simply put, Dingus is a music snob — a ridiculous audiophile who buys *only* OLD "missionary position" black vinyl by tragic prog dinosaurs. However, I prefer living in the now. While I still crave that old-school vinyl crackle, I also buy *a lot* of NEW, factory-sealed, colored vinyl by pop-rockers on the rise. Dingus always has maintained that vintage black vinyl is superior to current black (and colored) vinyl releases. He claims that from authentic musicianship to organic recording techniques to the actual manufacturing process, retro vinyl is king.

Believe it or not, I hadn't owned a turntable personally since the early '90s, until 2023. The GF and I would venture out together to various garage sales, thrift stores, and flea markets in pursuit of affordable vinyl treasures. Then, we'd spin 'em down at *her* place, on *her* turntable.

So, imagine my dismay and disappointment when I finally scored and set up my own new hi-fi (with turntable) at my own abode, only to discover that most of my shiny new (and very pretty), pink, purple, yellow, orange, green, red, white, and blue LPs sounded less than pristine — a smidge distorted, like there was dust build-up on the stylus. I'd noticed this frustrating factoid when playing some of the GF's new colored vinyl on her home system. I merely attributed it to her turntable being like Dingus — wonky and outdated. But soon, I realized that even several of my newly-released black vinyl records also sounded less than pristine — compressed and often muffled-sounding.

Upon reporting this modern sonic annoyance to Dingus, he explained to me in a subtle, yet decidedly "I told you so" tone, that it wasn't just my imagination running away with me. Apparently, when compared to old-school albums that were recorded (and produced) by *humans*, in analog studios with actual microphones and then mastered, properly, most new vinyl just doesn't make the cut. But Partridge Family vinyl checks ALL of the *right* boxes.

If people realized how little many of their worshiped crooners and idolized pluckers actually contributed to their beloved albums over the years, they might be less eager to malign those old Partridge Family releases. In fact, to dismiss them merely as disposable records that provided the sterile soundtrack to some campy sitcom would be to reveal one's naiveté regarding proper quality pop songwriting and world-class record production.

Partridge Family tunes were crafted pretty consistently by several of the leading songwriters of the day and they followed a very specific formula, but it was a fabulous formula that worked every time. The tracks were performed by some of the era's most sought-after session players. Pulled primarily from the legendary Wrecking Crew, this team of qualified music vets played quite frequently on most of the Partridge Family albums, including *Up to Date*.

Produced by music industry vet, Wes Farrell, *Up to Date* owned a slew of seductive earworms created by such celebrated songsmiths as Gerry Goffin, Tony Romeo and Mike Appel. As a result, Buick-sized hooks were bountiful throughout. *Up to Date* birthed TWO irresistible hit singles; the sunny-sounding "Doesn't Somebody Want to Be Wanted" (#6) and the toe-tapping "I'll Meet You Halfway" (#9). As a guy who ain't scared of a massive hook, "You Are Always on My Mind," "Umbrella Man" and "That'll Be the Day" still rank among my personal faves. Even Cassidy himself contributed to the record's songwriting, collaborating with Farrell on the crunchy, coliseum-caliber, "Lay It on the Line."

Awash in lush backing vocals provided by the Ron Hicklin Singers and the Love Generation, and polished to perfection with some gorgeous orchestration, *Up to Date* embraced the soft pop vibe of the late '60s and early '70s. But what gave the record extra cred was the potent cocktail of Cassidy's powerhouse vocals and Shirley Jones' angelic backups, combined with Hal Blaine's signature-style, precision drumming and the versatile ace guitar work of Dennis Budimir and Louie Shelton. Truth be told, even on 50-year-old vinyl, Joe Osborne's super-punchy bass parts still want to pop straight out of speakers. And whether it was a result of Farrell's master production skill or Blaine's total understanding of his instrument, HE had THE *perfect* studio drum sound — from the snare crack to the kick pop to the tom tuning.

As I said, I'm now a little old man. And I'll confess openly that without the aid of my talented salon tech, my (remaining) hair would be snow white. My eyesight is fading by the day, my hearing is totally toast, my schmeckle hasn't functioned properly in more than a decade, AND I gotta pee every 15 minutes! So, recently, I *hobbled* into a local used record joint, and spotted a Near-Mint condition vinyl copy of *Up to Date* — for $10. *SOLD!* Clearly, the shop owner had no idea what she had. I'd replaced my original battered and abused LP copy with a CD reissue back in the '80s. However, I was over the moon to have scored *this* vinyl copy. And instantly, I noticed how the (slightly crackly) vinyl format has remained FAR superior to the digital format. *C'mon! Get Happy!*

Up to Date

Track List

SIDE ONE

1. I'll Meet You Halfway (Farrell, Goffin) – 3:47
2. You Are Always On My Mind (Romeo) – 2:53
3. Doesn't Somebody Want to Be Wanted (Farrell, Cretecos, Appel) – 2:46
4. I'm Here, You're Here (Farrell, Goffin) – 2:51
5. Umbrella Man (Farrell, Cretecos, Appel) – 2:44
6. Lay It on the Line (Farrell, Cassidy) – 2:34

SIDE TWO

1. Morning Rider on the Road (Romeo) – 3:01
2. That'll Be the Day (Romeo) – 2:45
3. There's No Doubt in My Mind (Farrell, Goffin) – 2:29
4. She'd Rather Have the Rain (Cashman, West) – 3:17
5. I'll Leave Myself a Little Time (Dossick) – 2:27

36
The Pretenders

The Pretenders
"Pretenders"
(Sire Records / January 1980)

Pretenders

Okay, true confession time. I never owned this lil' nut cracker on vinyl until the GF and I started spotting used copies popping up seemingly everywhere in town somewhere around 2019. But, be sure, I *had* bought a *cassette* copy for the ol' boom box promptly upon its release. Years later, I replaced that squeaky old tape with a shiny new CD. Don't judge me!

..

The '70s had produced a wide array of exciting, engaging, and eclectic artists who made some of the most beautiful, truly timeless feel-good records ever. That's just a fact. However, as the decade tried coming to a cozy conclusion, fresh and often brash-sounding break-out acts, such as the Ramones, the Clash, and the Police, all were DEMANDING *their* turns at the mic. Hence, the '80s appeared destined to be an exciting new musical era. And that soon-to-be decade of decadence was detonated by a doozie when the debut from US / UK hybrid, the Pretenders, first exploded globally via Sire Records in early 1980. Leading the charge was Chrissie Hynde, the band's alluring, tough-as-nails American-born singer / songwriter and guitarist.

Groundbreaking all-girl group, Goldie & the Gingerbreads, had disbanded by the late '60s and Fanny had fizzled by the mid-'70s. The Runaways also had come and gone by 1980. None of these ill-fated female combos had exactly set the charts on fire. However, Runaways frontchick / guitarist Joan Jett was revving up to become a major rock force as a solo artist, and little Pat Benatar was prepping to give it her best shot — a bit later. So, with only a few exceptions, we hadn't really seen anything quite like the badass, leather-clad Hynde when images of her band first began showing up in the pages of international magazines and on the rare late-night cable TV programs that aired those crazy new music videos that weren't likely ever to catch on.

Sporting dark, shaggy bangs and spackled with super-thick, jet black eye makeup, Hynde oozed mystique as she slashed away at her Telecaster. She was dirty and dangerous, bold and beautiful. And her songs were crunchy and catchy.

A production collab between Nick Lowe and Chris Thomas, the *Pretenders* first three singles, "Stop Your Sobbing," "Kid" and the iconic hit "Brass in Pocket" all packed infectious pop appeal. But the edgier, riff-driven tracks, "The Phone Call," "Up the Neck," "Tattooed Love Boys" and the abrasive album opener, "Precious" were the more urgent of the million-selling 12-song set. *Wait. Did she just say, "fuck off?"*

My personal pick of the litter was the seductive, mid-tempo, reggae-inspired, dysfunctional love song, "Private Life." Hynde's scathing lyrics and honest vocals were compelling — "I just feel pity when you lie, contempt when you cry." James Honeyman-Scott's sparse and tasteful guitar licks colliding with his sexy soloing were spectacular. Dripping with true blue rock and roll swagger, Pete Farndon made the song sizzle with his smooth and slinky bass lines. And despite being known as a bona fide beast, Martin Chambers framed the track famously with mere minimal drum work.

In sum, *Pretenders* was an irresistibly brutal record that punished the rock scene like a naughty schoolboy, just when it really deserved a good paddlin'. Decades later, it remains a glorious aural assault — a heart-stopping treasure.

So, I'll go ahead and make *another* confession. I scored my current vinyl copy of *Pretenders* in 2022 at a South Florida joint for just $2 — it *was* in pristine condition, when I bought it. Well, as I was finishing this chapter, chicken-pecking on the laptop at my home work station, surrounded by stacks of vinyl, I reached over and grabbed the record to double check a couple of the credits. It only was an arm's length away, but it was out of its cover *and* the protective inner paper sleeve at that moment. I *thought* that I had a reasonable grasp on the LP, but my (undiagnosed) early-stage Parkinson's knew better. The *once* pristine record slipped from my grasp and crashed to the floor. It didn't shatter, but it skated across the less-than-smooth, stone-like tile.

Ring-Ring! Ring-Ring!

"Thanks for calling Savvy Vinyl Records! How can we help you?"

"Hey, it's me. Um, I did it again. So, can you find me *another* copy of the first Pretenders record, on vinyl, right away? Please?"

"Ha-ha! No worries, you dumbass!"

Pretenders

Track List

SIDE ONE
1. Precious (Hynde) – 3:34
2. The Phone Call (Hynde) – 2:27
3. Up the Neck (Hynde) – 4:24
4. Tattooed Love Boys (Hynde) – 2:58
5. Space Invader (Farndon, Honeyman-Scott) – 3:26
6. The Wait (Hynde, Farndon) – 3:34
7. Stop Your Sobbing (Davies) – 2:38

SIDE TWO
1. Kid (Hynde) – 3:04
2. Private Life (Hynde) – 6:23
3. Brass in Pocket (Hynde, Honeyman-Scott) – 3:01
4. Lovers of Today (Hynde) – 5:50
5. Mystery Achievement (Hynde) – 5:23

37
Bonnie Raitt

Bonnie Raitt
"Streetlights"
(Warner Bros. / September 1974)

Streelights

Oh, the frustration I've faced, as a result of being placed on the same planet with Bonnie Raitt — her super-sultry voice, her blues-injected music, and her — well, you know.

As an admitted, addicted Bonnie Raitt lifer, one of my greatest joys in recent years has been the pursuit and successful re-discovery of her classic albums — on vinyl, of course. Even cooler, I always find 'em, for "a song!"

In the introduction to this book I mentioned how *Streetlights* is the record that inadvertently ignited an exciting, all-new chapter in my writing career. During the 2022 holiday season I'd reached out to my longtime *Ink 19* editor, Rose Petralia, to inquire whether she had any interest in running a one-time little squirt of a retro review on a 50-year-old record that I'd just found at a neighborhood garage for less than a buck. Rose loved the idea and encouraged me to take it further. And in January 2023, my accidental "Garage Sale Vinyl" music column debuted at Ink19.com. It ran for a full year — 50 consecutive weekly installments that revisited an array of vintage LPs from an eclectic crop of artists that I'd found on the cheap.

As the GSV audience grew larger, installments were expanded to include more cozy personal stories, album cover images, music links, video links, and occasional interviews with the actual artists. Along the way I even hired a talented graphics guy to design professional related images to keep the column looking crisp and sharp. Then, about halfway through the series, I got a wacky notion to take my budding new brand to the next level. What was that, you might ask? You're holding in your hands, silly!

••

As with most of her early catalog, Bonnie Raitt's fourth album, *Streetlights*, has aged beautifully over the years — as fresh-faced now as it was the day the class photo was snapped way back in 1974.

The honest remake of the 1969 Joni Mitchell album cut, "That Song About the Midway," made for an engaging opener — "I met you on a midway at a fair last year. And you stood out like a ruby in a black man's ear." Now, *that's* some solid word crafting right there. With "Rainy Day Man," Raitt claimed complete ownership of the James Taylor tune without compromising his signature-style feel.

Streetlights earned three of its four stars simply as a result of housing Raitt's heart-stopping original studio version of the John Prine classic, "Angel from Montgomery." The Joey Levine / Jim Carroll-penned, "I Got Plenty," was a sexy, sax-soaked, gospel-tinged highlight that exemplified why Raitt has thwacked me so bad, for so long.

The Allen Toussaint number, "What is Success," as well as the (producer) Jerry Ragovoy song, "Ain't Nobody Home," both were powerfully soulful — revealing early glimpses of the authentic R&B-fueled street-style pop that continues to be present in Raitt's records to this day. Another standout, "Got You on My Mind," smiled with the feel-good charm of a '70s-era Wednesday night ABC "Movie of the Week."

Raitt reportedly was less than enthusiastic about label restrictions and producer direction on *Streetlights*. But, that's plain foolish. *Baby, sweet baby, you gotta believe me. This was a beautiful record, baby.* It remains a bright and shiny beacon in a very impressive, 50-plus-year catalog.

When I first discovered Bonnie Raitt (circa '75), I was a geek — a four-eyed freak. But, even as a naïve pre-pube navigating through my Beaver Cleaver world, I "got" the whole Bonnie Raitt package. A hopelessly music-crazed kid during those incredible shag-covered days, I snatched up a slew of LPs from the likes of Carole, Carly, Linda and Karla. However, those gals just couldn't scratch my itch quite like... you know who.

Decades later, I'm now a decrepit, albeit well-groomed little old man who enjoys romantic, moonlit walks on the beach and who also experiences uncontrollable, involuntary tremors and a frequent need to pee. Yet, Bonnie Raitt records STILL own the ability to make my heart race and to put me in the fetal position, sobbing in a corner like an inconsolable 37-year-old box store deli server who can't shake off misplacing their Chiefs jersey.

Streetlights

Track List

SIDE ONE

1. That Song About the Midway (Mitchell) – 4:39
2. Rainy Day Man (Taylor) – 3:38
3. Angel from Montgomery (Prine) – 3:55
4. I Got Plenty (Levine, Carroll) – 3:05
5. Streetlights (Payne) – 5:02

SIDE TWO

1. What Is Success (Toussaint) – 3:26
2. Ain't Nobody Home (Ragovoy) – 3:01
3. Everything That Touches You (Kamen) – 3:27
4. Got You on My Mind (Willis, Lasley) – 3:49
5. You Got to Be Ready for Love (Courtney) – 3:03

38
Ramones

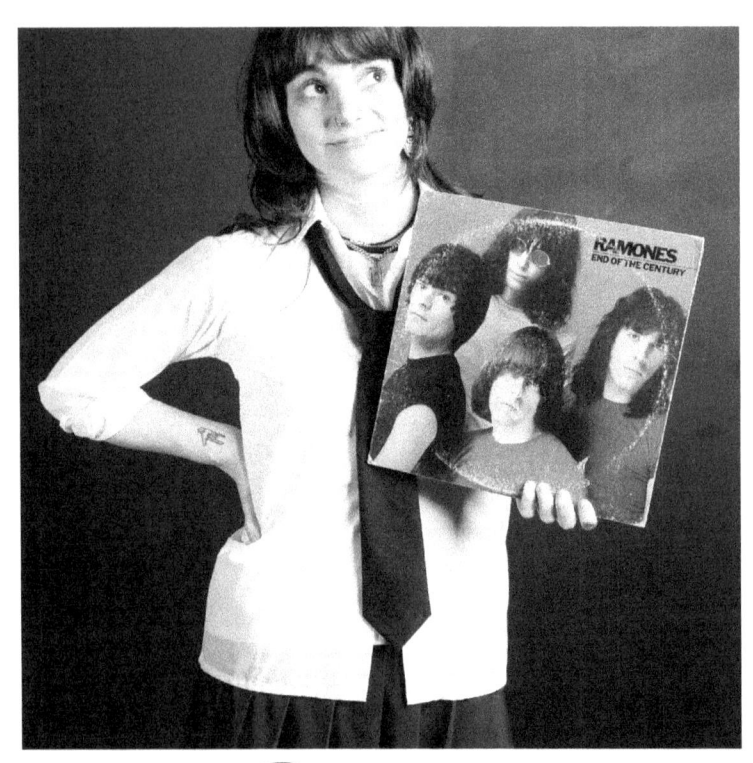

Ramones
"End of the Century"
(Sire Records / February 1980)

End of the Century

It has been argued over the years (by me) that the Ramones wasn't a *punk* band. Despite a well-crafted image — blue denim jeans and black leather jackets, and neck-break songs about being sedated, going mental and getting well, the Ramones actually was a brilliantly disguised *pop* band. I said what I said. And I'll stand by it.

••

As a teen growing up on Florida's Space Coast during the late 1970s, I was a committed consumer of 8-track driven corporate rock from a line-up of the day's usual suspects; Styx, Journey, Foreigner, Kansas, Boston, ELO, and of course, the turbo-charged Speedwagon.

However, my high school surf buddy, Dave Fife, rarely settled for rock's status quo and he always was looking to what was coming next. Dave was an amazing scholar when it came to educating me about a particular "New Wave" movement that was on the musical horizon. Frequently, he would come over to my house after school and bring his (vinyl) records by what I perceived as odd and unknown acts, including Joe Jackson, the B-52s, and Gary Numan. Dave also was the first guy I knew who owned albums by a brash new British metal band called, Motörhead.

One day in early 1980, Dave played a record for me by an underground group from New York. The band's songs were fast, short, and sounded like buzz saws. The lyrics were minimal and often rather tongue-in-cheek. But the strangest thing of all was that there were NO guitar solos! The album was *End of the Century*, the group was the Ramones, and my life was changed forever.

Containing such punk-injected gems as "Rock 'N' Roll High School," "Do You Remember Rock 'N' Roll Radio?," "Chinese Rock," "I'm Affected," and the Phil Spector-penned, '60s-pop inspired "Baby, I Love You," *End of the Century* proved to be personally irresistible and ultimately addictive — grabbing and appealing to my senses like aural cocaine. The songs were every bit as catchy as most of my FM faves, yet, they were decidedly edgier than "Bennie and the Jets." From that moment I sought out every Ramones record — even their hard-to-find live import releases.

This was still a couple of years before the arrival of MTV, so when the Ramones starred in the full-length, 1979 feature film, *Rock 'N' Roll High School*, it was a big deal. Hence, Dave and I attended weekend midnight showings of the movie religiously at our hometown draft house theater throughout the spring of 1980. With its quirky storyline, less than award-winning acting, and amazing soundtrack, the film has since gone on to achieve cult classic status.

July 29, 1981 not only was the day when Prince Charles wed Princess Diana, but it also was the day I finally got to see the Ramones live in concert for the first time.

I had just graduated from high school a few weeks earlier and a couple of my pals, Scott and Pat, wanted to live it up at least once more before heading off to college the following month. So, we piled into Pat's late '60s, black Ford Mustang and made the 90-minute journey from our beachside neighborhood to a nightclub called SPIT which was located just outside of Orlando. At the time, we only ever had been to a handful of live shows in proper concert venues, and we were completely surprised to discover an empty parking lot when we arrived at SPIT around 6:30pm. Had this been a typical enormo-dome concert, fans would already have been lined up around the building. However, this little rock and roll faux pas worked to our advantage.

We parked under a shade tree next to the nightclub as the sun was still brutal and the sweltering temperature remained in the 90s. We then pulled a couple of lawn chairs out from the trunk of Pat's car and tried to make the best of what was to be a long wait before we could enter the venue. Clearly naïve regarding the rock concert scene, we didn't really pay attention to the bus that just happened to be parked a few feet away.

Before long, we heard a commotion coming from the club's rear exit. The next thing we witnessed was the sight of bassist Dee Dee Ramone and drummer Marky Ramone carrying visibly impaired lead singer Joey Ramone from the club out to the bus. Apparently the band members had just finished their pre-show sound-check and presumably were headed back to their hotel until show time. Was this little pre-show "performance" genuine? Who knows? But it truly mirrored a scene out of their movie. And in the moment, we "bought" the bit hook line and sinker. While Dee Dee and Marky struggled to load Joey's limp body onto the bus, guitarist Johnny Ramone approached me and my buddies.

"Hi, I'm Johnny. I play guitar," he announced as he shook my hand. Little did he know that such introductions were completely unnecessary. This guy was THE Johnny Ramone — I knew darn well who he was. But before further pleasantries could be exchanged, a guy with a briefcase who I now realize was probably the band's road manager singled me out. He'd spotted the Ramones T-shirt that I was wearing and with considerable gusto, he articulated his disapproval. "That shirt is a bootleg! It's no good!" he scowled as he poked me in the chest. "You need a *real* one." I informed him that I'd happily take a "real one" if he was giving them away, but he seemed more concerned with getting the band members on the bus than listening to my wise-ass comments.

Although the evening's opening act Holly and the Italians were kinda lame, the Ramones were totally intense. They played loud, fast, and delivered a blistering set packed with one amazing, neck-breaking, two-minute song after another. I witnessed the show from what the kids today call "the pit." It had to have been at least 100° up front where I was. In fact, I actually had difficulty breathing during most of the band's set and my body literally was lifted off the ground more than once by the ocean-like movement of the near-riotous crowd. But I didn't care. I figured that if I was gonna die at 18, being crushed to death at a Ramones concert would be a pretty cool way to go.

As with many albums included in this book, I've owned *End of the Century* in various configurations over the years. However, in 2023, I set out to replace my long-lost vinyl copy. Having no luck locating it in my typical rummage sale excursions, I resorted to paying a whopping $12 for a copy at one of my proper go-to used record joints. The cover was a bit worn, but the vinyl looked really clean. But, when I got home and popped it on my turntable, it sounded like complete ass. And the search continues.

Despite the departure of Dee Dee and Marky in ensuing years, the Ramones remained a respected and prominent music force until disbanding officially in the late '90s. As of early 2024, only Marky has survived from the *End of the Century* lineup. They were one of the most influential bands in the history of rock and roll, and their music continues to touch, punch, and inspire fans worldwide. I sure miss the Ramones. *Gabba Gabba Hey!*

End of the Century

Track List
(All songs written by the Ramones)

SIDE ONE
1 Do You Remember Rock 'N' Roll Radio – 3:50
2. I'm Affected – 2:51
3. Danny Says – 3:06
4. Chinese Rock – 2:28
5. The Return of Jackie and Judy – 3:12
6. Let's Go – 2:31

SIDE TWO
1. Baby, I Love You (Spector, Barry, Greenwich) – 3:47
2. I Can't Make it On Time – 2:32
3. This Ain't Havana – 2:18
4. Rock 'N' Roll High School – 2:38
5. All the Way – 2:29
6. High Risk Insurance – 2:08

39
Boots Randolph

Boots Randolph
"Sweet Talk"
(RCA / 1965)

Sweet Talk

The front yard at my grandmother's house was enormous. The backyard was even bigger — or so it seemed at the time to five-year-old me. Granny Helen already was *really* old. Heck, in 1967 she was freaking 46, for cryin' out loud. *Give it up, lady! You're in your final days!*

As a little kid I loved going on our semi-annual family weekend excursions from our modest house in Springfield, Missouri to Granny's sprawling estate in Milan, Tennessee. The visits were fantastic; it was the commute that sucked.

In those days, it was quite permissible and perfectly normal to seal children in a rolling, four-wheel, solid steel death tomb — windows rolled up tight, dad chain-smoking up front, and the youngins trapped in back; breathing in the nauseating stench of the nicotine-saturated re-circulating air conditioning. And as our family vessel wound around, up and down the Ozark Mountains like a Pall Mall-sponsored rollercoaster hell ride, the end game was inevitable. *Ugh, Mommy! I think I'm gonna...*

But we always made it to Granny's and back, safe and sound, except for that time in 1968 when my dad took a rural road bridge a bit too fast. Our 1964 baby blue Cadillac became briefly airborne before crashing into a wooden guardrail, and then bursting into flames. The five of us — me, my eight-year-old sister, my baby brother (who was still in diapers) and my mom and dad — barely escaped tragic, fiery deaths that day. And I ain't playing "drama queen." There are actual photos. But I digress.

In addition to a groovy 19" black and white TV set (with rabbit ears), Granny had a impressive, self-contained hi-fi — a massive, solid wood unit on four stout wooden legs with sliding top lids, built-in speakers, AM / FM radio, record player, and ample vinyl storage space — a compartment that housed some incredible classic LPs; traditional Gospel, family-friendly comedy, and several pop-hybrid titles from instrumental artists, including trumpeter Herb Alpert and saxophonist Boots Randolph.

These records would provide the soundtrack to many Saturday soirees, with the adult folk wedged like the Culhanes of Cornfield County on Granny's barely-big-enough living room couch. It was the late '60s, but I remember it all like it was yesterday. Pretty much.

••

It's a seasoned axiom — "You can't judge a book by its cover." The same can be said for an album cover — especially in the case of *Sweet Talk*. While Boots Randolph's clean cut, suit and tie appearance might create the perception of his music being "square," that certainly would be a misnomer. In reality, the conservative-looking sax player (and his music) owned as much street cred as just about any other artist featured in these 50 chapters. But, don't feel bad. I might not have realized that either, had I not rediscovered this 1965 classic buried in a crate, stashed away in my family's beachside storage garage back in 2022.

The "Pride of Paducah," Randolph released his signature tune, "Yakety Sax," in 1963. Although it barely grazed the Top 40 at the time, more than a decade later, it would be recognized and embraced internationally as the perky theme song for the *Benny Hill Show*. Trust me, even many of today's most avid, hyper-sensitive, super-complicated TikTokers would (or should) know the tune if he, she, or they heard it.

> "Boots Randolph's magnum opus has proven to be a song which spans the generations; known by few, yet heard by all. Whether as the recurring background music to the sped up chase scenes at the end of every episode of UK comedian, Benny Hill's TV show, or the American TV classic, *The Muppet Show*, 'Yakety Sax' is always showing up when and where you least expect it — usually in a comedic setting."
> —Chris DeAngelis
> Stage and studio session bassist, audio engineer
> Miami, Florida
> August 2023

Aside from his exhaustive body of work as a celebrated solo artist, the World War II US Army vet also claimed a distinguished rep as an in-demand session cat. As a result, Randolph may be best known for contributing sax tracks on such iconic records as the timeless 1958 Brenda Lee holiday treasure, "Rockin' Around the Christmas Tree," the 1962 Elvis Presley staple "Return to Sender," and the 1964 Roy Orbison chart-topper "Oh, Pretty Woman." Now, if that's all a smidge "square" for my fellow Gen X-ers, let it be known that Randolph also played on "Little Queenie," the 1972 album cut from long-haired heartland rockers, REO Speedwagon.

Likely due to his relationship with RCA Records, Randolph was connected to the label's A&R guru and Nashville guitar great, Chet Atkins, on various projects. This also may have prompted the country-flavored pickin' style that was prevalent on many of Randolph's recordings. That down-home authenticity would lead Randolph to making frequent appearances on the top-rated TV program, *Hee Haw*, as a valued member of the show's distinguished Million Dollar Band.

Owning minimal vocals, yet delivering maximum melody, the *Sweet Talk* record checked all the boxes required to be cool back in the day — crisp, clean, old-school production that complemented brave guitar tracks, no-nonsense drum work, and LOTS of sax. Some 60 years later, *Sweet Talk* is still fun to revisit, as it remains a faithful audio time capsule from the kinder and cozier era of flat tops, malt shops, and sock hops.

> "I listen to Boots Randolph when I want to think back to a simpler time — watching *Happy Days* as a kid and aspiring to be the next Fonz. It really is my go-to, feel-good music."
>
> — *Steve Keller*
>
> Radio host, WFIT 89.5 FM
>
> Melbourne, Florida
>
> (January 2024)

The title track was a flirty, sassy little stinger — *Gimme a little of that sweet talk, baby. Oh, you crazy thing!* "Estrellita" was a slow and sultry standout, while "Blue Guitar" boasted the plunky, reverb-glossed guitar sound and style that's still sought by many of today's top players. Sexy and jazzy, the Randolph-penned "Little Big Horn" was a sax-soaked, smoky go-go bar delight — arguably the shiniest stone of this ten-gem treasure trove.

My grandmother passed away in 2018, at the fulfilled age of 97. When I flew to Tennessee to attend her funeral, I also revisited her old house in Milan. She hadn't lived there for decades, but I *had* to see it again. I hadn't been there since I was nine or ten and I was immediately taken aback by how *small* her yard actually was. Her aforementioned Buick-sized hi-fi somehow found its way to my dad's place in Florida. I'd been dispatched to transport the contents of his house to a family storage garage when the house was sold in 2019. After Dad died in 2022, I found myself rummaging through the unit, and there it was, that old Boots Randolph record from Granny's place, buried in a crate, stashed away in the back of the storage garage. I took it home, cleaned it up, and gave it spin. Surprisingly, nearly 60 years on, the cover was in pristine condition. And even without the protective inner paper sleeve, the vinyl also had remained pretty clean and quiet.

Although I'd forgotten how small Granny's yard was and how sweet *Sweet Talk* was, way back then, the record now rekindles some wonderful, vivid memories — of this amazing music, and of my beautiful relationship with my grandmother. Confidentially, I was always her favorite grandkid!

Sweet Talk

Track List

SIDE ONE
1. Sweet Talk (Reynolds, Fiocca) – 1:59
2. Estrellita (Ponce) – 2:00
3. Blue Guitar (Fotine, Stanton) – 2:32
4. Little Big Horn (Randolph) – 2:12
5. The Happy Whistler (Robertson) – 1:55

SIDE TWO
1. Greenback Dollar (Morris) – 2:19
2. Percolator (Morrow) – 2:01
3. Difficult (Atkins, Rich) – 2:07
4. I'm Getting Your Message Baby (Rich, Dooley) – 1:58
5. Red Light (Randolph) – 2:17

40
Charlie Rich

Charlie Rich
"Behind Closed Doors"
(Epic / 1973)

Behind Closed Doors

Mmm! Smell that? That's my mom's afternoon roast. It's been simmering in the crockpot since before church this morning. The cohabitating carrots and potatoes are pretty spectacular, too. It's any given Sunday — winter '73-'74. The wholesome scene at the family dinner table mirrors any *Leave it to Beaver* episode. While the authentic polyester is pretty groovy, the equally authentic bowl cuts are completely criminal. I just turned 11, but my parents are super old. Heck, even my mom is now 30. They're also totally un-cool. And they listen to country music. *GROSS!*

CAH-CLANK! Hear that? That's the shiny new 8-track deck in the living room, pumping out the standard Sunday afternoon soundtrack. Midwest winters are brutal. As a result, many days find us stuck indoors. And with the Internet, Netflix, and the NFL Sunday Ticket still decades down the road, home entertainment options are limited. Recently, my dad brought home an in-the-box scratch-and-dent AM / FM hi-fi set with TWO stereo speakers, AND an 8-track deck. Posthaste, my parents made a pilgrimage to Record Town and acquired a massive stack of 8-track tapes by such country crooners as Eddy Arnold, Glen Campbell, and The Statler Brothers. Yet, despite my parents' un-coolness, they do occasionally bring home a cool tape or two from such heavy hitters as Bread, John Denver, and The Carpenters. But the most faithful family go-to Sunday super jam is *Behind Closed Doors*, the 1973 breakout release from "the Silver Fox," Charlie Rich.

Fast forward a couple of lifetimes. Over the years, the family 8-track copy of that Charlie Rich classic vanished to who knows where. However, I never forgot about it. As a young adult, I scored it on vinyl in the early '80s. Where that copy vanished to, I also have no clue. As a "seasoned" adult in the late '90s, I'd bought it on CD. I purchased it (again) it from iTunes in 2023, 'cuz Spotify is for cheapskate slackers with commitment issues.

Somewhere around 2020, I walked into the office of a local live music production company where I'd been doing business for a few years. I also enjoyed a long personal friendship with the company's co-founder and co-head honcho,

Thomas Tritt.

While I didn't "get" the beauty of classic country music as a kid, I absolutely DID "get" it as an adult. So, when I spotted a vinyl copy of *Behind Closed Doors* propped up on Tritt's desk that day, I couldn't contain my enthusiasm. Come to find out, the album also was one of Tritt's lifelong favorites. But, tragically, I'd overestimated the depth of our relationship. 'Cuz when I asked him to "gift" me his copy out of "friendship," he laughed in my face. While I can't remember Tritt's exact words, he may have encouraged me to do something to myself that (to me) seemed physically impossible. Hey — no asks, no gets.

A short time later, while on a vinyl expedition with the GF, I spotted a very well-cared-for LP copy of *Behind Closed Doors* at the flea market in Mount Dora, Florida — for just three bucks. *SOLD* — take THAT, Tritt! The record played beautifully. The slight warm cozy crackle only added to the authenticity of the experience, and I was reminded instantly of what I'd been missing all these years by consuming the album in other formats.

But, why Charlie Rich? I was raised on a healthy musical diet of amazing records created by near-countless incredible classic country artists. What made *Behind Closed Doors* so special? Well, that's a question that requires A LOT of unpacking.

During the early and mid-'70s, Rich was at the forefront of defining the new "Nashville Sound" — back when that implied something cool. Also, possessing a noticeable amount of leather-clad, rock and roll swagger, Rich resembled a shaggier, silver-haired version of Memphis Mafia-era Elvis, which, according to my then-30-something mother was pretty darn, "sexy." *Ugh! GROSS, Mom!* And musically, Rich had roots that ran deep through Gospel, jazz, pop, and R&B — influences that he had revealed in his various, moderately successful, pre-'70s singles. But, with *Behind Closed Doors*, Rich brought all of those components together and soaked 'em with a Floyd Cramer flavor that was as smooth as the half-diluted glass of Kentucky bourbon perched atop his grand piano.

Behind Closed Doors also owned two monster crossover chart-busters; the title track and the follow-up single, "The Most Beautiful Girl" — hits that would help propel Rich's career for the next couple of decades and ensure his icon legacy. The album has since sold more than four million units and remains one of the all-time best and most beloved country-rock LPs created during that magical "Memphis Mafia" era.

Behind Closed Doors

Track List

SIDE ONE
1. Behind Closed Doors (O'Dell) – 2:54
2. If You Wouldn't Be My Lady (Holiday, Reeves) – 2:51
3. You Never Really Wanted Me (A. Rich) – 2:25
4. A Sunday Kind of Woman (M. Rich) – 3:05
5. Peace on You (C. Rich) – 3:53

SIDE TWO
1. The Most Beautiful Girl (Sherrill, Wilson, Bourke) – 2:42
2. I Take It on Home (O'Dell) – 2:50
3. 'Til I Can't Take It Anymore (Otis, Burton) – 2:28
4. We Love Each Other (Killen) – 3:05
5. I'm Not Going Hungry Anymore (Hart) – 2:10
6. Nothing in the World (To Do With Me) (M. Rich) – 2:36

41
Linda Ronstadt

Linda Ronstadt
"Heart Like a Wheel"
(Capitol / November 1974)

Heart Like a Wheel

That was a bad day. If it wasn't the worst day of my life, it certainly was the most defining — the day when *everything* changed. Truth be told, the entire Easter weekend of 1975 proved to be one long tragedy. It all kicked off on Thursday afternoon when, Mrs. Logan, my 6th grade teacher at Horace Mann Elementary called me out of an assembly program in the cafeteria and into a private conversation in the hall. "Your grandfather just passed away," she informed me with a calm, kind tone. "You need to collect your things, because your mom is on her way to pick you up." And so it began.

Within the hour, my parents would be driving me, my older sister, and my younger brother in the new '75 olive-green, wood-paneled family Ford station wagon from Springfield, Missouri to my maternal grandmother's house in Dyersburg, Tennessee. Us kids would stay there for a couple of nights while my parents attended my paternal grandfather's funeral seven hours east, in Johnson City, Tennessee. But the story actually would get worse. For me — much worse.

As usual, I was holed up by myself in the guest bedroom at my grandmother's, listening to the current Top 40 hits on her AM / FM nightstand radio when my parents returned to pick me and my siblings up on Sunday afternoon. The imminent news would NOT be good. And it would require a master messenger to deliver the urgent info to us kids — especially to me. As a result, my dad passed the task to our family's most skilled diplomat — my mom.

God bless my mother. That woman was a saint. At the time, I don't believe that even she was "buying" what she was about to try "selling" me. But she gave it her best Tupperware Party pitch. "We have some exciting news!" *Jeepers, Mom! What's up?*

In short order, she explained how my uncle Bill had approached my dad at the funeral and offered him a position with his chemical business — in Florida. *What? WHAT? W-H-A-T?* My dad had accepted the job on the spot, and we'd soon be moving to Florida. In just TWO months, nearly *everything* that ever meant *anything* to me would be taken away — my friends, my school, my radio station, Teri Kinser — *everything*!

Immediately, I became hysterical. Inconsolable. Wildly experienced in the game of wise, compassionate parenting, my mom quickly played her best card. "Hey, let's go to Kmart! I'll buy you *that record* you've been wanting." *Well-played, Mom!* "That record" was *Heart Like a Wheel*.

A captivating lil' pop-rocker, "You're No Good" had become a massive (surprise) #1 hit in early '75. But it wasn't until I *saw* Linda Ronstadt performing on *The Midnight Special* that I became completely wrecked — or at least as wrecked as you can get when you're a 12-year-old, four-eyed, super-geek (with a *really* awesome bike). Let's just say that after that TV appearance, my passion for Laurie Partridge was exterminated (sorta). Hence forth (or at least until I discovered Bonnie Raitt), Linda Ronstadt would be the *only* woman who *truly* could satisfy my steaming pre-pube desires. And I'd continue spending untold amounts of time standing in the record department at Sears, coveting the *Heart Like a Wheel* album. *Ugh! If I only could get my hands on $4.98!*

Sure, my life as I'd known it was quickly coming to a crashing conclusion. But as a consolation prize, I finally got, "that record." Thanks, Mom.

• •

"Just look up!" It's what us "seasoned" folks find ourselves saying frequently these days in an effort to compel the young people to pull their attention away from their emotionally crippling iGadgets and take a peek (for a sec) at the real world around them. *Like, OMG! Like, Briana! Like, watch out for that bus!*

In 2022, the GF and I traveled south about 45 minutes from her funky abode in Palm Bay, Florida, to Wax Records Inc. — a groovy little record store in Vero Beach. There I was, "just looking up," gazing at the shiny NEW just-released $40 LPs displayed prominently high across the shop walls. Then, I did something absurdly trendy, I looked down. And there they were. Under the main record bins, we discovered endless crates filled with disorganized, musty-smelling, "seasoned" LPs. "Everything down there's a dollar each," came the voice from behind the shop's front counter. *WOW!*

For the next hour, the GF and I remained crouched down, rummaging through the seemingly secret stash of treasure. *Oh, my freaking knees!* And as the shop owner apprised us of "closing time," we had massed an impressive pile of reasonably healthy-looking vintage slabs from the likes of John Denver, Bette Midler, Rod Stewart, Larry Gatlin, and The Oak Ridge Boys, as well as untold copies of Linda Ronstadt classics, including a well-loved copy of "that record," her 1974 breakout release, *Heart Like a Wheel*, the third of four copies I've purchased over the years.

A big brown-eyed doe of a beauty draped in shawls and donning micro denim cutoffs, Ronstadt possessed what was considered one of the finest, most versatile and powerful voices on the planet throughout her iconic recording career. However, back in 1974, after several baffling "walks," she really needed at least a "double," this time at bat. And with album #5, she smacked that muther clean outta Dodger Stadium.

> "Linda Ronstadt sings her 5th solo studio album with as much velvet in her voice as that Elvis painting your uncle had in the basement!"
> —*Kimberly Morgan York*
> Singer, songwriter
> Athens, Georgia
> December 2023

It was the record that checked all the boxes: white-hot performances, impeccable songs, and perfect arrangements. It also defined Ronstadt's soon-to-be very bankable signature country-rock sound. As a result, remove all-star producer Peter Asher and ace studio switch-hitter Andrew Gold from the roster, and *Heart Like a Wheel* may have been merely just another largely overlooked bench warmer sitting in Ronstadt's growing catalog. *Mmm, smells like team spirit.*

Although Ronstadt's cozy congregation had been inspired a smidge by the moderately successful 1967 Top 20 single "Different Drum" and the 1970 Top 30 hit "Long, Long Time," *Heart Like a Wheel* stirred a nationwide revival as it roared into 1975, spending nearly a solid year on the *Billboard* album chart, where it soared to the top slot. High-energy live concert performances on popular late-night TV shows helped make Ronstadt an "overnight" sensation while propelling the fiery-feeling "You're No Good" to #1 and the sassy-sounding "When Will I Be Loved" to #2.

> "With the more 'poppy' hits; 'You're no Good' and 'When Will I be Loved' juxtaposed with the country classic, 'I Can't Help It If I'm Still In Love With You,' it's a no brainer that this album earned so much critical attention and commercial success."
> — *Kimberly Morgan York*
> Singer, songwriter
> Athens, Georgia
> December 2023

In today's super-sophisticated music world, "albums" are created (typically) simply as "singles sets" to be sliced up Apple-style and piecemealed on streaming platforms. Conversely, *Heart Like a Wheel* was an eclectic, yet cohesive COMPLETE body of work. While the two singles both were (and still are) turbo-charged heart-stoppers, others cuts remain bona fide heartbreakers.

The Paul Anka tune "It Doesn't Matter Anymore" was a particularly moving track. The solitary acoustic guitar strumming of Bob Warford pinned to Ronstadt's honest vocals made this version considerably more compelling than the sunnier-sounding 1958 Buddy Holly version. Jimmie Fadden's harmonica work coupled with the pedal steel contribution of ol' Sneaky Pete Kleinow complemented the breakup ballad beautifully.

Ronstadt delivered one of her all-time most magical studio moments with the JD Souther song "Faithless Love," an honest and pure performance enhanced further by Souther's own heartfelt harmonies — "Faithless love like a river flows, like raindrops falling on a broken rose..." Doggone it man, that's good stuff. The garden-fresh banjo work of Herb Pedersen made the tune all the tastier. BRAVO.

A telling tale of forbidden love, "The Dark End of the Street" slid its way into a front pew, courtesy of the Sunday morning backups of famed gospel singer Cissy Houston. Andrew Gold's "Gladrags"-style piano track combined with Warford's dire guitar work intensified the tune's taboo factor.

In a room filled with so many A-Listers, it's pretty darn tough to point to a particular MVP. However, a strong case can be made easily for the title track. Smeared with the stylistic DNA of the traditional bridal march, it was a delicate heart-crusher, to be sure — "But my love for you is like a sinking ship. And my heart is on that ship out in mid-ocean." C'mon man! If that don't getcha, you might wanna run out back in search of your lost soul. The skin-tight backup vocals of Maria Muldaur together as one with Ronstadt's passionate lead vocals made for one holy union. Then, you got Andrew Gold on piano, in cahoots with the legendary David Lindley on fiddle, plus the sweet strings of Dennis Karmazyn on cello, and David Campbell on viola — brilliant, just brilliant.

Ronstadt owned the Lowell George staple "Willin'," outright — "I've been warped by the rain, driven by the snow. I'm drunk and dirty, don't you know. But I'm still, willin'." So solid! At age 12, I had no idea what "weed, whites, and wine" even meant, but I was a quick study.

With the qualified assist of Emmylou Harris' sweet backups, the revamped 1974 edition of the 1951 Hank Williams classic, "I Can't Help It If I'm Still In Love With You" remains a perfect, timeless example of why everything that's peddled today as "new country" actually is pure pabulum.

From start to finish, *Heart Like a Wheel* never ran out of steam, as the Paul Craft-penned "Keep Me From Blowing Away" was a lonely, yet engaging, "two-minute warning" highlight, and the James Taylor composition "You Can Close Your Eyes" brought the record to a soaring crescendo.

In an era when albums made warm, engaging, artistic statements, *Heart Like a Wheel* had a lot to say. It still reads like a page-turning novel, and it remains an important, relevant must-have for any comprehensive roots-rock music library.

Heart Like a Wheel

Track List

SIDE ONE
1. You're No Good (Ballard) – 3:40
2. It Doesn't Matter Anymore (Anka) – 3:26
3. Faithless Love (Souther) – 3:13
4. The Dark End of the Street (Moman, Penn) – 3:55
5. Heart Like a Wheel (McGarrigle) – 3:08

SIDE TWO
1. When Will I Be Loved (Everly) – 2:52
2. Willin' (George) – 3:01
3. I Can't Help It If I'm Still In Love With You (Williams) – 2:44
4. Keep Me from Blowing Away (Craft) – 3:10
5. You Can Close Your Eyes (Taylor) – 3:10

42
Bob Seger

Bob Seger
"Night Moves"
(Capitol Records / October 1976)

Night Moves

What an inspirational character! David was a grade ahead of me when we first met at Stonewall Jackson Junior High in Orlando, circa '76. When you're 14, one year is a big spread and I kinda looked up to David like an older brother. Unlike many of my delinquent schoolyard pals at the time, David was focused on academics and he never got into trouble (at least not that I know of). He played sports and earned money mowing lawns. David also was passionate about rock and roll — and I had a MAD crush on his younger sister, Donna. Hence, David definitely was a guy who I wanted to hang around with.

After struggling for months to prove myself as being at least kinda cool and slightly astute when it came to rock and roll, David finally invited me to his house one day after school — and yes, Donna was home. Upon entering David's bedroom I was in immediate awe of his vast music collection. He had crates and shelves full of vinyl LPs, as well as stacks of both 8-track AND cassette tapes. David's stereo system was equally amazing. It had AM and FM capabilities with TWO types of tape players and a built-in turntable. PLUS, his speakers were MASSIVE — way more impressive than ones we had attached to the rinky dink family hi-fi at my house.

I don't know if it was because he was cool, or that perhaps he was afflicted with some kind of attention deficit issue, but David only referred to musical acts in abbreviated terms. For example, he referred to Jethro Tull only as "Tull." Aerosmith merely was "Smith" and so on. During that first visit, David revealed how he was gonna school me on an artist who he referred to simply as "Seger" — and he wasn't talking about folk musician Pete Seeger.

Hot on the heels of his double-live 1976 breakthrough LP, *Live Bullet*, veteran Detroit rocker, Bob Seger (along with his Silver Bullet Band), had released the follow-up album in late '76. And by early '77, *Night Moves* was racing up the charts.

Also by this time, I'd become well-known at school as being an over-the-top KISS Freak. "Seger blows KISS away," David informed me, posthaste, and with a bit of a snarl, as he removed his vinyl copy of *Night Moves* carefully from the album jacket and placed it gently onto the turntable.

As the opening track, "Rock and Roll Never Forgets," began blasting from David's enormous speakers, I realized quickly that I'd never heard such blistering, authentic rock and roll. The popular radio hit title track already had been speaking to me for a few weeks, and I became more enraptured with each ensuing tune.

But, I soon got a sort of queasy feeling in the pit of my stomach, as if I was cheating on a girlfriend. I thought to myself, what would I say if KISS guitarist, Ace Frehley, actually walked in David's bedroom at that moment and caught me listening to Bob Seger, and with such delight? I could only imagine my defense. "Oh, Ace — uh, you're home early. This isn't what you think! I swear it was only this one time. Seger means nothing to me!"

Then, I was struck with an absurdly unspeakable notion. Could it possibly be that KISS was NOT in fact, "The Hottest Band in the Land?" *Say it ain't so!* Be sure, I was unwilling to dethrone my kabuki-faced heroes. However, I did have to concede by the conclusion of *Night Moves* that I would at least have to *consider* making room for TWO at the top of my "Hottest Band(s)" list. It didn't take long before I'd bought my own *Night Moves* LP.

When it comes to music, nothing is unanimous. Music speaks differently to different people on different levels. One consumer's cray-cray vanilla sludge is another's "Doth saith the Lord." Often, it's the *when*, *where*, and *how* music finds us that makes it magical, or at least memorable.

Upon my family's relocation from Orlando to Satellite Beach in March 1977, I redirected my personal passion from David's sister, Donna, to a particular girl at my new junior high school — an olive-skinned, dark-eyed beauty with a flower in her long brown, golden-streaked hair — a stunning surf angel named Dawn.

One spring night while walking through my new neighborhood, I happened by Dawn's house. At that moment, I could smell the blooming seasonal flowers as I heard the *Night Moves* track "Mainstreet" piping through the open windows of her house. I just stood there on the corner at midnight, tryin' to get my courage up. But I never did. To this day, nearly 50 years later, whenever I hear "Mainstreet," I'm transported to that warm, full moon night at age 14. I'm reminded of that floral fragrance. And I'm reminded of Dawn. Music is magical, like that.

My original vinyl copy of *Night Moves* disappeared decades ago, but I replaced it on CD in the late '80s. In 2023, I read an online music feature from a couple of years earlier about how rare Bob Seger albums are in the modern-day used vinyl world. Personally, I've never found locating his used catalog titles to be terribly challenging. In fact, I discovered my current LP copy of *Night Moves* somewhere around 2021 at a local thrift joint for just a couple of bucks. "Come to Poppa," indeed!

Night Moves

Track List

SIDE ONE
1. Rock and Roll Never Forgets (Seger) – 3:52
2. Night Moves (Seger) – 5:25
3. The Fire Down Below (Seger) – 4:28
4. Sunburst (Seger) – 5:13

SIDE TWO
1. Sunspot Baby (Seger) – 4:38
2. Mainstreet (Seger) – 3:43
3. Come to Poppa (Randle, Mitchell) – 3:11
4. Ship of Fools (Seger) – 3:24
5. Mary Lou (Jessie, Ling) – 2:56

43
Shalamar

Shalamar
"Three for Love"
(Solar / December 1980)

Three for Love

"This ain't no Who concert!" the linebacker-sized man announced to the crowd of early bird fans who were pressing in. I'd become enveloped by a sense of panic as my three compadres and I were getting crushed against a security barricade just prior to the venue's doors opening at 6PM. Like a mother hen protecting her four little (white) chicks, the Nate Newton look-alike then commanded the crowd, "Ya'll back the fuck up!" Thanks largely to our rather large "mother hen," we ultimately made it into the arena unharmed.

..

Memorial Day weekend, 1981. We were four wide-eyed teenagers piling into my parents' 1980 Pontiac, setting sail on what would become a fantastic voyage. In a matter of days, Ray, Connie, Rich, and I would be graduating from the hallowed "party hardy" halls of Satellite High School, located in the quaint little community of Satellite Beach, just south of Cocoa Beach on Florida's famed Space Coast. How on earth I ever managed to wrangle my mom and dad into allowing me to borrow the family station wagon for a bi-coastal Sunshine State excursion such as this escapes me still. Perhaps they deserved more credit than I gave them at the time. This would be our last HURRAH! — our final gasp of high school glory — and I guess that my tragically un-hip folks actually recognized and appreciated the potential immeasurable value in the experience.

This movie possessed all the key characters of a classic John Hughes blockbuster: the jock, the princess, the model student, and me — the rock and roll wannabe. We were an unlikely, mismatched crew — random kids with seemingly little in common. At least that would have been true in today's super-sensitive, hyper-critical iUniverse. But these were simpler times — an era before communication advancements built up walls that actually push people away from each other. It was an age of innocence when being different, being unique was endearing. And back then, we communicated with each other, face to face, and with real words that formed complete sentences, unlike today. *OMG, Ashley! Like, the new Tay Tay is like, cray cray!*

In today's "enlightened" culture, Ray and I would be the last two guys who would discover common ground. Destined for greatness, Ray was good-looking, well-dressed and well-liked — an athletic over-achiever who had amassed impressive academic stats. Conversely, I was a rather unkempt, long-haired rock dude who typically sported slightly stretched-out bootleg concert T-shirts. My personal academic schedule included two student aide classes, two drum classes, and a student government class. In 1971, I was a second grade super-geek with a certain bright future. By 1981, I'd become a bona fide under-achiever, now destined for a certain future filled with professional disappointments, personal heartbreak, and an endless string of low-paying beer joint gigs.

But, Ray and I did have one thing in common, our love for music — particularly our passion for R&B. As a kid growing up in Springfield, Missouri during the truly enlightened, shag-covered early '70s, I couldn't "hear" race. As a result, I identified with such classic R&B artists as the Ohio Players, Rufus, and the O'Jays as much as I did with the chart-busting rock acts of the day. Although by my senior year, I'd fully embraced hard rock — Van Halen, Ted Nugent, and KISS, Ray had been reigniting my former R&B fire by blasting *Three for Love*, the latest release by Shalamar, on his massive boombox cassette player in the practice room during our daily chorus class. So, when he suggested that we venture out together across the state to see Shalamar in concert at the legendary Bayfront Center in St. Petersburg, it actually was a pretty easy sell. "COUNT ME IN," I replied, with little persuasion.

When we arrived at the Bayfront Center, our lifelong reality was turned upside down in very short order. The concert was a high-profile showcase for the hottest current SOLAR (Sound Of Los Angeles Records) artists: Carrie Lucas, Lakeside, the Whispers, and of course, Shalamar. Approximately 7,000 enthusiasts were in attendance for this indoor R&B "Woodstock" — 6,996 Black teens and 20-somethings from a less-than-privileged area on Florida's west coast, and us four White kids from a rather affluent community on Florida's east coast.

While there were several African-American students who attended Satellite High, the sudden leap from being in the 99% majority to instantly being in the less than 1% minority provided my crew with quite a culture shock.

This was during the days when General Admission concert seating still was a thing. So, despite this particular show's sell-out status, I relied on the skills I'd honed recently at the Cheap Trick concert to make my way down to the front row. At one point, I was encouraged by the "Beat It"-era Michael Jackson look-alike who was seated next to me to shotgun a joint. Tragically, I did it all wrong and wound up blowing smoke all up in the dude's face. Fortunately, "Michael 2.0" was cool about my naïveté regarding such dope-smoking techniques, and he shared the rest of his weed with me, generously.

Following a concise and catchy opening set from Carrie Lucas, Lakeside stormed the stage. Promoting their current chart-busting album, *Fantastic Voyage*, the band members all were adorned in outrageous, colorful pirate costumes, while delivering a blistering, high-energy, theme-related production. Boasting near-non-stop Hendrix-style guitar solos, the Lakeside show was (almost) more metal than it was Motown.

I'd discovered a dangerous new band in Lakeside, and the subsequent headline set from the Whispers was smooth-groovin', indeed. But my crew had traveled a great distance to see only ONE act tonight — Shalamar. Simply put, the So-Cal combo did not disappoint.

Oozing supermodel-caliber appeal, soon-to-be solo superstar Jody Watley dazzled and delighted in her white, skintight, floor-length gown, while Howard Hewett's powerhouse live vocals took our favorite *Three for Love* tracks to a whole new level. And Jeffrey Daniel's moon waklin' and body poppin' dance moves were completely mind-boggling — a full two years before they got grabbed by the "glove."

Our excursion was a magical, once-in-a-lifetime experience. And as we shared several first-ever adult-type conversations along the way, I realized, perhaps for the first time that night, that the four of us no longer were kids. We'd grown up and now were moving on with our lives. Even after all these years, I NEVER will forget our fantastic voyage.

As for that Shalamar record, *Three for Love* was infectious, funky, and sunny, back when R&B artists had permission to make those kinds of records. It also dropped during the pre-Auto-Tune days when musicians sang (with their real voices) and played actual instruments. And be sure, Hewett, Watley, and Daniel were NOT pop puppets, as their songwriting credits appeared prominently throughout the album liner notes. The album has since sold in excess of a million copies.

More than 40 years later, *Three for Love* tastes as fresh as the day producer Leon Sylvers picked it from the tree in his backyard. And I was completely amped when I located a well-cared-for used vinyl copy down at my local flea market in 2019, for just a buck.

Three for Love is still full of fire, and you can take that to the bank. It remains one of the crown jewels of my classic R&B vinyl collection.

But, what about Ray? I'm SO glad you asked. I still hear from my old high school friend every now and again. And I'm pleased to report that he was leading the life at 60 that you'd expect from a fella who made ALL of the *right* decisions at 17. While he technically doesn't own the world (yet), he's only a couple of payments away from possessing the deed to the entire property, outright.

Three for Love

Track List

SIDE ONE
1. Full of Fire (Watley, Gallo, Randolph) – 6:20
2. Attention to My Baby (Shelby, Spencer, Potts) – 4:32
3. Somewhere There's a Love (Stokes, Shelby, Reed) – 4:23
4. Some Things Never Change (Shelby, Meyers) – 4:55

SIDE TWO
1. Make That Move (Spencer, Shelby, Smith) – 6:15
2. This Is for the Lover in You (Hewett, Meyers) – 5:04
3. Work It Out (Watley, Beard) – 4:24
4. Pop Along Kid (Daniel, Hewett, Beard) – 4:48

44
Nancy Sinatra

Nancy Sinatra
"Nancy's Greatest Hits"
(Reprise / 1970)

Nancy's Greatest Hits

As a near-50-year resident, I've learned that I don't need one of those schmancy metal-detecting gadgets to locate buried treasure on Florida's sunny Space Coast — at least not when I'm searching for *vinyl* treasure. I just gotta be aware, and be in the right place at the right time. While I consider thrift stores, flea markets and garage sales to typically be the "right" places, occasionally, some treasures "find" me — in more traditional retail settings.

In 2023, I'd ordered a bunch of shiny new Lillie Mae 12-inchers and 7-inchers from my preferred traditional indie outlet, Savvy Vinyl Records, in Melbourne. My principal "dealer" at the shop is a turbo-charged, red-head who often sports a rather fashionable pair of Clark Kents. Known to her faithful flock simply as "Snap," the former Roller Derby queen also knows me. Perhaps too well.

Given that Snap's shop is located a good 30 miles south of my cozy Cocoa Beach condo, I usually call ahead of time to apprise her of my impending tumultuous arrival and to ensure that she hasn't sold my stuff off to some other 60-year-old creeper.

Simply put, Snap is a crafty one. Possessing the savvy of a skilled dealer endeavoring to tempt Steven Tyler with a tray of fine Peruvian blow, she often "accidentally" leaves certain *other* newly-arrived records out in the open where she knows darn well I'm gonna see 'em.

"Oh, goodness! I 'forgot,' you have a 'thing' for Jenny Lewis. What a coincidence, I just happened to be pricing this translucent 'Green Jello-O' vinyl edition of *Joy'All*, with the semi-nude, pullout rubber poster. What are the odds?"

Ugh! Save it for the Feds, Snap. I'm on to you!

When I arrived to pick up the aforementioned Lillie Mae LPs, I noticed that a "random" record was laying next to my stash on the front counter — a just-arrived, original vinyl pressing of *Nancy's Greatest Hits*, the 1970 compilation LP from Nancy Sinatra.

The album checked all the initial boxes necessary to grab my attention: an iconic name, a bright pink cover and a funky, retro-style font. The 50 years' worth of cover wear only added to the allure. As for Sinatra herself, she got EVERY-

THING right too: big blond hair, painted pouty lips, thick black lashes AND a tight, tasty-looking tummy. *YUM!* But most importantly, *Nancy's Greatest Hits* oozed exactly that — GREAT HITS.

Produced by Sinatra's longtime musical partner, songwriter Lee Hazlewood, the catchy 11-track cavalcade owns a slew of biggies from Sinatra's red-hot '66-'68 Reprise Records run — packing all the appeal of a Tarantino movie soundtrack, decades before that even was a thing.

"These Boots Are Made for Walkin'" remains one of Sinatra's Top Two signature staples. Performed by the legendary Wrecking Crew session collective, the 1966 chart-topper serves as something of an audio Polaroid depicting a beautiful bygone era that birthed great songs, groovy riffs and go-go girls galore. Written by Hazlewood, it also owned some pretty splendid lyrics — "You keep lyin' when you ought to be truthin'." Doggonit, that's great stuff!

Another Hazlewood-penned track, "Some Velvet Morning" reached a measurably lower Top 40 altitude. A duet between Sinatra and Hazlewood, the production and arrangement reflected the times. However, the lyrics were kinda awkward, even by 1967 standards. Today, they feel downright creepy — "Some velvet morning when I'm straight, I'm gonna open up your gate."

As the saying goes, "If it ain't broke, don't fix it." Hence, Hazlewood's "Boots" soundalike, "How Does That Grab You, Darlin'?" also was a mighty Top Ten smash for Sinatra in '66. Another massive '66 Sinatra chart-buster, Hazlewood's "Sugar Town" was a bona fide, bouncy delight.

A Hulk-like non-album single, "Something Stupid," is Sinatra's other staple. A lovely, heartfelt duet with her famous father, it powered to #1 in 1967. While "Things" wasn't a charting single, the 1968 duet between Sinatra and her pop's Rat Pack compadre, Dean Martin, was another super-tall standout.

Magical music, gobs of mascara, exposed midriffs and Aqua Net for days — *Nancy's Greatest Hits* still scratches all of my personal (and private) itches. BTW, Snap hooked me up with this timeless tissue tosser for just $6. Bring on the go-go girls!

Nancy's Greatest Hits

Track List

SIDE ONE
1. These Boots Are Made For Walkin' (Hazlewood) – 2:43
2. Some Velvet Morning, w/ Lee Hazlewood (Hazlewood) – 3:42
3. How Does That Grab You, Darlin'? (Hazlewood) – 2:31
4. Something Stupid, w/ Frank Sinatra (Parks) – 2:40
5. Friday's Child (Hazlewood) – 2:25
6. Jackson, w/ Lee Hazlewood (Wheeler, Rogers) – 2:46

SIDE TWO
1. Sugar Town (Hazlewood) – 2:24
2. Summer Wine, w/ Lee Hazlewood (Hazlewood) – 3:40
3. You Only Live Twice (Barry, Bricusse) – 2:57
4. Things, w/ Dean Martin (Darin) – 2:46
5. Lightning's Girl (Hazlewood) – 2:59

45
Rick Springfield

Rick Springfield
"Success Hasn't Spoiled Me Yet"
(RCA / March 1982)

Success Hasn't Spoiled Me Yet

For me, it's been more vital than at any other time of year, the music that has bookmarked my personal summer experiences — sunny days at the beach, smoky cookouts in the backyard, and moonlit nights with "you know who." Decades later, those unforgettable "summer jams" still possess the power to transport me instantly back to magical times, wonderful places, and amazing people. In 2023, my undisputed #1 "summer jam" thwacked me as only very few have before. The crazy thing is, it dropped more than 40 years earlier.

∴

There I was, hanging out at one of my local go-to music joints one afternoon earlier in the season, watching with bated breath as my "dealer," dug on her hands and knees through a creaky old crate of musty new arrivals — "Ugh, these are gonna go cheap." Then, hidden within the nearly 100 tattered-looking, tired butt rock albums, she spotted a true treasure — "Hey, check this out!" Peaking up from her crouched position on the floor, she handed me a surprisingly pristine LP — "Are you into Rick Springfield?"

As a proud graduate of Nick Gilder Power Pop University (summa cum laude), I certainly was "into" Rick Springfield, kinda. I mean, I at least knew and appreciated his string of catchy '80s hits. But also, as a faithful subscriber of *Cock Rocker Monthly*, I naively always sorta thought of him as that too good-looking soap opera guy who "did music" on the side. As a result, I'd never owned a full-length Rick Springfield album. That was about to change.

Back in the old days, many, if not most of my LP purchases were based on one crucial criterion — a cool cover. The follow-up to Springfield's massive 1981 breakout record, *Working Class Dog*, the pseudo sophomore set, *Success Hasn't Spoiled Me Yet* arrived in the spring of 1982. The now classic cover depicts Springfield's own Bull Terrier, Ron, "rollin'" in a private limo, "Pimp

Daddy"-style, while cozied-up with a couple of canine cuties, and being served champagne by Springfield himself as the handsome limo driver. Punched up with fun shades of pinks, blues and purples, the eye-catching cover somehow now was speaking to me as I gave it a close examination. The cover of this particular copy was clean and the record itself was in what many vinyl aficionados might consider "Near-Mint" condition.

"How much?"

"Six bucks."

"I'll take it!"

Produced by Keith Olsen (Fleetwood Mac, Benetar, Heart, Ozzy), the infectious 12-track collection hooked ya from the tippy, and it kept ya reeled in for a full 37+ minutes. While Springfield has received a slew of well-deserved personal acknowledgments and accolades over the years, *Success Hasn't Spoiled Me Yet* arguably shines brightest as his most exceptional and influential piece of work.

> "Riding high on the success of his smash album, *Working Class Dog*, Springfield's all-important follow-up delivered with AM radio hit precision."
>
> –Ken Sharp
>
> Musician, songwriter, producer, author
>
> Encino, California
>
> June 2023

TIMELINE IS EVERYTHING. So, when Springfield proclaimed, "I want to see it on the video tonight," in the opening tune, "Calling All Girls," it showed some pretty forward-thinking awareness, as MTV only had launched a couple of months prior to the record's release and relatively few homes had access to the fledgling music video channel. Also, honest lyrical rock star swagger such as "She was insatiable, you know the type. And she was young, but she was ripe" never would be tolerated by today's "enlightened" influencers. DON'T apologize for a freaking thing, dude — you're Rick Springfield!

Those who have been around long enough and possess proper "vision," can see with 20/20 clarity how the record inspired future music from a menagerie of up-and-coming '80s artists — from the lyrics ("Yeah we talk about the *girls, girls, girls*") to the song titles ("Still Crazy for You") to the phrasing that'll "wham" ya every time. In "Tonight," Springfield revealed how Patty and Jesse seemingly were "living on a prayer" as they struggled in their working-class reality, years before that *other* song came along.

But *Success Hasn't Spoiled Me Yet* didn't merely inspire a crop of '80s icons, it also would inform a cast of gunky '90s rockers. I know, bro — "say it ain't so," right? Heck, "The American Girl" alone is only one bad haircut and a spritz of BO away from having you craving "cake," for goodness sake. In fact, there's a scene in the 2013 documentary, *Sound City*, in which Foo Fighters frontman Dave Grohl is prepping for an in-house, all-star recording session. Despite a guest list that included the likes of Sir Paul McCartney, Tom Petty and Stevie Nicks, Grohl looks into the camera with schoolgirl-like glee and announces, "Rick Springfield is coming over tonight!" Furthermore, I shudder to think how Spuds' future would have played out if not for Ron's inspirational prosperity message presented on the album cover.

With a track list that owned this much WOW factor, it's tough to hit just a few highlights. However, I'd be remiss in not pointing out how Springfield's reworked collab with Jim Vallance on "Kristina" jumped way higher than the original version ("Jamaica") did for Bachman-Turner Overdrive in 1979. Also, "What Kind of Fool Am I" (still) serves as a three-minute crash course in perfect pop songwriting — mic drop.

> "Hooks aplenty abound on such jewels as 'Calling All Girls,' 'Tonite,' 'Kristina,' and 'How Do You Talk to Girls.' A Sweet success!"
> –Ken Sharp
> Musician, songwriter, producer, author
> Encino, California
> June 2023

Thanks to my friendly "dealer," I now can count *Success Hasn't Spoiled Me Yet* among my personal all-time favorite "summer jams." And my poor GF has proved to be quite a good sport about it, as she too "experienced" the album over and over (and over) again in 2023. As a result, I know that it takes exactly two full passes of the album (via my trusty iGadget) to mow her entire lawn. "Pass me the sunscreen, sweetie — Big Daddy's gots man's work to do!"

Success Hasn't Spoiled Me Yet

Track List

SIDE ONE
1. Calling All Girls (Springfield) – 3:26
2. I Get Excited (Springfield) – 2:32
3. What Kind of Fool Am I (Springfield) – 3:19
4. Kristina (Springfield, Vallance) – 3:01
5. Tonight (Springfield) – 3:19
6. Black is Black (Hayes, Grainger, Wadey) – 2:52

SIDE TWO
1. Don't Talk to Strangers (Springfield) – 2:59
2. How Do You Talk to Girls (Springfield) – 3:17
3. Still Crazy for You (Sanford) – 3:56
4. The American Girl (Springfield) – 3:09
5. Just One Kiss (Kelly, Steinberg) – 3:14
6. April 24, 1981 (Springfield) – 1:33

46
Stryper

Stryper
"The Yellow and Black Attack"
(Enigma Records / July 1984)

The Yellow and Black Attack

Summer 1984. At 21, I was working full-time as the merch buyer for the chain of seven independently-owned Florida Record Mart stores. The music buyer for the Record Mart chain, Carl, was a rather large and jolly fellow in his mid-20s. Carl prided himself on being something of a music aficionado and he took considerable delight in turning me on to some of the latest and greatest rock bands of the day.

"You're gonna love this!" Carl exclaimed one afternoon, leaping from his back room work station while checking in a shipment of July new releases. "I ordered it just for you!" Then, quite enthusiastically, he shoved a copy of an album in my face. The record that had Carl so wound up was the debut EP by a then-unknown Southern California-based band called, Stryper.

Simply put, Carl was right. Given my acknowledged affinity for glam rock, the image of Stryper presented on the back cover of *The Yellow and Black Attack* grabbed my full attention immediately — four dudes, dolled-up like chicks, wearing skin-tight black and yellow-striped leather outfits with sky-high coifs. And considering my up-front faith perspectives, Carl informed me, with a peculiar grin, "These guys are like Mötley Crüe, but with Jesus lyrics." I thought he was joking.

> "I remember hearing about this new Christian metal band named Stryper. In fact, they may have been the only one anyone knew about at the time. I went and picked up *The Yellow and Black Attack* and wore it out."
>
> — *Scott Itter*
>
> *Dr. Music* podcast host, concert photographer
>
> September 2023

Stryper's look was every bit as outrageous as any other band coming out of the LA metal scene at the time and I hardly could wait to hear their music. I placed the yellow vinyl, six-song record onto the in-store turntable, posthaste. Michael Sweet's piercing opening scream and Oz Fox's massive guitar chunk on the lead-in track, "Loud N' Clear," were heart-stopping. But then, I noticed the lyrics — "No matter how we look, we always praise His name." *Uh, what?* "And if you believe, you've got to do the same." *Hang on now, just one dadgum minute here.*

Carl wasn't joking — these guys were singing about Jesus and one of them was a dead ringer for my fiancée! What could be better? To me, *The Yellow and Black Attack* was the greatest thing since those Reese's guys came up with that "chocolate on my peanut butter" combo.

As the record played out, each ensuing track was as bone-crushing and inspirational as the next — from the infectious hook of "From Wrong to Right" — *All say, 'Jesus is the way!'* to the chub-worthy chug of "You Know What to Do" to the fist-pumping sing-along "C'mon Rock" and the arena-sized record-closer "Loving You," *The Yellow and Black Attack* hit like a spandex sack of concrete Bibles.

> "I wasn't sure it was 'cool' to like a band that yells out 'Jesus is the way,' but I knew that it rocked as hard as anything else at the time. I saw a lot of kids picking up Bibles, looking for Isaiah 53:5. And some never put their Bible down again."
> — Scott Itter
> *Dr. Music* podcast host, concert photographer
> September 2023

As an aspiring drummer at the time, the band's powerhouse "Visual Timekeeper," Robert Sweet, had become my latest musical hero. And Tim Gaines' rock-ribbed basslines added a smidge more icing on the cake. Plus, as I mentioned, he looked (almost) exactly like my fiancée.

Stryper was, as *they* say, "the whole enchilada." They possessed the perfect visual, the perfect sound and they seemed to be right on for Jesus. Soon, spreading the word about these outrageous metal missionaries became a top personal priority.

I saw to it that *The Yellow and Black Attack* received (near) non-stop in-store airplay. In fact, Carl became so annoyed by my over-the-top Stryper obsession that he often would hide the in-store copy of the record. One day, Carl engaged another one of our co-workers in a game of cruel Keep Away — tossing the record back and forth to each other, over my head. I retaliated by taking my Bic to Carl's beloved in-store copy of King Crimson *Three of a Perfect Pair* and torched the shit out of it. I realized quickly what a dick move it was and I offered Carl a genuine, heartfelt apology. Yet, things were never again the same between us.

After contacting a rep at Stryper's label, Enigma Records, I received 100 full-color *Yellow and Black Attack* promo posters — ALL of which I displayed prominently throughout Record Mart's primary location in Indian Harbour Beach. My efforts met with enormous success, as the IHB store began selling Stryper records and tapes, casefuls at a time.

> "With this record, Stryper opened the door to the church of heavy metal and offered Jesus a seat."
> — Scott Itter
> *Dr. Music* podcast host, concert photographer
> September 2023

I soon became interested in also stocking Stryper-related merch for the Record Mart stores. Our Enigma rep suggested that I contact Daryn Hinton, who at the time had a close personal association with the band. Although Daryn couldn't connect me with Stryper merch, she did put me in contact with the band's manager, Janice Sweet.

Janice also just happened to be the mother of the band's frontman Michael Sweet and drummer Robert Sweet. I called Janice in California one night from the Indian Harbour Beach store. Initially, she was so taken aback by my enthusiasm for Stryper that she insisted I actually was a rock writer, attempting to dupe her into getting an interview by masquerading as a retail guy. After finally assuring her of my genuine motive, I asked if she'd heard from her sons recently. "They still live at home," she replied. "That was Robert who answered the phone. Wanna talk to him?" *Gulp!*

All I wanted was to order some Stryper T-shirts — suddenly I was "in" with their mom and my newest drum hero was coming to the phone! Robert immediately had the same reaction to me as his mother did, and I also had to convince him that I really was just a retail guy who liked his band and that my call wasn't a ruse. Robert Sweet proved to be quite easygoing. While it certainly was NOT an interview, our brief 10 or 15-minute conversation taught me a lot about how to do a proper interview in the future.

The Yellow and Black Attack was a raw, in-your-face, heavy rock record from a raw, in-your-face, heavy rock band that at the time still oozed street cred. Sadly and shamefully, the record was castrated sonically when it was re-mixed and re-released with two bonus tracks in 1986. *Please forgive them Father, for they knew not what they did.*

In sum, *The Yellow and Black Attack* was a ground-breaking "sledgehammer" for the Christian heavy metal genre. Several decades after its initial release, it remains a rib-cracker. And for old school '80s hard rock purists, locating or re-locating a copy of the *original* 1984 vinyl version is a worthwhile venture, indeed. Although I still owned my original (now scuffed) yellow vinyl version, I did score another copy in 2023, on annihilated, unplayable black vinyl, for $4.

The Yellow and Black Attack

Track List

SIDE ONE
1. Loud N' Clear (M. Sweet) – 3:38
2. From Wrong to Right (M. Sweet, R. Sweet, Fox) – 3:52
3. You Know What to Do (M. Sweet, R. Sweet, Fox, Gaines) – 4:58

SIDE TWO
1. C'mon Rock (M. Sweet) – 3:49
2. You Won't Be Lonely (M. Sweet) – 3:47
3. Loving You (M. Sweet) – 4:18

47
Pat Travers Band

The Pat Travers Band
"Heat in the Street"
(Polydor Records / 1978)

Heat in the Street

Oh, the things that teenage boys have done through the ages (and continue to do today) just to impress a teenage girl. In my dopier days, I was one the most desperate and shameful of these hormone-fueled offenders.

∙ ∙

She wasn't just a local beach beauty or a high school hottie. At 15 or 16, she already was *sexy*. Relax, "cancel" cretins — I was only 15 or 16 years old myself at the time. But, Jeanie wasn't *just* stunning. She also was super-cool. This rather alluring combination put her completely out of my league and I knew it. However, that didn't stop me from at least trying to make a connection.

Jeanie seemed to attend every major rock show that came through Central Florida in those days and she always was ahead of the curve when it came to discovering cool new bands. As a result, I hung on her every rock-related recommendation and observation. Prior to becoming producers of platinum-selling pop provolone, Jeanie told me that REO Speedwagon was one of her favorite bands. In short order, I snatched up a copy of their faultless then-latest album, *You Can Tune a Piano, But You Can't Tune a Fish*. Instantly, REO became one of my favorite bands as well. *'Cuz, there ain't nobody who talks with their gi-tar the way Gary does!*

So, my heart kinda skipped a beat when I spotted Jeanie at the Van Halen concert, motioning for me and my buddy, Doug, to come over and sit with her. Eager to impress this rock and roll princess with my incredible coolness, I thought nothing of taking several strong hits off her Marley-sized joint when she passed it my way, just prior to the opening act, Talas, taking the stage.

"Wow!" she confessed, a smidge surprised. "I had no idea you were so cool."

Eeer!

"There's a lot you don't know about me," I replied smugly, trying desperately not to drool on the end of her doobage.

Five minutes or so later, as Talas took the stage, I began feeling "weird." Then, all the sounds and colors began swirling together. Then I went blind. Then I went deaf. Then I hit the pavement like a wall of crashing Marshall amps. Fortunately, Doug picked me up and dragged my semi-limp body up the stairs to the concession area where he revived me with much-needed ice-cold A/C and a fresh, bubbly Coke. Thank goodness I got myself together in time for Van Halen's set. The takeaway from this tale: I could always trust Jeanie's music. But I could never trust her dope.

It was around this time when Jeanie began cooing praises for a particular new rocker on the rise — 24-year-old Canadian singer, songwriter, and guitarist, Pat Travers. As a front seat passenger on the PT bandwagon, Jeanie made clear that I *really* needed to check out his then-current record, *Heat in the Street*, pronto. *As you wish, my fair maiden!*

By 1978, Pat Travers' career was zinging along, having released three previous modest-selling record's worth of compelling guitar-driven cock rock — an impressive brand of blues-based bar band boogie. But what made Travers' fourth LP, *Heat in the Street*, superior to his past efforts was that it was the record where all the dots connected — the musicianship, the production, the arrangements, and the *songs*. Additionally vital, the moniker pasted on the album cover now read, Pat Travers *Band*.

> "*Heat in the Street* — so hot,
> my Sony Walkman caught fire."
> — Tommy Craig
> Drummer, Pat Travers Band (2016-2021)
> January 2024

Not only had Travers established an acknowledged rep as an ace guitarist, he also possessed one of rock's most powerful voices. His songwriting chops had become razor-sharp and his gift for crafting a magical melody was undeniable. But the project now was being billed as a *band*. And what a band it was!

Prodigy Pat Thrall proved to be a perfect guitar partner for Travers. While Travers and Thrall both also contributed keyboard tracks to *Heat in the Street*, they were *cool* keyboard tracks. Even before moving on to Ozzy's band, as well as to Whitesnake later, one-time Black Oak Arkansas drummer, Tommy Aldridge, already had become a recognized heavy hitter. And bassist, Peter "Mars" Cowling, provided extra punch.

> "With *Heat in the Street*, Pat continued his path of delivering great hard rockers."
> —Michael G. Yanko
> Concert photographer
> Cocoa, Florida
> October 2023

As a 16-year-old underachiever, my typical weekends were spent doing much of the same stupid stuff that teens (still) do. Then, come Sunday night, I'd be holed up in my bedroom — head buried in my hi-fi headset as I struggled to complete my neglected homework assignments before the Monday morning school bell. The soundtrack to those Sunday night cram sessions always featured *Heat in the Street*, on vinyl, of course.

I even had the good fortune of seeing the Pat Travers Band LIVE on the *Heat in the Street* tour — one my all-time most memorable concert experiences. The band was a ball of fire and fury — Aldridge's tuft of red hair bouncing about, just over the top his massive white Sonor rack toms, bashing away, bare-handed during his punishing drum solo, and Travers punching out his mic, knocking it to the ground (stand and all) during the brutal set-closing, "Boom Boom (Out Go the Lights)."

A red-hot, eight-song seduction, *Heat in the Streets* has aged beautifully over the years. Although my original vinyl copy had vanished over the years, I'd picked up a Japanese import CD edition in the early '90s. Despite the audio perfection of the digital format, you can NOT beat *Heat in the Street* on vinyl.

> "Three minutes of nonstop excitement and catchy riffs,
> 'Hammerhead' oozes that '70s rock and roll attitude.
> The guitars hit you hard as soon as the track starts."
> —Bella Perron
> Plush
> January 2024

In 2019, I discovered and scored a reasonably clean and quiet replacement vinyl copy at a local thrift joint, for $8. However, we wouldn't truly consummate our re-union until I purchased and set up my new personal home audio system (with turntable) in 2023. Bathed in warm, mild crackle, the vinyl version sounded even bigger and badder than I had remembered. While much of that credit certainly is owed to renowned producer Jeffrey Lesser (credited on the back cover as Jerry Lesser), I point the finger of blame for that badass brutality directly in the faces of Tommy Aldridge and the late Mars Cowling. Not only was their musicianship superb, but their individual *sounds* were freaking lethal. In fact, based simply on the drum and bass sounds, I'd *still* put ALL of my money on *Heat in the Street* to win *any* bar fight against *any* rock contender, particularly from that era.

> "When I heard the songs on *Heat In The Street*, I really saw what that band could do and appreciated them as a unit. Those basslines still wake me up in the middle of the night."
> — *Scott Itter*
> *Dr. Music* podcast host, concert photographer
> September 2023

Back in my 20s, my slapstick-inspired, hard-core band, Dead Serios, opened for more national acts than I can even remember, from Anthrax and Marilyn Manson to Hootie and the Blowfish and Faith No More to Cinderella and Slaughter. Then, there was the night we opened for Pat Travers at a nightclub in Palm Bay, Florida. The billing was a total stylistic mismatch, but somehow, we crushed it that night. And apparently, Mars Cowling had watched our entire performance from stage left.

"Um, excuse me," I began nervously, when I manned-up and approached the bass legend, a few minutes before *he* went onstage. "You don't know me, but I was in the band that opened for you tonight."

"Oh, I know who *you* are," Cowling replied warmly, with his distinctive British accent. Leaning in to be heard over the backstage clatter, he added, "I stood *right there* and watched *your* whole set. I wish I was in *your* band!"

I couldn't believe what I was hearing. Mars Cowling was one of my all-time rock heroes, and the words of praise gushing from his mouth were beyond surreal to me. I didn't know whether to laugh, cry, or piss in my pants. So, I just took a deep breath, shook the man's hand, gave him a lil' side hug and went on my way, 'cuz after all, *he* had a show to play that night too, ya know!

> "It was such an honor to be friends with Mars Cowling for nine years. No matter how I tried, I could never get a bass to growl like Mars could. He had such a unique tone and an unorthodox way of playing."
> —*Rodney O'Quinn*
> Bassist, Foghat / former bassist, Pat Travers Band
> March 2018

From the rib-cracking title track to "Go All Night" and "Killer's Instinct" to the skull-crushing instrumental "Hammerhead," the album still hits, hard! Truth be told, if forced at gunpoint to make a decision, I'd take *Heat in the Street* over *Van Halen I*, any day. I once had an actual former Pat Travers Band member question my mental stability for making that statement.

Heat in the Street

Track List

SIDE ONE
1. Heat in the Street (Travers, Lesser) – 4:28
2. Killer's Instinct (Travers, Lesser) – 5:10
3. I Tried to Believe (Travers) – 5:06
4. Hammerhead (Travers, Cowling) – 3:05

SIDE TWO
1. Go All Night (Travers) – 3:57
2. Evie (Russell, Van Horne) – 4:14
3. Prelude (Travers) – 3:42
4. One For Me and One For You (Travers) – 6:18

48
Stevie Wonder

Stevie Wonder
"Innervisions"
(Tamla Music / August 1973)

Innervisions

This was one of those elusive little buggers I'd been pursuing for quite some time. So, when I popped in at a popular local used record joint in the summer of 2023 and discovered that a garage sale-caliber original pressing copy had just arrived, I was jazzed, to say the least — especially given the very appealing sticker price of just $6. *SOLD!*

Of the many entries in the impressive and exhaustive Stevie Wonder music catalog, *Innervisions* remains one of his most explosive bangers — a bona fide "hip diddler," as the kids say. And for good reasons. To begin with, artistically, the album covered more ground than an Olympic triathlon champion — taking home multiple gold medals.

Any qualified creative writing coach will teach you two things, straight out the gate: write what you know, and *show* DON'T *tell*. As a world-class word craftsman and master storyteller, Stevie Wonder checked both of those boxes with a big fat Sharpie throughout his multi-platinum-selling run during the early and mid-'70s. And with *Innervisions*, he *showed* us EVERYTHING, revealing the often harsh realities of authentic inner-city life, while also reflecting a heartfelt sense of hope, peace, and love.

A supremely gifted artist, Wonder wrote all nine songs on this self-produced masterpiece and played most of the instruments, including drums. He also explored new frontiers within his acknowledged keyboard comfort zone. The result was a powerful statement that was so relevant and real, you (almost) can still smell the fragrance of strawberry incense as the needle burns across the grooves.

Oozing a smooth vibe and peppered with a dash of scat, "Too High" made for a sweet opener glossed with engaging vocals, punched up with a smidge of scorching harmonica and beaming sparkly images — "She's a tangerine," indeed! Equally beautiful, the acoustic guitar-driven "Visions" resided in a magical place where pop meets jazz, not far from "the land of milk and honey."

One of the record's three *Billboard* Top 40 bruisers, "Living for the City" stunk from the funk. As a ten-year-old, pop-bottle-goggled geek from the 'burbs, even I felt the funk. The minute-long vignette that played out in the middle of the full-length LP version painted a vivid portrait of the prevalent racial injustice of the time.

Despite primarily being a fabulous funkfest, *Innervisions* owned a couple of significant, magnificent ballads, including the shiny, piano-fueled gem "Golden Lady" and "All in Love Is Fair" — a timeless treasure that soon would become a modest hit, and a massive staple for Babs.

I scored my personal copy of the record for "a song." Hence, the cover clearly had done some living over the years, and the condition of the vinyl was kinda shabby. But it plays pretty well, especially when played wet. Yes, that IS "a thing." Yet, as often is the case with cozier-feeling, seasoned LPs, a lil' warm crackle actually can add a bit more authenticity to the music. Two prime examples of tunes (on my copy) undeterred by some scuffiness — the iconic, bass-slappin' Top Five smash "Higher Ground" and my all-time #1 Stevie Wonder power jam, "Don't You Worry 'Bout a Thing."

Nothing's new, man. Cultural clashes, political unrest, social tension, racial injustice — it's always been with us, ever since that time when "you know who" took a chunk out of that juicy red Fuji. Let's face it, humans are a consistently imperfect, downright dopey species that craves conflict. And with *Innervisions*, Stevie Wonder proved to have his thumb placed firmly on the pulse of world culture. As a result, the record remains as fresh and relevant today as when it dropped at my neighborhood Kmart, more than a half century ago.

Innervisions

Track List
(All songs written by Stevie Wonder)

SIDE ONE
1. Too High – 4:36
2. Visions – 5:23
3. Living for the City – 7:22
4. Golden Lady – 4:58

SIDE TWO
1. Higher Ground – 3:42
2. Jesus Children of America – 4:10
3. All in Love Is Fair – 3:41
4. Don't You Worry 'Bout a Thing – 4:44
5. He's Misstra Know-It-All – 5:35

49
Frank Zappa

Frank Zappa
"Joe's Garage Acts II and III"
(Zappa Records / November 1979)

Joe's Garage Act II and III

They say that often in life, things happen in threes. Regarding Frank Zappa, that theory certainly proved true in my world as I navigated through 2023.

In 2019, I discovered *Adventures of a Metalhead Librarian*, the riveting debut from author Anna-Marie O'Brien. As an avid reader and an admitted retro rock geek, I found O'Brien's conversational memoir to be an irresistible page-turner. Truth be told, except for sleeping and performing particular personal tasks that required more than one hand, I literally did NOT put her book down until I'd burned through it from cover to cover — a joyous process that took four days. As a writer, I found *Metalhead Librarian* to be a TOTAL game changer — the magic key that unlocked the door that led me to finally *truly* finding my own writing voice. #BubblegumSaint

So, what on earth does that have to do with Frank Zappa? Well, as I revisited O'Brien's book in 2023, I was reminded of a certain fun-factor that had faded from my memory in the four years since I first read it. A fellow retro rock fan, O'Brien also is known as something of a poster chick for free speech. As a result, *Metalhead Librarian* was full of Zappa references, pulling the irreverent music artist back into my current creative conciseness.

Around the same time, I found myself with a very special green-haired friend, visiting Monster Music & Movies in Charleston, South Carolina. As we perused the store's near-endless racks and bins of vintage records, CDs, DVDs, VHS tapes, and books, I discovered an $8 used copy of *The Real Frank Zappa Book*, the 1986 autobiography from, Frank Zappa. *SOLD!* Upon returning to Florida, the book instantly became part of my morning reading regimen for the next month. *Can I get a blueberry scone with that Grande dark roast?*

Those two experiences triggered a hat trick, reminding me of a crate of musty old records that my nail tech, Melody, had gifted me a couple of years earlier. In that creaky crate were scratchy vinyl classics from such rock legends as Humble

Pie, Elton John, and Alice Cooper, as well as a copy of Frank Zappa's *Joe's Garage Acts II & III*.

I soon made the 30-minute commute from my place in Cocoa Beach to the GF's house in Palm Bay to retrieve my near-forgotten treasure. Lickety-split, I rummaged through her garage, fished the record out from the crate, and brought it back with me to its new forever home. To my surprise, the record was in *pristine* condition. In fact, the album sounded so clean, it didn't come off my turntable for a week. In 2023, Frank Zappa (once again) had become my favorite new "Artist of the Year."

Rewind — summertime 1980. A perfect pink sunrise was just peeking out atop the rugged Ozark Mountains when my wily crew finally rolled in after another memorable all-nighter brimming with misguided teenage exploits. And as our cruising vessel sputtered to a stop on my buddy's parents' driveway with tires (and engine) smoldering, the Orwellian insights of the Central Scrutinizer blasted from my buddy's Jensen Triaxial car speakers. We were music-crazed high school misfits who excelled exceedingly well at making poor life choices, and for us, Frank Zappa was THE MAN! *Our criminal institutions are full of little creeps like you who do wrong things!*

One of the coolest aspects of growing up during the simpler, wide-eyed, pre-Internet, pre-"enlightened" era of the 1970s was living in a world seemingly free of musical and expressional boundaries. From popular TV shows including *The Midnight Special* and *Don Kirshner's Rock Concert* to Casey Kasem's weekly Top 40 radio countdown, to various music-related magazine publications that actually embraced (of all things) free speech, constant, free-thinking pop culture content was available readily to young consumers like me.

As a result, I hung on the words of such music writers as Lester Bangs as much as I did on my parents', teachers' and preachers'. To this day, even as a little old man, I'm not afraid of words. I might be afraid of the IRS, divorce attorneys, and agitated 30-year-old Tay Tay fans, but I'm not afraid of *words*. And musically, I still can't hear *genres* — I simply hear *music* as my personal iGadget shuffles randomly from Carly Simon and Motörhead to Loretta Lynn and Buddy Guy to King Crimson and Debbie Gibson. And that's probably what appealed to me most when I first discovered the music of Frank Zappa — his artistry knew no limits and it wasn't afraid of anything or anybody. For me personally, Zappa's lyrics weren't "funny," and they certainly weren't "dirty." They were *interesting*. And his chaotic music wasn't "weird." It was brilliant and *inspiring*.

> "Zappa had his own language. When my cousin played *Joe's Garage* for me, he pointed out all of the musical things that Zappa was doing in the background of those songs. When I started to pay attention and tune into all of those nuances, it changed the way I listened to music."
> — Scott Itter
> *Dr. Music* podcast host, concert photographer
> (September 2023)

I first became acutely aware of Zappa when he performed on *Saturday Night Live* in late 1978. I was only 15 at the time, but I took note. However, it wasn't until early 1979, when we received a promotional, in-store copy of *Sheik Yerbouti* at the record shop where I worked after school that I became actually obsessed with the iconic avant-garde artist.

The compositions contained within that two-record *Sheik Yerbouti* set were orchestrated meticulously. Yet to me, the music still felt dangerous, spontaneous. The blistering, urgent guitar playing on "I'm So Cute," "Rat Tomago," "The Sheik Yerbouti Tango" and "Yo' Mama" was unlike anything I'd heard before. For a young aspiring drummer, Terry Bozzio's frustrating tracks also had a profound impact. And it was *Sheik Yerbouti* that first introduced me to up-and-coming guitar phenom, Adrian Belew. All of these components added up to one massive musical statement — one that thwacked me completely. I can't even count the hours I spent holed up in my bedroom during the summer of '79, processing, analyzing and savoring every song. *Why don't you take it down to C-sharp, Ernie?*

In September, Zappa dropped *Joe's Garage Act I*. I snatched up an initial cassette copy of the single-album, posthaste. The double-LP, *Joe's Garage Acts II & III* would follow in November. I also bought that one promptly, on vinyl.

Telling the compelling and conflicted tale of a troubled rock star-in-training (Joe), and his groupie-in-training girlfriend (Lucille), the first installment of Zappa's soon-to-be three-record rock opera educated me about the correlation between music, heartbreak and "unpronounceable diseases." Assuming the role of the story's prophetic narrator, "the Central Scrutinizer," Zappa cautioned listeners of how the government ultimately would criminalize music, while also revealing in graphic detail everything a kid needed (or didn't need) to know about "alternative lifestyles." *Jeepers, Mom! What the heck is a "golden shower?"*

> "If you get to heaven expect to hear *Joe's Garage*
> when you walk through the pearly gates."
> — Chuck Lazaras
> Songwriter, session guitarist
> Cocoa, Florida
> December 2023

The *Joe's Garage* saga further introduced me to several of my future all-time favorite musicians, including guitarist Warren Cuccurullo, vocalist / guitarist Ike Willis, drummer Vinnie Colaiuta and an exciting new blond bombshell back-up vocalist named Dale Bozzio. Subsequent Zappa records, such as *Tinsel Town Rebellion*, *You Are What You Is*, *Ship Arriving Too Late to Save a Drowning Witch* and *Broadway the Hard Way* also would all wind up in my ever-expanding music library over the next several years.

As I reflected on Zappa's decades' worth of recorded work and his life in general during 2023, I wagered a bet with a buddy that we likely wouldn't be living in such a sissified, hypersensitive, politically correct world of coerced, weepy public apologies if Zappa still was around to take the piss out of today's "tolerant" cultural objectives — which reminded me of my favorite Zappa quote — "There's a big difference between kneeling down and bending over."

It could be said that Frank Zappa was quite an inventive "mother" — a visionary, a prolific genius. A truly brilliant artist, he was a gifted composer, a master musician, and an extraordinary producer who didn't take any shit from anybody. Of his many career highlights, I'd personally point to the entire three-record *Joe's Garage* series as his most impressive musical achievement.

It might seem wacky, but the guy who was known for making "crazy," "weird" music was the same guy who created "Watermelon in Easter Hay" — the soaring ten-minute opus that appeared on Side Four of *Joe's Garage Acts II & III*. A simply splendid production, the song felt like a melancholy dream. To this day, Zappa's sparkling, ambient guitar tone on "Watermelon" remains the most intoxicating I've ever heard. The track continues to be regarded by many aficionados as Zappa's finest work.

> "'Watermelon in Easter Hay' is a brilliantly moving song. The beautiful melody seems to put you in a trance, blissfully unaware that nine minutes have passed. Zappa's phrasing is incredible. With his impeccable timing and vibrato, the guitar sings out all of the emotion in the piece."
> —Bella Perron
> Plush
> February 2024

But, what's really ironic is that this beautiful piece of *instrumental* music was composed by the same "offensive" character who wrote all those "dirty" lyrics that caused Tipper Gore, Fritz Hollings, and all the other distinguished tight-asses such anxiety during the infamous 1985 PMRC hearings. Decades later, relatively few folks remember Paula Hawkins, however, many enthusiasts still remember *and* revere Frank Zappa. *He used to cut the grass. He was a very nice boy!*

Joe's Garage Acts II & III

Track List

ACT II
SIDE ONE
1. A Token of My Extreme (Zappa) – 5:28
2. Stick It Out (Zappa) – 4:33
3. Sy Borg (Zappa) – 8:50

SIDE TWO
1. Dong Work For Yuda (Zappa, Smothers) – 5:03
2. Keep It Greasey (Zappa) – 8:22
3. Outside Now (Zappa) – 5:52

ACT III
SIDE THREE
1. He Used to Cut the Grass (Zappa) – 8:34
2. Packard Goose (Zappa) – 11:38

SIDE FOUR
1. Watermelon in Easter Hay (Zappa) – 10:00
2. A Little Green Rosetta (Zappa) – 7:25

50
ZZ Top

ZZ Top
"Fandango!"
(London Records / April 1975)

Fandango!

One cool thing about being a little old man in today's brave new world is that I can still remember rock and roll, before it became extinct — or least before it became relegated primarily to "classic" radio outlets, nostalgia package tours, theme-related cruise ship experiences, and local rib fests.

It's fun for the whole family! Get ready for...
THE CLASSIC ROCK REVIEW
Starring: Ronnie Van Zant's original hat
With Special Guest: Kip Winger's original tights
LIVE — TONIGHT @ 7:00!
On the BBQ, Blues & Brews Main Stage
Don't miss it, Des Moines!

∴

Driven by iconic riffs, the list of records that defined rock and roll and *forced* me to skate FAST was seemingly endless — "Taking Care of Business," "Frankenstein," "We're An American Band," and so many others. But there were certain records that *owned* sounds, particularly *guitar* sounds that SCREAMED "rock and roll" INSTANTLY — the crisp first two or three Rickenbacker twinks of "Ticket to Ride," the psychedelic punch of "Purple Haze" and the opening gunk of "Smoke on the Water," to name just a few. However, very few records informed my wide-eyed rock and roll awareness like the very first note of "Tush," the chart-busting ZZ Top banger from the 1975 LP, *Fandango!*

As *they* say, "less IS more" — especially when it comes to rock and roll. In 1970, "That Little Ol' Band from Texas" high-tailed outta Houston, cranking out a wall of blues-based boogie woogie clatter that would have required a larger collective of mere mortals to create.

Although their 1971 debut and 1972 sophomore effort each landed with a resounding chart thud, guitarist / vocalist Billy Gibbons, bassist / vocalist Dusty Hill and drummer Frank Beard were in it for the long haul. Fueled by their breakout radio single, "La Grange," ZZ Top's third record, *Tres Hombres*, blasted onto the *Billboard* Top Ten in 1973 and in the process, it transformed the unlikely trio into world-class contenders.

> "ZZ Top was quietly, and at times not so quietly, the most badass band of the '80s. Although I do believe that in the modern era, 'Sharp Dressed *Man*' would have to be called, 'Sharp Dressed *Them*.'"
> —Jimmy Failla
> TV / radio host, comedian, author
> December 2023

With longtime manager / producer Bill Ham at the helm, ZZ Top recreated the Top Ten success of *Tres Hombres* with the fab follow-up slab, *Fandango!*

At the time when such up-and-comers as KISS, Peter Frampton and Bob Seger were revving up with full-length, double-live records, ZZ Top once again proved the "less is more" theory by releasing *half* of a *single* live album. Side One of *Fandango!* featured blistering live tracks recorded at New Orleans' renowned Warehouse, while Side Two offered six blazing new studio tracks.

The band cut to the chase in short order, offering a simple battle cry — "Get high everybody, get high" on the record's opener, "Thunderbird." Oozing raw, nitty gritty energy, this one combined Hill and Gibbons' early signature blown-speaker-sound with their skin-tight blended vocals — all wrapped up in one beast of a package. Clocking in at under two minutes (yes, less is more), the raucous remake of "Jailhouse Rock" was leaner, and (so much) meaner than the beloved Elvis version. Yeah, I said what I said. The nine-minute, barn-burning "Backdoor Medley" bordered bravely on sloppy, while serving as a massive and effective showcase. In fact, it was "badder than Shaft, Super Fly, James Bond and Kung Fu all put together." *Hmm, better, let them boys boogie woogie!*

> "ZZ Top, *Fandango!* — I saw this tour! An outstanding three-piece band that just keeps cranking out the hits! 'Backdoor Medley' is still one of my favorite live jam memories."
> —*Michael G. Yanko*
> Concert photographer
> Cocoa, Florida
> October 2023

Side Two featured arguably the band's all-time best work. Each clocking in at just two minutes and change, "Nasty Dogs and Funky Kings" and "Balinese" both were get-to-the-hook, dirty little nut-busters. "Mexican Blackbird" introduced us to a gal they call Puta, 'cuz no one really knows her name. However, we *do* know that she "works" at the cantina — her mama was Mez'can and her daddy was a ace of spades. "Heard it on the X" is still THE definite ZZ Top track — EVER. Yeah, I just said that, too. Frank Beard unleashed his tastiest chops, and the shared lead vocals between Gibbons and Hill were just spectacular. *Fandango!* came to a break-neck conclusion with the aforementioned, time-tested Top 20 treasure, "Tush."

Several chapters back, I revealed how I discovered an old box of musty LPs out in my home garage. *This* was one of those near-forgotten records in that box. Despite being scratched and scuffed-up as can be, it actually still plays great — just crackly enough to feel legit. Once again, it just goes to show that you don't always have to go other people's garages to discover vinyl treasure.

Fandango!

Track List

SIDE ONE

1. Thunderbird (Gibbons, Hill, Beard) – 4:10
2. Jailhouse Rock (Leiber, Stoller) – 2:01
3. Backdoor Medley – 9:45
 - Backdoor Love Affair (Gibbons, Ham) / Mellow Down Easy (Dixon)
 - Backdoor Love Affair No. 2 (Gibbons)
 - Long Distance Boogie (Hooker)

SIDE TWO

1. Nasty Dogs and Funky Kings (Gibbons, Hill, Beard) – 2:37
2. Blue Jean Blues (Gibbons, Hill, Beard) – 4:42
3. Balinese (Gibbons, Hill, Beard) – 2:37
4. Mexican Blackbird (Gibbons, Hill, Beard) – 3:04
5. Heard it on the X (Gibbons, Hill, Beard) – 2:23
6. Tush (Gibbons, Hill, Beard) – 2:14

Afterword

For me, the sunniest aspect of *Garage Sale Vinyl* is that it was conceived, carried, and birthed naturally. The seed was planted accidentally during a rather reckless 2022 Christmas season. *Oopsie!* I ignored all of the initial warning signs in early 2023. *Um, maybe it's just indigestion.* But, by the spring, I could feel my unexpected column now kicking at Ink19.com. Then, in June, an unscheduled examination revealed something beautiful. *Congratulations, Mr. Long! It's a baby — BOOK!* Holding my hand lovingly, editor Anna-Marie O'Brien proved to be a faithful, qualified literary Lamaze coach as I entered the third trimester in early 2024. *Hoo-Hoo! Hee-Hee!* And by May, my newborn baby had been delivered in bookstores and at online retailers. *Hooray! Cigars for everyone!*

Although *Garage Sale Vinyl* is *based* on my Ink19.com column, many of these 50 chapters were created specifically for the book. Even the content that was published previously has been revamped and expanded, edited and re-edited. While I did have a bit of a head start, the project took off pretty much from square one — an honest and pure labor of love that required my full attention. So, it's not an overreach to say that I spent nearly every wakened moment pouring in my heart and soul for more than a year — kinda like a fresh, googley-eyed romance — *before* the restraining order. *I don't know what happened, Your Honor. One day, she took my breath away. The next day, she keyed my Kia!*

Along the way, vintage LPs were finding me quicker than I could write about them. As a result, even if I never buy another rummage sale record ever again, I'll still have enough ammo stockpiled to fire off a half dozen sequels. *Hmm!*

I'm from the past. I don't deny it. In fact, I'm *proud* of it. Truth be told, I wouldn't want to be a young person in today's super-complicated, hyper-sensitive, uber-critical iGadget world for *anything*. Looking back, I feel extremely fortunate to have lost my virginity in a lava-lit, shag-carpeted bedroom with Ted Nugent wallpaper. But, I don't want to *live* in the past, nor do I want to be defined by the past. So, even as a little old man, I keep an ear to the ground and an eye wide open, seeking exciting records from authentic new bands and with catchy and crunchy songs that scratch my sonic itch.

Based on this fully disclosed passion, during the *Garage Sale Vinyl* book birthing process, I was contacted by a Florida-based editor to write a column revealing my favorite *new* records. Thanks to the assistance of Snap, my ever-ready and valued confidant at Savvy Vinyl Records in Melbourne, Florida (that's us in the photo), I'm *always* able to snatch up the latest and greatest music releases on sparkly, factory-sealed, colored vinyl. And in January 2024, my monthly *NÜ GROOVZ* column was picked up and published by a couple of different Florida Space Coast arts and entertainment print publications.

Onward and upward, baby!

—Christopher Long
Cocoa Beach, Florida
May 2024

Acknowledgements

My personal author journey got rolling rather late in life, 20+ years ago. In fact, I was freaking 40 when I first began peddling my thinly written early proposals to various literary agents and book publishers. Fortunately, as with so many things in life, after years of dedication and development, my chops got a bit beefier. And before long, the frequent "no's" I'd been receiving from within the publishing world became *less* frequent. I now have a total of five different published titles under my belt. Yet, despite this fun fact, the anxiety and frustration I experience from navigating through the bowels of the book biz each time another pitching phase revs up remains downright soul-crushing. And be sure, it's like that for ALL authors. *UGH!* However, with *Garage Sale Vinyl*, the

ACKNOWLEDGEMENTS

process proved to be completely different. Truth be told, the entire experience was fantastic AND fun. *Wait! What? Why?* Well, it all boils down to two key components; people and relationships.

One of the wisest men I've ever had the honor and privilege of knowing and working with is former KISS business manager and adjunct NYU music and marketing professor, Chris Lendt. While advising me on a particular writing project, Lendt once said, "If you're *explaining*, you're *losing*." I've clutched that golden nugget tightly for decades.

My longtime Ink19.com editor, Rose Petralia, didn't need any kind of explanation. Neither did the magazine's founder, Ian Koss. I'd emailed Rose in late 2022 with a simple one-time story idea about an old Bonnie Raitt record that I'd found at a neighborhood garage sale for a buck. Rose "got" my little story, but she also saw something bigger — something even I had missed. Without Rose's encouragement and Ian's support, *Garage Sale Vinyl* would never have launched as a weekly music column in 2023 and there certainly never would have been a book in 2024. And to think it all started with a one-paragraph email reply I received from someone with vision, someone who required no explanation.

When I ran the *Garage Sale Vinyl* book concept past my longtime writing partner, Bryan Dumas (aka Dingus), he "got" it immediately. No explanation needed. Then, I began reaching out to an array of celebrated music artists in hopes that they might offer additional commentary for various chapters. Even the (cool) rock stars "got" it — especially, co-founding Anthrax drummer, Charlie Benante. While ON TOUR, Benante actually took the time to craft and send me a THREE-PAGE Word doc packed with his personal perspectives on *Led Zeppelin III*. NOW, *that* guy is a TOTAL rock star! And speaking of "rock stars," FOX News TV and radio poster boy, Jimmy Failla, fired a few signature-style quotes off to me in short order.

Then there's my seventh-favorite person in the whole wide world, Bella Perron. The then-20-year-old ace guitar slinger for the rising arena rock band, Plush, "got" the *Garage Sale Vinyl* vibe SO perfectly (and without explanation), that she wound up contributing the book's beautiful, heartfelt foreword. Based on her world-class talent, unmatched professionalism, and being an all 'round badass, I've now decided that when I grow up, I actually wanna be Bella Perron!

It was extremely important to me that Bella sparkled in this book like the shining star she is. So, lickety-split, I contacted renowned concert photographer, Scott Itter, because not only am I a huge admirer of his work in general, but also because I knew he had THE perfect, ass-kicking live shot of Bella. And *that* shot *had* to accompany her foreword. Now, I ain't gonna lie, I kinda expected the guy to be a prick. After all, he's "the great" Scott Itter. But, he totally "got" *Garage*

Sale Vinyl and he was psyched about having his photo in the book. Simply put, the dude was a straight-up bro, man!

I wasn't exactly sure how the *Garage Sale Vinyl* mission was going to play out, but I believed in the project. So did many others. Proper promo images wouldn't be needed right away, as I hadn't even begun pitching the proposal to prospective publishers. But, I'm a pretty proactive guy, and early in the fall of 2023, I reached out to my dear friend, Sarah Karp, about using her local venue, Arts for All Studio, for an official photo shoot. Sarah also "got" it — no explaining needed. In fact, Sarah was so excited about the book that she rented her venue to me for a day, along with a dozen of the talented, fresh-faced actors, actresses, singers, and dancers who frequented her facility. Then, I called up Florida photographer, Lenin Rodriguez. Son of a gun, Lenin "got" it all too.

Opening each chapter with a plain image of the respective album cover felt sorta flat to me. So, I thought I'd kick it up a notch by opening each chapter with a fun shot of gorgeous people modeling each album. Sarah put the word out to her "kids" that the shoot was gonna be more like a party. *Hey, y'all! We got snacks and sodas over in the next room!* She also let them know that I wanted everybody to look as wild as they wanted. And when Noelle showed up on the set wearing a blue and white jammy-style bear suit onesie, I was over the moon. *Yes! Even the 12-year-old "got" it!*

As Dingus always says, "Choose those who choose you." Wise words, indeed, even if they come from a guy who thinks *Born to Run* is overrated.

Dingus' words would really hit home when I hired two specific adult-aged Cocoa Beach honey's as lead models for the book's promo photo shoot. Actually, my intention was that they'd be on the *front* cover. After *explaining* the premise to them fully, they definitely "got" it. Or so I thought. That is, until they messaged me to cancel, just 13 minutes prior to the shoot. I'd chosen *them*, but apparently, they really hadn't chosen *me*. After sharing a few choice expletives with a couple of my production team members, I pivoted quickly and embraced Dingus' words of wisdom and "chose the ones" who *truly* had "chosen me." I snapped my fingers posthaste and hollered out to the ever-reliable teenage sisters who were standing by, waiting for the shoot to commence in the next room. *Rylie! Brooke! Get in the hair and makeup chairs! You're my new lead models! BTW, here's some extra cash, for being total pros!*

Speaking of hair and makeup, I'd hired my personal nail tech, Lisa Johnson, from Karma Hair and Nail Lounge to do makeup, her in-house stylist Alisa Deeley to do hair, and her assistant Cheryl Weber who actually was as helpful to me as she was to Lisa. Their work was impeccable. I even coaxed the tech trio to get in a few of the shots as well. *Let's do some fun shit, y'all!*

ACKNOWLEDGEMENTS 275

At one point following the shoot, somebody said something to me along the lines of, "those kids probably don't even know anything about the albums they were holding." *Au contraire!* Believe it or not, 14-year-old Rylie actually had the cojones to call me out — maintaining that *her* band, Led Zeppelin, somehow was greater than *my* guy, Harry Styles. *Bless her little heart.*

Sarah's "kids" possessed more professionalism than most of the "seasoned" talent I'd hired for projects over the years. And I was psyched that that *they* "chose" to work with *me*. They also all looked even more fab, sporting limited edition *Garage Sale Vinyl* fashion accessories — earrings and necklaces, designed and created by Florida Space Coast outfit, Art Bydandl.

One of the most impressive people involved with *Garage Sale Vinyl* was Christina Weaver. I'd "discovered" Christina in 2022 when she was my daily morning barista at my neighborhood Starbucks in Melbourne. There was just something special about Christina. She genuinely seemed like "the girl next door" — if the girl next door lived at Vans Warped Tour. I "chose" Christina to be in a music video I directed in 2023. Fortunately, *she* "chose" *me* too, and she stole the show! As a result, I hired her again for a couple of other projects over the next few months, including the *Garage Sale Vinyl* photo shoot. She arrived on the set as always; prompt, prepared, professional, and brimming with energy. And when she noticed the need, she jumped in to assist both me and photographer, Lenin Rodriguez. I'd fall on a sword for that girl, any day!

After the photo shoot fun and games, it was time to dive deep into the business of the book biz. Unfortunately, if you're developing and pitching a book, at some point, you gotta deal with agents and publishers — and they require A LOT of "explaining." The *Garage Sale Vinyl* project was zinging along, "winning" at every turn. Everybody involved "got" it. But, the notion of having to suddenly start *explaining* everything to agents and publishers ad nauseam, just felt like "losing." Enter Bibliozona Books.

By late 2023, I was blessed to have developed a professional relationship and a personal friendship with Tempe, Arizona-based author, Anna-Marie O'Brien. When I mentioned to Anna-Marie my anxieties regarding the impending *Garage Sale Vinyl* pitching phase, she revealed how she'd been planning to launch her own imprint, Bibliozona Books. Anna-Marie "got" *Garage Sale Vinyl* and she WANTED *Garage Sale Vinyl*. The passion and interest that she showed for the book and the encouragement she offered me personally as writer meant SO much. In the course of just a 30-minute conversation, I'd sidestepped the entire pitching process and *Garage Sale Vinyl* had found a cozy home. *Welcome to Tempe!*

Although it's been said that you can't judge a book by its cover, a crisp, eye-catching, professional-looking book cover is extremely important. Florida graphics guru, Squeegie Carson had done such an incredible job designing some of my previous book covers that it was a no-brainer who to hire for *Garage Sale Vinyl*. The results once again were, *spectacular*!

    I once heard somewhere that, "it takes a village." In the case of *Garage Sale Vinyl*, that certainly proved true. Much heartfelt gratitude for all of the "villagers" — the talented pros and great friends who "got" it and helped make a vision become a reality.

— C.L.

ACKNOWLEDGEMENTS

CREDITS

Editor:
Anna-Marie O'Brien (bibliozonabooks.com)

Cover design:
Squeegie Studios (squeegie.net)

Chapter photos / Acknowledgements photo:
Lenin Rodriguez (leninrodriguez.com)

Foreword photo:
Scott Itter (scottitterphotography.mypixieset.com)

Afterword photo:
Martha Pessaro (facebook.com/savvyvinylrecords)

About the Author photo:
Amber Clarke (amberleephoto.co @amberlee.photo)

Hair and makeup:
Karma Hair and Nail Lounge (instagram.com/karma_hair.and.nail)

Fashion accessories:
Art Bydandl (instagram.com/art_bydandl)

Photoshoot resources:
Shawn Dourrieu, Diana Cannon, and Michelle Pessaro

CHAPTER MODELS

Kendyl Allison / Chapters 49 and 50
Katie Boyd / Chapters 19 and 24
Nex Boyd / Chapters 25 and 40
Alisa Deeley / Chapters 7, 21, and 45
Jamie Greene / Chapters 8 and 22
Lisa Johnson / Chapters 1, 17, 29, 31, and 42
John Karp / Chapters 11, 26, and 32
Symme Keim / Chapters 10 and 28
Joell Legge / Chapters 5, 39, and 44
Noelle Maginness / Chapters 6, 18, and 47
Trey Maginness / Chapter 23
Ace Matteson / Chapters 36 and 46
Alex Thipsingh / Chapters 4 and 34
Sierra Traver / Chapter 35
Brooke Tucker / Chapters 15, 27, and 41
Rylie Tucker / Chapters 2, 12, and 30
Christina Weaver / Chapters 9, 14, 20, 38, and 43
Cheryl Weber / Chapters 16, 33, and 48
Jordan Wiley / Chapter 13

About The Author

Christopher Long is a show biz analyst, TV / radio / podcast contributor, award-winning musician, and entertainment personality. Referred to once as "the rock and roll Erma Bombeck," Long is known for his conversational, common sense writing style and passion for sharing his unique perspectives on pop culture.

The author of three previously published non-fiction titles; *A Shot of Poison* (CG Publishing 2010), *C'MON!* (Digital Books International 2012), and *Shout it Out Loud* (Digital Books International 2014), Long released his fiction debut, the Christian-themed *Superstar* via Moonshine Cove Publishing in 2019. A 10th Anniversary Edition of *A Shot of Poison* was released in 2020. Based on his popular weekly Ink19.com music column, Long's fifth release, *Garage Sale Vinyl*, arrived in stores and at online retailers via Bibliozona Books in May 2024.

Since 2007, Long has contributed lively content to the entertainment news outlet, Ink19.com. He also has written for V13.net, MuenMagazine.net, and the Florida-based print publications, *Brevard Live*, *The Buzz*, and *JAM!*

As an in-demand DJ, Long often can be found in an array of nightclub settings throughout Central Florida and on various concert stages, fronting his high-octane rock combo, DL Serios.

When not writing or performing, Long makes frequent guest appearances on TV / radio shows and podcasts. He also has enjoyed roles in global missionary work and local youth ministry programs.

Raised in Missouri's rugged Ozark Mountains and on Florida's sunny Space Coast, Christopher Long currently lives in Cocoa Beach with three other humans and four furries; two loveable Goldens and two rambunctious Berne Doodles.

CHRISTOPHER LONG CONTACT & SOCIALS:

www.garagesalevinyl.com
facebook.com/AuthorChristopherLong
instagram.com/author_christopher_long
linkedin.com/in/authorlong
goodreads.com/author/show/91134.Christopher_Long
AuthorChristopherLong@yahoo.com

About The Co-Author

Known to his closest colleagues and confidants as "Dingus," co-author, Bryan Dumas, is a former professional touring musician, audiophile geek and admitted all 'round music snob. Despite being a (really good) bassist, Dumas' equipment actually has wheels, he's always on time, and he's gainfully employed. *Ugh, day gigs!* However, he's still hoping to get a call from Bruno Mars. Yeah, he's *that* good.

Dumas has maintained a Tupperware-tight personal friendship and creative partnership with Christopher Long since their wild-eyed days of making poor life choices during the mullet-mandated early '80s.

In 2012, Dumas came onboard as a consultant for Long's second book, *C'MON!* His full-time post-touring career in Christian ministry combined with his vast music industry background made him the ideal co-author for Long's faith-based 2014 book, *Shout it Out Loud*, as well as their Christian-themed 2019 release, *Superstar*.

A bona fide military "brat," Dumas grew up on an array of Air Force bases in various locales across the country throughout the rock-crazed, disco-driven '70s. Bryan Dumas currently lives in Bella Vista, Arkansas where he serves on the worship team and tech team at NEWLIFE church. In his spare time, Dumas can be found loitering in his hometown record joints with his savvier and better looking teenage son, Daniel — eagerly anticipating the arrival of new (used) Captain Beyond and Atomic Rooster LPs.

Bibliozona Books was conceived in 2019 under the creative vision of Anna-Marie O'Brien, who is known as The Metalhead Librarian. With a lifelong passion for both books and rock-n'-roll, Anna-Marie spent two decades as a librarian and the last seven years as a dedicated writer and writing coach, helping other writers give life to their unique stories.

At Bibliozona Books, our specialty lies in publishing eclectic narrative non-fiction, compelling memoirs, thought-provoking essay collections, and captivating cultural histories — especially when infused with a rock n' roll twist.

Want to know more?

Visit us at: www.bibliozonabooks.com

Bibliozona Books

Tempe, Arizona
2024

If you enjoyed this book, please consider leaving a review on Amazon and/or Goodreads. It really helps connect other readers to the types of books they like, and it helps writers find their audience.
We appreciate your support!

www.ingramcontent.com/pod-product-compliance
Lightning Source LLC
Chambersburg PA
CBHW052133070526
44585CB00017B/1804